ANCIENT EUROPEAN COSTUME AND FASHION

HERBERT NORRIS

DOVER PUBLICATIONS, INC.
Mineola, New York

Copyright

Publisher's Note copyright © 1999 by Dover Publications, Inc.
All rights reserved under Pan American and International Copyright Conventions.

Published in Canada by General Publishing Company, Ltd., 30 Lesmill Road, Don Mills, Toronto, Ontario.

Bibliographical Note

This Dover edition, first published in 1999, is an unabridged republication of the Second Edition of the work originally published in 1924 by J. M. Dent and Sons Ltd., London, under the title *Costume & Fashion, Volume One: The Evolution of European Dress through the Earlier Ages*.

Library of Congress Cataloging-in-Publication Data

Norris, Herbert.
    [Costume & fashion. 1, Evolution of European dress through the earlier ages]
    Ancient European costume and fashion / Herbert Norris.
        p.   cm.
    Originally published: Costume & fashion. Vol. 1, The evolution of European dress through the earlier ages. London : J. M. Dent and Sons Ltd., 1924.
    ISBN 0-486-40723-3 (pbk.)
    1. Costume—Europe—History.   I. Title.
GT720.N62   1999
391'.009—dc21
                                                          99-42697
                                                             CIP

Manufactured in the United States of America
Dover Publications, Inc., 31 East 2nd Street, Mineola, N.Y. 11501

To the Memory of

LADY RANDOLPH CHURCHILL

To whose encouragement the writing of this book is due

PUBLISHER'S NOTE

Herbert Norris was renowned in his time as a costume architect and archaeologist. He designed historical and theatrical costume and stage sets for one hundred plays in England and America, as well as for a number of British films and pageants. Nevertheless, his series of books, *Costume and Fashion,* is considered his finest achievement.

Originally intended to be a six-volume series that would tell the story of costume and fashion from the time of ancient Greece until the end of the nineteenth century, only four volumes were completed and published before his death in 1950. They include *Volume 1: The Evolution of European Dress through the Earlier Ages* (1924); *Volume 2: Senlac to Bosworth, 1066-1485* (1927); *Volume 3: The Tudors, 1485-1603*, 2 vols. (1938); and *Volume 6: The Nineteenth Century* (1933). The fourth and fifth volumes, if completed, would have covered the Stuart and Hanoverian periods of fashion history, respectively. This book is the unabridged reprint of Volume 1 of the series—*The Evolution of European Dress through the Earlier Ages*—originally published in 1924. The reader may notice a few references to the other volumes in the text of this work.

This republication of Volume 1 is something of an event. For the first time in many years, all four of the volumes in the series that Mr. Norris completed before his death are back in print. Volume 2 is available in a 1999 Dover reprint entitled *Medieval Costume and Fashion* (ISBN-486-40486-2). Volume 3 is available in a one-volume (unabridged) Dover edition published in 1997; it combines Books I and II, and is entitled *Tudor Costume and Fashion* (ISBN-486-29845-0). Finally, Volume 6 of the series is available in a Dover reprint published in 1998. It is entitled *Nineteenth Century Costume and Fashion* (ISBN 0-486-40292-4).

FOREWORD

DESPITE the multiplicity of books on Costume already available, I found frequently in the early days of my professional work the greatest difficulty in securing authentic *dated* information to enable me to portray faithfully the modes and fashions of a chosen period. Many years ago, therefore, I started to compile a chronological list of dated notes and sketches on Costume and accessories, and have continually added to the list examples of unquestioned authenticity. It has been of the greatest value in the supervision of costumes for historical plays, pageants and films, and formed the basis of my course of lectures on Costume.

Much of the information given in this volume has been published before, and is available elsewhere, in fragmentary form, to anyone who has the industry and the time to pursue the details in a hundred books (in half a dozen languages) and a thousand illuminated MSS., pictures, statues, mosaics and frescoes scattered throughout Europe, together with the knowledge to extract therefrom the facts of design and period which they record.

At the suggestion of several clients who have tested the value of my collection, a selection from the notes, so far as they relate to periods discussed in the present volume, are here expanded into a chronological sequence, tracing the origin and development of a garment and its relations to forerunners and successors. It is hoped that the arrangement will facilitate reference and enable the student to find what he seeks without waste of time; and this, rather than the production of a literary or artistic work, has been the aim in view. The chronological order sometimes produces a somewhat fragmentary result, as in The History of the Tunica of Rome (*see* p. 97); items which developed simultaneously are usually kept separate, but occasionally, as with the Tunica and Dalmatica, details of their progressive changes are alternated in historical sequence.

The evolution of Costume has been affected, throughout history, by the events and standard of culture of the times. For this reason I have prefaced each chapter by a list of historical data relating to the period concerned. Some events are chosen because in a measure they influenced Costume, but others which bore scarcely any relation to the subject are included because they are likely to assist the student to identify the period as contemporary with facts already known. This method has been used freely with regard to the less known periods;

and, for parallel reasons, brief accounts of some of the races who influenced civilisation are included in Chapters I., III., IV. and VI.

My survey is largely concerned with England and France, although the influences which affected these two countries are traced back to Greece, Rome, Constantinople, to the shores of the Baltic, and a passing glance is given to Ireland.

As regards Greece, it will be seen that the present volume starts with the Classic Period. I am, of course, aware that discoveries in Crete and Mycenæ during the last forty years have revealed the existence of a civilisation there many centuries before the time formerly regarded as the beginning of Greek history. Our present knowledge divides this civilisation into two distinct periods: The Cretan or Minoan (so called after Minos, King of Crete, a law-giver and organiser of a considerable maritime power), which existed approximately 3500–1400 B.C., and the Mycenæan, 1600–950 B.C.

One curious result of this enlargement of our knowledge is that some of Homer's accounts of men and matters, regarded half a century ago as picturesque legends, have been found to be careful narrative of facts; and the discoveries have opened up a new source of information with regard to Culture and Costume of these far-distant times and their bearing on subsequent arts and manners. As regards Costume, fashions entirely different from those previously known appear to have dominated the world of dress, until superseded by new styles evolved at the beginning of the Classic Period. Information of an authentic character is naturally scanty at present, but I hope to find time, as soon as sufficient data have been collected, to write a history of Costume of these two periods as an addendum to Chapter II. of this volume.

I believe that the Costume of Republican and Imperial Rome has been treated here more fully than in any previous work, and to the best of my knowledge the chapter on Byzantine Costume is the first work on the subject in English. Space only prevents me from dealing with it in a more comprehensive manner.

In such a book as this, illustrations are an important feature—and thanks to my publisher they are numerous. The figures are simply drawn—they are designed to show the appearance of people at different periods, not as works of art; nor do they compete with a modern style of "costume drawing," full of beautiful inaccuracies and useless as a practical guide to dress. Attention to pose and composition is subordinated to display of the dress and accessories. Many of the drawings in the letterpress have no relation to clothing; they are inserted as useful details for the guidance of producers in search of authentic properties—for example, a drinking-vessel proper to almost every period will be found.

Diagrams illustrating the cut of certain specific garments are included for practical purposes. These have been worked out to scale on models, and the results given should be fairly accurate. The same procedure has been followed with regard to the intricate arrangement of draperies described in the text and shown in the illustrations.

I have it in mind that the book may be found useful to—

Students of the literature and history of European nations, and the large numbers of students who are taking up the study of Costume, now an integral part of the course for the University of London's Diploma in Dramatic Art;

Artists who paint historical pictures;

Producers and actors in historical and Shakespearean plays and films, helping them to create the right atmosphere, to wear their costumes correctly, to use the right make-up, and to assume the correct deportment of the period, for Costume exercised a considerable influence on manners and customs;

Teachers of History.

From an artistic standpoint it is disastrous that, with few outstanding exceptions, the theatrical profession know little about historical costume, and, worse still, care less! How many British actors wear the toga correctly? What actresses look as if born and brought up in the period of their parts? Invariably some detail jars—a touch of modernity, or some item (perhaps "becoming") from another period creeps in, and the effect is marred beyond redemption. If this book helps to foster a closer approach to accuracy in the stage representation of costumes of long ago, I shall be amply repaid for the labour of its composition. I urge those who regard the authentic costume of the age they are to portray as "unbecoming," or "ugly," to believe that *consistent* adoption of its modes in every detail will achieve a triumph which will reward their courage and concentration more generously than any hybrid makeshift, or "pretty pretty" collection of oddments from all ages.

Anachronism is always ugly!

In conclusion, I wish to express my grateful thanks to Mr. C. Wilhelm, whose pupil I was in everything but name, for the encouragement he showed me in my youthful days; to my wife for translating the various French and German authorities; to Major D. S. Paterson for his help in editing the MS., and to his wife for her assistance with the illustrations; to the Publishers for all the trouble and expense to which they have been put over this work.

HERBERT NORRIS.

London, 1924.

FOREWORD TO SECOND EDITION

THIS book was produced originally as a handbook designed to provide a summary of information about costume in a period hitherto not thoroughly explored, and to fill the gap in books on the subject prior to the Norman Conquest. It was intended to be complete in itself, but its principles of arrangement and classification were found so useful and convenient for reference that the success of this departure from previous practice led to the compilation of a second volume (1066–1485) on similar, but more ample, lines.

It is very gratifying that the steady sales of Volume I should have justified a further edition, prior to the publication of Volume III (the Tudor Period).

One or two distinguished critics have suggested that it would have been preferable had I reproduced the original sources on which my interpretations were based—whether sculpture, mosaic, or miniature—rather than translated their information for the benefit of the busy student, in the manner adopted in the first edition. My intention was to produce a handbook as comprehensive and comprehensible as possible. This object would have been defeated, rather than furthered, by adopting the means suggested by my critics, especially in view of the limits of space at my disposal.

Many drawings were derived, not from one source alone, but from half a dozen, thus assembling the various details and concentrating the results of my own researches in a labour-saving presentation for the student's benefit.

To clinch the argument, it is only necessary to refer to the few faithful reproductions of medieval art given in Volume II in order to see how little may be deduced from one isolated authority by students at the elementary stage.

Unfortunately it is impossible to amplify this volume to any great extent, but a few minor corrections have been made.

HERBERT NORRIS.

London, December, 1930.

Fig. 17A

CONTENTS

10th Cent.

LIST OF ILLUSTRATIONS

COLOURED PLATES

NOTE: For this edition, all color plates marked by an asterisk (*) appear between pages 170 and 171.

LIST OF ILLUSTRATIONS

IN HALF-TONE AND LINE

xii

LIST OF ILLUSTRATIONS

COSTUME AND FASHION

CHAPTER I

FROM THE EARLIEST TIMES TO 78 A.D.

HISTORICAL DATA

B.C.
*550,000. The end of Pliocene Age.
First Race. Fig. 1. Pithecanthropos Erectus Type.
*110,000. Second Race. Fig. 2. Eoanthropos Type.
*50,000. Third Race. Neanderthal Type.
*35,000. End of Early Palæolithic Age and beginning of Late Palæolithic Age.
Fourth Race. Fig. 3. Cro Magnon Type.
*15,000. End of Late Palæolithic or Old Stone Age and beginning of Neolithic or New Stone Age.
3,000. The Bronze Age.
The Coming of the Gauls.
The Coming of the Phœnicians.

B.C.
600. The Iron or Celtic Age.
150. The Coming of the Belgæ.
55. First Roman Invasion of Britain.
54. Second Roman Invasion of Britain. Cassivellaunus.

A.D.
4. The Year of Our Lord.
5-41. Cunobelin.
43. Third Invasion of Britain. Caractacus.
51. Capture of Caractacus, who is sent prisoner to Rome.
61. Boadicea, Chieftainess of the Iceni.
62. Her defeat and death.
78. Complete subjugation of Britain.

EARLY PALÆOLITHIC AGE

To understand thoroughly *the evolution of Costume* it is necessary to go back many hundred thousand years before the Christian era to that period in the world's history called the

PLEISTOCENE AGE (River Beds)

or the beginning of the Early Palæolithic Age, when mankind was emerging from his earlier stage of ape.

The first race of Man (*circa* 550,000 B.C.) is called the " Pithecanthropos Erectus," or Ape Man (*see* Fig. 1). They were powerfully built individuals, with low foreheads, prominent bony ridges above the eyes, and retreating chins. Their forearms were heavy and clumsy, their thigh-bones bent and their shin-bones short, so they must have been bow-legged and awkward in gait. This type of human being became differentiated from animals because development of the faculty of primitive speech enabled them to sustain thought and created memory.

A second race of Subman, named " Eoanthropos " or " Dawn Man," was in existence (*circa*) 110,000 B.C. Their only weapons were branches torn from the trees (*see* Fig. 2).

* These dates are given by several authorities on the subject of Early Man, as indicating approximately the periods mentioned.

I

A third race, also Subman, Neanderthal Type, existed approximately 50,000 B.C. These people lived in caves and under the shelter of rock ledges. Their implements were made by chipping flints and stones into required shapes.

No clothing of any kind was worn by this still subhuman, half-animal people: not even the skins of animals, for they had not acquired sufficient skill to utilise them.

The taming of animals had not yet begun. Man was still at war with the creatures that inhabited his savage surroundings; his potential friends and servants he regarded merely as food, and most animals were classified in this simple manner. They were there to contribute to his physical support, by providing flesh, blood and the marrow of their bones, to satisfy his appetite. Self-preservation, and, later, the business of food-getting, developed man's skill as a hunter; and his skill was essentially a mental quality, for he planned the destruction of beasts that were physically infinitely superior to him.

Pits and snares were his counter to teeth and claws; and such primitive mental efforts developed the power, and ultimately increased the scope and outlook of the early men of those far-away times, laying the foundation of primitive culture and opening up possibilities of progress. Reliance on instinct was replaced by definitely constructive mental effort, and thought progressed. Thought widened racial experience.

The Late Palæolithic Age or Old Stone Age

Circa 35,000–15,000 B.C. This date, 35,000 B.C., is given as the end of the Early Palæolithic Age and beginning of the Late Palæolithic Age.

A fourth race, the Cro Magnon or " True Man " Type (*see* Fig. 3), lived during this period, and was akin to the Eskimo of the present day. These people occupied the cave-dwellings of their predecessors, but led a much freer life in the open.

First sense of art. Even in these wild and crude surroundings, a dawning appreciation of the embellishments of life is apparent in the carving and decoration of weapons and implements still extant; and, as seen in cave wall paintings, indicates a distinct sense of beauty, and the ability to copy beauty in nature.

Garments. During the whole of this period, weaving was entirely unknown. Garments, *when* worn, consisted of the skins of animals wrapped round the body of the wearer.

The Neolithic or New Stone Age: *Circa* 10,000 B.C.

The people of this period constituted a *fifth race of mankind,* of moderate stature and slender proportions. Those who resided on

Fig. 1. A man of the Palæolithic Age (first race)

Fig. 2. A man of the same (second race)

Fig. 3. A man of the same (fourth race)

Fig. 4. A man of the Neolithic Age

the western side of the island now known as Great Britain were dark, and of the Iberian type. Those on the eastern side were fair, and very like the Gauls (*see* Fig. 4).

Arms and weapons. Flints and other hard stones, worked into fine points and edges by a process of chipping, formed the spear-heads and knife-blades with which these prehistoric warriors fought their adversaries and hunted their prey.

The *spear-heads* were bound by thongs of hide to strong wooden poles. *Axe-heads,* with holes for their hafts, were treated in the same way. The *knife-blades* had holes worked into them, and were fastened to wooden or bone handles by wooden pegs (*see* Fig. 4).

Javelin-heads were made of horn, either with smooth, sharp edges finishing in a point, or barbed in several places. These were bound to poles by threads of sinew.

Bows and arrows were extensively used, especially in the chase. Arrow-heads were very skilfully shaped out of flint and bone, with grooves for fastening them on to the shafts. It is even suggested that these people poisoned their arrows, as grooves, apparently for that purpose, have been found in some of them.

In the later Stone Age, spear-heads, knife-blades, and so forth, were no longer sharpened merely by chipping, but by grinding, and finished off with a polish, and were made in various technically perfect forms. Suitable handles were regarded as especially important, and the stone implements were provided with a hole, notch or groove for fixing.

Dwellings. This race made dwellings by digging pits. The earth was thrown up all round, forming a small breastwork. In the centre of the pit a stout upright, or branch of a tree, was raised, and this supported other branches, radiating from the centre to the top of the mound to form a roof, which was covered or thatched with bracken, twigs, etc., and often covered with earth. From the outside these pit-huts had the appearance of molehills. The burying places (tumuli) were similar in outward appearance. The more important tumuli enclosed chambers built of colossal blocks of stone piled one upon another, and these were the temples, as well as the burying places, of these prehistoric people. The admirable construction of these tumuli proves that the builders of the time were little less dexterous than the Egyptians in transporting and piling masses of stone.

Dawn of domestic crafts. Many things have been found in these tumuli which reveal an advance in the evolution of clothing. Scrapers of flint and bone tell us that the men of the Stone Age knew how to dress skins for use as clothing. Bone needles with eyes, and fine awls, are evidence of a knowledge of the art of sewing. They knew how to make cords, by twisting the sinews of the reindeer, and impressions and indentations made by cords are conspicuous on their horn and bone implements.

The art of plaiting was understood, and this is seen in the design of primitive ornaments.

From the same sources we find many implements for domestic use, mostly made of bone and reindeer horn, including groove-like or hollow spoon-shaped pieces which were used evidently for cooking and eating.

Reindeer horn was very skilfully worked into shape and decorated by a tool which was simply a blunt-edged, saw-shaped stone.

Leather bottles, made of the skins of small animals stripped off whole without a seam, were no doubt in use to carry liquids.

First garment: the shirt. Their scanty clothing, formed of the skins of animals, now began to assume some shape, the skins being sewn together by needles of bone and threads of sinews (*see* Diagram I); and so we arrive at the first TUNIC, the oldest article of apparel, and ancestor of the shirt of to-day.

Dia. 1

How the tunic was made. During the late Stone Age the tunic was simply two pieces of skin, with the hair worn either inside or out, laced together on the shoulders by sinews, and fastened round the waist by another piece of hide. Later, the two pieces were sewn along the top, leaving a hole for the head and a slit in front. After this, the sides were sewn up, completing the tunic. If the skin was large enough, only a hole was cut in the centre for the head, one portion of it hanging in front, the other behind. A girdle of hide or sinew-cord confined it at the waist.

Arms and legs were left bare, but ornaments were very important and characteristic. These were the teeth of dogs, wolves, horses, oxen, bears and boars, threaded on cords of sinews into necklaces and bracelets. The popularity of such ornaments may be gauged by the fact that imitations of them were often worn; and bones and reindeer horn were carved into ornamental plaques, circular and square, and basket-shaped, shuttle-like and chisel-shaped beads. These were also fashioned into eardrops.

Hair. Both men and women wore their hair long and flowing; and although there was no attempt to arrange it in any particular style, they took care of it, presumably, as many neat little combs made of boxwood, and hairpins of bone, have been found in the remains of the dwellings of these primitive people. It was the general habit for the men to wear long beards and moustaches.

THE BRONZE AGE

3,000 B.C.–600 B.C.

" The Bronze Age " denotes the period that began when bronze replaced stone in the making of weapons. The classification of various ages as Stone, Bronze, and Iron should not be regarded as a strictly accurate division of definite epochs. There must have been much over-lapping in the use of different materials, and stone implements of superior finish are often found in association with early bronze work.

At this period the men were tall of stature and round-headed. Later, these British savages, as they still were, got into communication with their neighbours on the other side of the water—the Gauls, a race of superior culture, who were in closer touch with Eastern civilisation.

Fig. 5   Fig. 6

The Gauls in France were called by the Romans Galli or Celtæ=Celts, Greek Galatæ (*see* Greece, p. 27). Originally the Gauls came with the rest of the great drift of Celtic races from Asia, at some remote period, and in their journey overran and ultimately occupied a part of Western Europe.

In the sixth century before the Christian era they settled in the section of Europe we know as France; and their settlement involved the subjugation of the Iberian peoples who had been the previous holders of the land.

These Gauls were of fair complexion, blue-eyed and light-haired, brave and intelligent; and they favoured brilliant colours and barbaric display. They were ruled by a body of priests called Druids (Drui=the Celtic for oak tree), and were divided into small tribes or clans, headed by chiefs.

The Phœnicians (600 B.C.) were a people of higher culture than the Gauls, and are supposed to have visited Britain for tin; and, in return, they bartered the goods they had brought from their native country at the eastern end of the Mediterranean. This is practically the first instance of the import of merchandise into Britain.[1]

The *art of weaving* now began to be understood, and many primitive weaving implements of this age have been found; but the distaff

and loom do not seem to have been yet introduced into Britain. However, the British were able to produce a certain coarse material from the flax which they had but lately learnt to grow, so by now they were not wholly dependent on the skins of animals for clothing (*see* Figs. 5 and 6).

The *potter's art* was known throughout Europe during this period; but at first it was practised entirely by hand, without the aid of the potter's

Primitive Pot

wheel.[2] The simple decoration in use consisted merely of incisions or impressions made with the fingers on the upper edge. The clay of the outside of the vessels acquired a bright red colour through burning, whereas the inside remained a greyish black. Towards the end of this period pottery was distinguished by an artistic finish and beauty of form, and geometrical designs were generally incised on the surfaces.

These clay vessels are elementary examples of *coloured decoration,* the incised dots and strokes being filled in with a white substance in contrast with the bright red ground-work and black interior.

A handle of the simplest form now appears like a wart projecting from the side of the vessel, pierced with a narrow opening to allow a cord to be passed through.

Later Pottery, Bronze Age

[1] Some authorities believe that Phœnician commerce with Britain dates from the fourteenth century B.C.

[2] The potter's wheel was known in Egypt 2,500 B.C.

THE CELTIC OR IRON AGE

600 B.C.–A.D. 78

[Reginald Hughes says the date of the coming of the Celts to Britain is a matter of some controversy, and that the Iron Age could not have been many centuries old at the time of Cæsar's landing, for bronze was not wholly superseded.]

When Pytheas, the Greek explorer (the first educated visitor to these shores), arrived in the middle of the fourth century B.C., the Celts were in occupation of the country.

The *British Celts* had migrated from Gaul, and were split up into two races. Those living in the southern part of Britain were as civilised as their neighbours and kinsmen, the Gauls or Celtæ of France; those living in the north were in the wildest state of nature, and their descendants came to be known as the Caledonians and Picts.

There do not seem to have been many differentiating features in the dress of the various races of Continental Celts. The Gauls were the chief peoples of the Celts, so a description of the Gaulish dress must suffice. Their costume differed chiefly from the classic dress by the addition of a covering for the legs.

It must have been at this period that the Gaulish element was greatly diffused by intermarriage with the Britons, as we are told by classic writers of the time that " the Britons in their manners partly resemble the Gauls " (Strabo), that they " are near " and " like " them (Tacitus), and " fought armed after the Gaulish manner " (Pomponius Mela).

Henceforth the Gauls and their descendants living in Britain will be designated

THE CELTS

Pytheas tells us that they were a tall people, with red or fair hair, whose implements were made of iron instead of bronze. He noticed many indications of a culture greater than he had expected. But until shortly before this time there can be little doubt that their dress was conspicuous by its absence. In fact, they went absolutely naked in the warmer seasons of the year, staining their bodies with a kind of blue dye called " woad "; in the winter months only, the skins of animals were used as clothing. Tattooing, in lines and curves, was an ornamentation much in favour, and was considered a mark of nobility.

Dwellings. The Celts dwelt in huts made of wattle-work and daub, above ground, circular in shape, and with pointed roofs. They tilled the earth and were proficient in agriculture, their wealth consisting chiefly of great herds of cattle. Navigation began to be understood; and the rivers, lakes and sea were traversed in canoes of definite boat-shape, propelled by oar and sail.

Vehicles. The first vehicle in Britain makes its appearance during this age, in the form of a primitive two-wheeled wooden chariot, open in front, having, between two small shaggy ponies, a wide pole on which the driver or charioteer stood. In battle, scythes were attached to the axles of the wheels.

Coinage, copied from that used in Eastern Europe, was in use about 200 B.C.—an indication that the Celts had advanced to a considerable degree of civilisation through their intercourse with the Gallic and Phœnician merchants, a fact noted by Posidonius the Stoic two and a quarter centuries after Pytheas visited the land. Although somewhat primitive, these coins afford details of portraits and headgear of officials of the time.

Their *cloth,* woven from wool and flax, is described by Pliny (50 A.D.) as being of the texture of thick, coarse felt, and some of much finer make.

By this time the Celts in Britain and the Gauls in France excelled in the art of dyeing cloth in many *colours:* purple, scarlet, yellow, brown, and, above all, flaming red.

Celtic Ornament

Celtic Jug

Celtic Drinking-vessel

Their bronze and iron *ornaments* and utensils were very artistic, curves and scrolls and intertwined work being the chief characteristics of early *Celtic Art.*

Enamelling in red colours was much used on metal work, and studs of coral and pearls, or some bright pebble, were worked into their breastplates, shields, and helmets.

THE BELGÆ (150 B.C.)

The Belgæ, a tribe occupying one of the three great divisions of Gaul, arrived in Britain about the middle of the second century B.C. They had a reputation for bravery beyond all the other tribes of Gaul, and were a cultured race, bringing with them, no doubt, improvements of every kind; for we learn later on from Cæsar that the Celts were a stage behind their Continental kinsmen in general development, with the exception of the Belgic Britons. These Belgic Britons, like the Gauls, were not only completely dressed, but splendidly attired, and had a great affection for finery and jewellery.

We are told by Pliny (100 B.C.) that the belief that Britons of this period went about unclothed is quite wrong. It *was* the custom for warriors to take off their clothing when they took part in the fight.[1]

Cæsar (55 B.C.) tells us that " all the Celts " (meaning warriors) " stain themselves with woad, which gives them a frightful aspect in battle." They displayed their bodies tattooed in a very elaborate manner, not only in lines and curves, but in the forms of beasts and birds. But this was not the general rule in times of peace, for even the least civilised in the country went clad in skins.

COSTUME

The chief garments worn by personages of importance toward the latter part of this period were:

THE TUNIC—THE CLOAK—and THE DRAWERS.

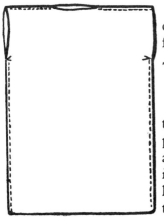

Dia. 2

These three garments are the oldest articles of dress, and the models on which successive fashions are founded.

THE TUNIC.

Called in the Celtic language " Crys."

Diagram 1 gives the first crys, formed of two skins, and its evolution is described on p. 5. It was at this time that the crys assumed the shape of a modern vest, cut as in Diagram 2 from one piece of stuff, with a hole in the middle for the head, and sewn up the sides, leaving a portion open for the arms. The portion from the neck to the outer edge formed short sleeves. Sleeves to the wrist were very general also among

[1] This practice continued among their descendants, the Scots, right up to the year 1689, for we are told that the Highlanders at the Battle of Killiecrankie stripped themselves of their plaids when they made an attack.

the Celts and other barbarian tribes. These could be joined easily to the crys at the arm opening.

As a rule the crys only descended half-way down the thigh.

THE CLOAK or SAGUM.

During the Bronze Age, the headman or chief of a tribe wore the skin of some large animal as a distinctive garment of authority. It was hung from the shoulders, and secured by tying the two front legs together: later, a bronze fibula answered the same purpose.

During the Celtic Age this cloak was called in the Celtic language " Saic," meaning a skin or hide, and Latinised by the Romans into " Sagum."

Now that the art of weaving was thoroughly understood, a piece of cloth was often used in place of a skin. It was of various shapes, square, oblong, circular, and semicircular, and was generally worn fastened on the *right* shoulder by a *fibula*. This left the right arm free for action.

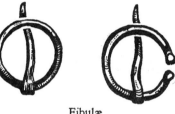

Fibulæ

For the use of the highest personages of the late Celtic Age, it was customary to line a large skin of a bear, wolf, etc., with a material of some brilliant hue.

THE DRAWERS or BRACCO.

Celtic " Bracco," Latin " Bracæ," Old French " Braies."

These drawers, or, as they will be known, the bracco, were adopted by the British Celts after their first intercourse with the Gauls of France.

When the Romans conquered Gaul in the year 121 B.C., they considered this national dress so original that they named their newly-acquired province after it—" Gallia Braccata," or " Behosed Gauls," a description they used later for all Gaulish lands.

At Rome, politically pre-eminent, and at Athens, still the intellectual centre of the world, the bracæ were looked upon with contempt as a distinctive feature of barbarism.

Material. The bracco were made of woollen and linen material, and, for hard wear and riding, of hide. At this time they were chiefly made of a coarse hemp linen, and were cut like our modern trousers (*see* Diagram 3). They had a

Dia. 3

series of holes at the waist-line, through which a thong or strap of hide was passed to gather the material in and attach them round the waist. They were fastened round the ankles also by thongs, but these were not threaded through any holes. The leg part was not very wide round, measuring from eighteen to twenty-four or thirty inches.

The bracco did not always reach up to the waist. At some periods in their history, especially when they were bound to the leg by cross-gartering, they only came to just below the knee.

Colour. The crys, sagum, and bracco were often dyed, woven or worked in stripes or squares of various colours, and sometimes both. When the crys and the bracco were decorated with stripes, these always went across or round the garment.

The Gaulish name for this decoration was " Breach " or " Brycan," from " Breac " = striped, speckled or spotted.[1]

If the sagum was of a uniform colour, it was generally of scarlet, blue or black. A favourite and characteristic colour for the garments of the Celts was " saffron," a dye of a deep orange tone made from the stigmata of the crocus.

The *hair* was always worn long, brushed back from the forehead and flowing on the shoulders.

Men of rank amongst the Celts of Britain and the Gauls of France shaved the chin, and wore immense tangled moustaches, hanging down upon their breasts like wings.

A *Celtic British chieftain* of the latter half of this epoch wore a crys descending to just above the knees, with short sleeves, or, as was more often the case, long ones reaching to the wrists, of woollen material, checkered in various colours. On his legs, if they were not bare, he

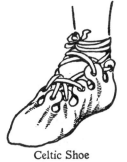

Celtic Shoe

wore the bracco, tied at the waist and at the ankles. Over his shoulders, and fastened on the right, he wore a sagum, of cloth, or the skin of some large beast—perhaps of both (*see* Fig. 7).

His *shoes* were of untanned hide with the hair inside, made in one piece, with a thong of hide to lace the edges over the instep. His *hair*, turned back on the crown of the head, was long and flowing on to his shoulders, and he wore a huge moustache upon his upper lip. The wearing of beards was not usual with persons of distinction, but was limited to old men and peasants. Round the neck he might have an *ornament* called

[1] The Gaelic " Tarstin," or " Tarsuin," meaning " across," was applied to this striped material. It is interesting to note that the word " tartan " is used to-day by the descendants of this race.

a " torque," composed of twisted gold wire, and bracelets of the same on the arms and wrists. These seem to have been worn only by chiefs, and were much prized by their Roman conquerors.[1]

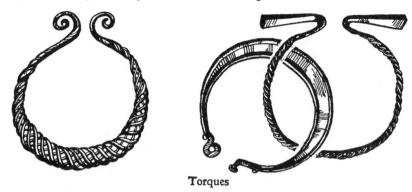

Torques

Arms and armour. As arms, offensive and defensive, formed the most important factor in the civil costume of these times, it

Fig. 8

Fig. 9

is necessary to give a few details on the subject. In addition to the garments already described, a chieftain would carry a knife and often a sword.

[1] *See* illustration of Roman general, Fig. 35.

A *chieftain* in full war-dress would wear a crys, and over it (*see* Fig. 8) a jacket of skin, with the hair outside, over which was placed the bronze breastplate. Over the shoulders a rectangular sagum of cloth was worn, fastened with a bronze fibula. His legs were bare, or, if necessary, he would wear the bracco, tied at the ankles or cross-gartered. His hair was long and flowing, and he wore long plaits on either side of the face and a moustache. A beard would be exceptional. On his head was a bronze helmet with a bronze comb to it. The sword-blade was of iron, in a leather sheath, and hung on the right side by a rope of twisted thongs over the left shoulder. He carried an oval-shaped shield of bronze, decorated in the Celtic manner, and an iron spear in the right hand.

Warriors in general would wear either the bracco and crys, the bracco and no crys, or the crys and no bracco. A belt for carrying the sword and a bronze helmet were worn, and a shield was carried.

Fig. 10   Fig. 10A

Sometimes a sagum was worn, and frequently it was the skin of an animal tied round the neck by its two legs.

A *man* of less importance would wear a costume similar to the one described in Fig. 7, but not so elaborately dyed, with less fine skins, and ornaments of polished bronze, iron, or copper instead of gold (*see* Fig. 10).

If he were hunting, he would wear the bracco cross-gartered with thongs of hide, and be naked from the waist upwards, and would carry a spear and knife only (*see* Fig. 9).

MIDDLE-CLASS MEN OF THE CELTIC AGE

Fig. 10A shows a cloth crys to the knees, with short sleeves cut as in Diagram 2. Over this is

Fibula

a rectangular striped sagum, fastened with a fibula on the right shoulder. On the legs are bracco, without cross-gartering, and shoes of coarse hide.

Fig. 10B is similar, but the crys has long sleeves, a plain rectangular sagum, and short bracco attached at the ankle and knee by thongs. His shoes are the same as described in Fig. 7. The most important feature about this man is the CAP he wears, which is fashioned on Greek lines (*see* p. 46).

Fig. 10B

Celtic Ornament

HISTORY OF THE CONQUEST OF BRITAIN BY ROME

Julius Cæsar (100–44 B.C.) invaded Britain in the year 55 B.C., but this was merely a reconnoitring visit. His second, in the summer of 54, was more formidable; and he met as his chief antagonist Cassivellaunus, a prince or chief of the important tribes of the Catuvellauni, whose stronghold was situated near the site of St. Albans. After some fighting, peace was made on condition that a yearly tribute should be paid to Rome. Cæsar then departed, and for nearly a century the Romans left Britain undisturbed.

THE YEAR  OF OUR LORD

During this period civilisation made considerable advance. Merchants from Romanised Gaul paid frequent visits to this island, bringing not only their wares, but the arts and culture of Gaul, far greater than before now that Gaul was under Roman rule.

A.D.  33

In the year A.D. 43, during the reign of the Emperor Claudius (41–54), a third invasion of Britain was made by the Roman army under Aulus Plautius. The ruling prince of Britain was Cunobelin, or Cymbeline, as Shakespeare calls him. He died about this date, and was succeeded by his son Caractacus. The stronghold of this Icenian prince was Camulodunum, identified by differing authorities with either Colchester or Maldon.

After seven or eight years' continual fighting, Camulodunum was stormed and captured, the Emperor Claudius himself being present —the fact is noteworthy as being the first occasion on which a Roman emperor set foot on our island—and forthwith a colony of Roman settlers was founded.

Roman life, with all its conveniences and luxuries, was soon established in this new Roman city. Roman temples, theatres, baths and villas quickly rose, and the famous Roman roads and bridges were constructed during this period of Roman occupation.

London (Llyn Din = the Fortress on the Lake) *Bridge* was built by them at this time. It was a wooden structure, upon solid oak and elm piles. The upper stories were burnt and rebuilt several times, but it lasted for close upon eleven centuries.

In the meantime, Caractacus had fled (A.D. 51) to the mountains of Wales, where he collected a formidable army among the descendants of the Celtic refugees who had retreated to this wild district when Julius Cæsar made his appearance on these shores. He made repeated onslaughts on the Roman garrisons, but was ultimately defeated at York, the stronghold of the Brigantes. Betrayed by his mother-in-law, Cartimandua, the chieftainess of that tribe, he was captured in the year A.D. 51 and, with his wife and family, together with many of his followers, sent prisoner to Rome.

The fame of this British hero had reached Rome, and its citizens were anxious to behold the barbarian who for so long had defied their power. A great concourse of people assembled to witness the procession of British captives led through the streets in chains to the Capitol, where the emperor, seated upon his throne with the Empress Agrippina by his side, received them.

The Praetorian Guards, Rome's crack regiment, were drawn up in line on either side, and the long train of captives, headed by the servants of the prince and the spoils, was followed by the brothers, the wife, and daughters of Caractacus, and last of all Caractacus himself, calm and undismayed by his misfortunes. The speech he addressed to the Emperor is preserved intact by the historian Tacitus, and it was so remarkable and moving that he won the favour of the Empress, who petitioned for and gained his pardon. The public life of Caractacus ended here, and he spent the remainder of his life as a peaceful Roman citizen.

We now pass on to the year A.D. 61. Meanwhile, the British people had been suffering much oppression at the hands of their Roman conquerors.

Hitherto, a woman of the ancient British or Celtic race had been but an accessory to man. From this point she takes a more prominent place in the life of the Briton, for a woman arose and became a great heroine —the would-be deliverer of her country, Boadicea—Celtic Boudicca— Chieftainess of the Iceni.

She was the widow of Prasutagus, reigning Prince of the Iceni, and with her two daughters had been subjected to the vilest outrages. It is said that she had been publicly flogged, and, in revenge, she called upon the whole Celtic population to rise against the Roman tyrants. Thousands answered her call, and after defeating the Romans in several engagements, an immense host took vengeance on the colonists at Camulodunum, slaying by the sword or by torture men, women, and children alike. The massacre spread wherever a Roman was found, and in a few days 70,000 of them perished.

The Roman general, Suetonius Paulinus, now determined on retribution, and advanced with his legions. He was met by Boadicea, riding in her war chariot at the head of a great horde of her infuriated countrymen, and a great battle ensued. Suetonius gained a decisive victory over the Britons at some unknown spot, probably not far from Camulodunum, and, after the defeat of her army, Boadicea committed suicide by poison (A.D. 62) to avoid being led captive to Rome.

Tacitus tells us that some writers state the number of Britons slain amounted to 80,000.

This event completed the conquest and firmly established Roman power in Britain. It became a province of the vast Roman Empire, under whose sway it made great progress in civilisation.

Women of the Nobility

We are fortunate in having a description of the great British chieftainess, Boadicea, as she appeared in battle, given by Dion Cassius, the Greek writer and historian.

She was very tall, grim in appearance, keen-eyed, harsh-voiced, with a wealth of exceedingly yellow hair falling below her waist, wearing a great golden collar and bracelets on her arms and wrists. She was attired in a tunica of several colours, blue, red, and yellow predominating, which hung in folds about her. A sagum was thrown over all, fastened by a fibula or brooch. This was her usual dress, and on this occasion she grasped a spear, so as to strike awe into all.

Fig. 11 (Inside front cover) is a design made after this description.

The wives of great British or Celtic chieftains wore a long robe, the GWN (Celtic "Gwn" meaning "that which is stitched"), reaching to the

Torque

Bracelet

feet, hanging straight, with or without a belt, dyed or worked like the men's crys in stripes or squares. Over this, a sagum of coarse cloth, or the skin of a large animal, was fastened on the shoulders with a fibula, brooch, or bosses of bronze, or gold and enamel.

A torque of gold was worn as a necklace, and bracelets of bronze or gold were worn on the arms.

The *hair*, parted in the middle and flowing over the shoulders, was bound by a circlet of gold and twisted wire.

Sometimes a sort of super-tunic, without sleeves and reaching to just below the knees, with a check border, would be worn over the long gwn.

Fig. 12B   Fig. 12   Fig. 12A

It was confined at the waist with a belt, fastened and ornamented with bosses of bronze or gold.

Women of less exalted rank wore the same style of dress, but of coarser cloth and less elaborately decorated. The ornaments of these women were made of bronze or iron.

MIDDLE-CLASS WOMEN OF THE CELTIC AGE

The women of what we should call the middle class wore quite simple clothes. The body garment consisted of a straight gwn, hanging from the shoulders to the feet, without sleeves, girded at the waist to keep it in place. When necessary, a rectangular sagum was draped around the shoulders, and fastened by a pin or brooch of bronze or iron (*see* Fig. 12). Long, close sleeves were or were not worn with this garment, according to individual taste. They also had little short jackets, cut square, which they wore over the long gwn. These jackets sometimes had short sleeves, reaching only to the elbow (*see* Fig. 12A).

Pin

A woman a little inferior, but not quite of the peasant class, would wear a straight garment like a skirt, fastened round the waist by a belt. Over the shoulders and round the neck was a sort of collar, or contrivance for suspending the skirt and belt (*see* Fig. 12B).

The *hair* for the most part was parted in the middle, and left to flow over the shoulders. In Gaul it was quite a general habit for women to plait their hair in two long tails, hanging either in front or behind.

When not bare-footed, the prevailing custom, the women wore shoes of untanned leather, drawn in at the ankle like those worn by the men. The wearing of the sandal was exceptional, and when worn it would have been imported from Rome.

Early in 1921, at Clermont-Ferrand, France, while digging, workmen discovered some coffins, one of which contained a beautiful woman of this period, in a complete state of preservation, with her long plaited *black* hair arranged round her head. In another was a young woman with fair hair, dressed in white linen, wearing beautifully made leather sandals on her feet. In a third lay an old woman wearing, with her own scanty locks, an artificial plait. Many other objects were found, including linen clothing, shoes and sandals, ornaments and toilet accessories.

Peasant Women of the Celtic Age

Women of the poorer class wore only a long skirt, fastened at the waist with a belt, and a bodice of skin, without sleeves, laced together with thongs of hide. The arms and legs were always bare, the former decorated by a few ornaments, such as their means would provide (*see* Fig. 13).

Fig. 13

For the most part the peasants dressed exactly as their ancestors of the Bronze Age had done—chiefly in skins, with the addition of some coarsely woven cloth.

Note.—After the final Roman conquest of Britain in the year 78 A.D., and when many Roman colonies had been established in this country, Britons of high rank became Romanised with an eagerness that led them to adopt not only Roman arts, but Roman fashions in dress.

This makes the consideration of *The History of Roman Costume* of particular importance.

THE CELTS OF IRELAND

A few words are necessary here to explain why this section is inserted before the account of Greek and Roman Costume. The reason is that the Irish Celts or Gaels were not affected seriously by events in Britain for more than thirteen centuries. Their costume, therefore, was more akin to that worn by the British Celts than to the dress of any later period, and although this note covers briefly so great a length of time, it has been thought better to insert it here than at any later juncture.

HISTORICAL INTRODUCTION

When we first hear of Ireland it is by the name of "Ierne" (pronounced "Eeirrny"). Dropping the first and last letters, we arrive at Ern, later "Erin," by which name Ireland is known to this day.

The Romans called it "Hibernia," their nearest approach to the name.

The earliest mention of Ireland is made in a Greek treatise written about 250 B.C.

The original inhabitants of Ireland were of the Iberian race, a people of low stature and swarthy complexion. The first colonists were the Phœnicians, and the Celts, during their migration from Asia, established themselves in the island. The usual intermixture of races took place, and the civilisation of the Phœnician-Celts predominated, permeating the social life, with the result that the welded races and their descendants became an ingenious, artistic, sensitive, and adventurous people.

The original language was entirely superseded by the Celtic or Gaelic tongue.

The earlier race was known to strangers as "Picts," because they stained themselves with woad. The blended race became known later as the Scots, for the same reason—"Scot" meaning the same thing, but in a different language.

Up to the time of Charles the Second of England, Ireland was known as "Scotia Major," while what we now know as Scotland went by the name of Scotia Minor. The Scots soon overflowed from the smaller island to the greater and, in Christian days, Irish missionaries spread culture into the Scotland of to-day through Saint Columba and his monks at Iona.

During the Roman and Saxon invasions of Britain in the early centuries of the Christian Era, Ireland was left undisturbed, owing to its remote and isolated position. In consequence, it retained its national independence as a Celtic kingdom, with its own institutions, laws, art, literature and costume, until it was brought under the sway of England in the reign of Henry II.

COSTUME OF THE CELTS IN IRELAND

From the Second Century B.C. to the Twelfth Century A.D.

Tacitus states that the Celts of Ireland, in their manners, customs and dress, differed but little from the Celts of Britain—a fact also confirmed by a writer [1] of the twelfth century.

An Irish epic of the latter part of the first century B.C. gives minute

[1] Giraldus Cambrensis.

details of the costume worn by warriors of a certain king of Louth named Cormac or Conaire. The *Táin Deirdre* and the *Táin Bó Cúalnge*, both ancient Irish poems dating between 30 B.C. and A.D. 39, give many particulars of civil dress.

They wore the crys of various lengths, some only reaching to the knee, some to the calf, and others to the ankle, and shaped as shown in Diagram 2. To the crys, long sleeves, a barbaric feature, could be added.

The characteristic garment of the Celts—the bracco—made of linen, was in use until the twelfth century, worn as already described. Another kind of leg-covering was the tight-fitting drawers, fastened by a strap under the foot, and belted at the waist. These garments were often decorated with spots and stripes or chequered in the same manner as the bracco.

It was a very usual practice with the Irish Celts to wear, instead of the bracco, a piece of cloth wrapped around the hips and thighs, and belted at the waist. This garment was called by them the "kelt," and is the original form of the *kilt*. A similar garment was worn by the Greek peasants (*see* p. 46), and by the Romans (*see* Subligaculum, p. 72).

With the kelt in times of peace, lengths of cloth or soft leather were worn bound round the lower part of the leg, and tied at the ankle and knee, leaving the latter bare. In times of war the legs were bare.

Belts of leather, ornamented with bronze, silver, or gold, were worn about the waist, and from them swords were hung.

Irish Celt

The sagum, in all the varieties already described, was in general use. Green, blue, purple, saffron "fairly bedizened," and "many coloured," often chequered, "composed of small pieces of cloth of different colours sewn together"—patchwork! They were also striped across or at angles, and sometimes spotted. Small cloaks of a semicircular shape were worn, closely enveloping the figure. The various cloaks were fastened on the right shoulder, or in front, by fibulæ, chiefly the penannular shape, of gold, silver, or bronze, much ornamented and set with stones. Loops and strings took the place of fibulæ at times. The lower classes used this means of fastening their cloaks. Smaller cloaks, nothing more than capes, were used with or without an attached hood shaped like a square bag.

The only other head-covering, worn occasionally, appears to have been a high conical hat without a brim.

The *materials* from which the Irish Celts made their garments were home-spun linen and a woollen fabric equivalent to serge, in various thicknesses. The most important and wealthy people sometimes used silk.[1] The furs of large or small animals (the seal, otter, badger, fox), sewn together, were used for the sagum, and also for the trimming of other garments.

The *decoration* of garments consisted of borders of Celtic design, appliquéd, worked, or woven, and often the garments of the rich were intermingled with threads of gold and silver. The women made a speciality of needlework and embroidery.

The Irish Celts were very fond of bright *colours* and they had great practical knowledge of the art of dyeing. Crimson, blue, purple and saffron were the colours most used. The several articles of dress were usually coloured differently, and the rank and position of the wearer was denoted by the number of different colours in his dress.

The wealthy Celts of Ireland wore *shoes*, called "brogs," of tanned hide, similar to those worn by the Celts of Britain, but of better workmanship, and frequently ornamented with cut leather. They even had a sole attached to them. People of the lower orders (unless they went bare-footed, which was often the case) had brogs of untanned hide, laced about with thongs, precisely as shown in the drawing on p. 12.

The *hair* of both men and women was worn long and flowing on the shoulders, often very elaborately curled and sometimes braided in long plaits. Exceedingly long hair on a woman was considered the height of beauty. In some poems of this period the hair of the men is described as being dressed in "hooks and plaits and swordlets."

In time of war many of the warriors wore their hair shorn. In colour it was "fair yellow," "deep golden," etc., typical of the Celtic race. Black hair was a proof that the wearer was descended from the Iberian aborigines.

Beards were worn bushy, long or forked, and some were trimmed square, a fashion of great antiquity among the Irish Celts, dating back to the time previous to their ancestors' migration from the East.

The moustache varied in length, according to the rank of the wearer. They were sometimes worn curled up and pointed at the ends.

Men and women of position frequently wore gold ornamental balls fixed to the ends of the hair. These balls varied in size from two to four inches in diameter, and were worn singly or in pairs, one each side of the face. They often enclosed the ends of the long plaits of hair.

The art of making-up the face was much indulged in by the Irish Celtic ladies—another habit acquired by them when in the East. They pencilled their eyebrows and eyelashes with black, and they coloured their cheeks with the red juice of the alderberry. Like Oriental women

[1] Unusual at so early a date. Its occasional use shows how advanced in culture and commerce these people were.

of very early and modern times, they had great admiration for finger-nails stained a deep crimson.

> I shall no more sleep, and I shall not crimson my nails.
> *The Lament for Usna.*

JEWELLERY

The jewellery of the Irish Celts was of considerable merit, com-bining excellent workmanship with beauty of design. Celtic ornament is characterised chiefly by the particular type of pattern known as "vermiculate," or interlaced. This was an intricate plaiting, twisting and knotting of one or more different-coloured, yet sometimes mono-chrome, bands, interwoven so as to cover the entire surface with a symmetrically disposed design. Two other features predominate in Celtic ornament—the spiral and the use of contorted and fantastic figures of human beings and animals.

Early chieftains and later kings wore an ornamental gold band or fillet as a diadem.

Personal ornaments worn by the wealthy comprised necklaces, ear-rings, bracelets, torques, fibulæ, brooches, rings, buckles and pins. They were of elaborate design and set with precious stones and polished pebbles. Ornamental pins or bodkins were used for fastening garments, as well as for ladies' hair. It was the custom for men of position to wear in their ears not only rings of gold, but frequently a large single pearl.

WEAPONS

Swords like those seen in Figs. 8, 9 and 10 were either slung across the shoulders by a strap, or hung from the waist-belt. Their hilts were of bronze, gold, or silver, and the guards of the same metal. "Swords they had, with round hilts of gold, and silver fist-guards."

Shields were either long or circular, shaped and carried after the manner seen in Figs. 8 and 9. They were made of wood, covered with leather secured with metal ornaments, or sometimes entirely covered with "shining" metal, with sharp edges.

Metal spear-heads ("grey," some "five-pronged") mounted on "slender-shafts" of great length were carried by the rank and file of the troops as they marched; "together they raised their feet, and to-gether they set them down again," like the measured tread of a regiment of to-day: an illuminating touch at variance with the common mis-conception that these people were a race of undisciplined barbarians.

LIST OF AUTHORITIES CONSULTED FOR CHAPTER I

Herodotus
Pliny
Caius Julius Cæsar
Diodorus
Strabo
O. M. Edwards
F. W. Fairholt
Oscar Fraas
Arthur Hassall

Reginald Hughes
Prof. Huxley
P. W. Joyce
Patrick Kirwan
Dr. J. C. Mahaffy
Prof. Oman
J. R. Planche
Prof. Johannes Ranke
H. G. Wells

CHAPTER II

CLASSIC GREECE, 600–146 B.C.

Greek Costume of the Classic Period exercised a great influence on Roman Costume, which in a large measure was based upon and copied from it.

The History of Roman Costume is therefore prefaced by the History of Greek Costume of the Classic Period.

The period of Greek civilisation called "The Classic"[1] is subdivided into three distinct periods:

The Archaic Age, 600–468 B.C. Including the Persian Wars.

The Age of Pericles, and the period of the Peloponnesian Wars, 468–404 B.C.

The Alexandrian Age, 338–220 B.C. Down to the fall of Greek independence (146 B.C.), including The Hellenistic Age, 330–146 B.C.

HISTORICAL INTRODUCTION, 600–146 B.C.

600 B.C. THE ARCHAIC AGE [2]

This date marks the rise of Greek civilisation and art.

The *Ionians* settled in Attica at the beginning of this period, and developed an individual art of their own. At the time, the dominant race was the *Dorians*, who had been established in Attica for two centuries.

The beginning of the fifth century saw the commencement of the Persian Wars.

In 490 Darius I. (521–483), King of the Medes and Persians, invaded the Peloponnesus with a large fleet, which was wrecked in a storm off Athos. A second attempt followed, and the enormous hosts of Darius landed at Marathon in Attica and made the first attack upon the Greeks, in which the Persians were hopelessly defeated.

481. The next invasion was conducted by Xerxes (485–465), son of Darius, who mustered a great army for that purpose.

480. Xerxes reached the Hellespont, and received submission from the Northern Greeks. The Greek army was defeated at the Pass of Thermopylae, and Xerxes occupied Athens. The Greeks won the most decisive victory known in history over the Persian fleet, off the Island of Salamis, and Xerxes retired.

479. Mardonius occupied Athens. On each occasion the city was sacked, and the temples and statues of the Acropolis were razed and burnt.

The Greeks gained a land battle at Platæa, and on the same day the Persian fleet suffered another defeat at Mycale.

477. When the Athenians regained possession of their city, they buried what remained of the statues in the Acropolis.

After renewed attacks upon the Greeks, ending in the battle of Eurymedon, 468, the Persians finally withdrew.

Æsop, the fabulist, and Æschylus (525–456), the father of Greek tragedy, lived during this Age.

---

[1] It must be borne in mind that Greek chronology is ever changing according to investigations carried out by archæologists of the day.

[2] The term "Archaic," meaning beginning or preliminary, must not be confused with "Archæan," being the name of a people inhabiting Achaia, situated north of Argos. They are the Heros of Homer.

26

463–431 B.C. THE AGE OF PERICLES

It is also called the Golden Age of Pericles, the most distinguished of Athenian states-men. Athens became the centre of Western civilisation, art and culture, and fostered the fullest and most perfect development of Classic Greek Art.

431–404 B.C. The three Peloponnesian Wars occurred between these years.

HERODOTUS (443), the historian; ARISTOPHANES (427), the only writer of Greek comedy; EURIPIDES (480–406) and SOPHOCLES (495–405), tragic poets; SOCRATES (469–399) and PLATO (429–347), philosophers; XENOPHON (443–359), the author; and LYSIPPUS (325), sculptor and bronze worker, are some of the learned men of the period.

338–146 B.C. THE ALEXANDRIAN AGE

Also spoken of as the HELLENISTIC AGE, 330–146 B.C., is the third subdivision, named after the great Macedonian king.

In the year 338 Philip of Macedon brought the Greek States under his sway, and his son Alexander succeeded him in 336 B.C. Two years afterwards, Alexander undertook his expedition against Darius III. (336–330), King of Persia. Alexander crossed the Hellespont, and after the battle of Granicus, captured Halicarnassus. It was here that the famous cutting of the Gordian Knot occurred.

He met Darius in 333 on the plains of Issus, and defeated him with great slaughter. He subdued Phœnicia 332, took Tyre and Gaza, and afterwards freed Egypt from the Persian yoke.

In 331 he founded the city called after him—Alexandria—which contained the most wonderful library of antiquity. His general and favourite Ptolemaios became the first of the Ptolemaic dynasty, who ruled Egypt until the death of Cleopatra VII. in 31 B.C.

A renewed attack was made on Persia 330, and the title of King of Persia was assumed by Alexander in 329.

The invasion of India commenced in the year 327. While residing at Babylon, he was attacked by fever, from which he died in 323. His sarcophagus at Sidon, now at Constantinople, was executed about 300 B.C.

The Gauls from the West raided Macedonia and Greece in the year 277 and afterwards crossed into Asia Minor, settling themselves in Phrygia. These Gauls became known as the Galatians, to whom St. Paul wrote his Epistle.

The Romans were the next oppressors of the Greek States, and the fall of Corinth in 146 marks the end of Greek independence.

This city of art and culture was destroyed by Lucius Mummius, who sent to Rome, as part of the spoil, the first fine paintings ever seen there. Some Greek cities, however, continued to be nominally free. These included Athens and Pergamum, the chief city of a Greek colony in Mysia, Asia Minor, and the most civilised State in the world at that time—a city possessing among other treasures of art and literature, a library second only to that of Alexandria. At his death, its king, Attalas III. (138–133), bequeathed the State to Rome.

ARISTOTLE (384–322), philosopher and tutor to Alexander the Great; DEMOSTHENES (385–322), the greatest orator of anitiquity; PYTHEAS, the explorer (330), APELLES (352–308), the most famous painter of antiquity; EPICURUS (342–272), the philosopher; ARCHIMEDES (287–212), the mathematician; POLYBIUS (204–122), statesman and historian; and POSIDONIUS (130), are among the many great men who distinguish this time.

To the Western civilised world, Athens was the centre of fashion from 500 to 146 B.C.

Fig. 13A.   (For description see p. 47)

GREEK COSTUME OF THE CLASSIC PERIOD

600–146 B.C.

THE art of the Greeks of this period is renowned for its great beauty and elegance. They were a nation of intellectual artists, and brought their art to such a high standard of perfection that it has never been surpassed.

As a race, their appreciation of truth was intense, and their art expressed a logical simplicity consequent upon that guiding enthusiasm, beautiful effects being attained by the simplest methods.

The costume of these people consisted practically of only two garments for men and women alike—nothing more than rectangular pieces of material—but the manner of wearing them required care, management and perfect taste.

These garments were called by the Greeks:

THE CHITON ($\chi\iota\tau\acute{\omega}\nu$) and THE HIMATION ($\acute{\iota}\mu\acute{\alpha}\tau\iota o\nu$), but are commonly known to us as "The Tunic" and "The Mantle."

The last six centuries B.C. *and* the nineteenth and twentieth centuries A.D. share a distinction in the history of costume, as being the only periods in which women have dominated the fashions.

By virtue of this fact, the costume of Greek women has first place in this section.

COSTUME OF THE WOMEN OF THE CLASSIC PERIOD, 600–146 B.C.

The Ionic Chiton, 600 B.C.–A.D. 200

The most important garment among women was the chiton. It continued in general use, with but slight modifications, from the sixth century B.C. until about the second century A.D., when Greek national traditions were submerged.

28

The advent of the chiton. The Semitic root from which the word "chiton" is derived signifies "a linen garment," and there is no doubt that the chiton came in the first instance from Babylon, that city of considered luxury and idle fashion, as the short and long chiton appear on many of the very oldest Assyrian bas-reliefs. From thence it probably passed on to the Asiatic coast of the Ægean Sea, and so on to Caria, the ancient name for Ionia and the Ionian Isles. Halicarnassus was the chief centre of Ionia, and the birthplace of Herodotus (484–408 B.C.) and Dionysius,[1] the historians.

Herodotus tells us that as a result of constant intercourse with the inhabitants of the Ionian Isles, the Athenians were led to adopt the Ionic chiton.[2]

As a matter of fact, the women were compelled by law to change

Pin

Fig. 14

their attire, as it was found that the large pins by which the earlier "peplos"[3] was fastened proved dangerous weapons in the hands of infuriated women, whereas the Ionic chiton generally required no pins.

---

[1] Flourished during the first century B.C.

[2] It was not called by this name until the fifth century B.C. Herodotus uses ἐσθής.

[3] The peplos was the chief garment of the Achæan women of the early Archaic Period (circa 1200–600 B.C.). In shape it was a rectangular piece of material, often heavily embroidered and consequently of a solid texture. It was put on in the manner described under the Doric chiton, p. 33, but being made of more substantial stuff it was wrapped tightly round the figure *without* folds, girded at the waist and open up one side, the top part falling back over the chest and back. It was fastened on the shoulders, and often down the side, by large pins (see p. 35).

Fig. 14 shows the Ionic chiton, which differed from the peplos in shape, its method of fastening, and in the material used.

Material. It was always made of linen or cotton of various textures.

How to wear it. The usual way of arranging the chiton on the neck and shoulders was to bring the back and front edges together on the shoulders, slightly gathering or pleating them, and fastening them with a clasp or brooch. For spacing the front portion between the shoulders, about two or three inches more than at the back was allowed. This gave the line of fall over the edge (*see* Figs. 14 and 17) so characteristic of the arrangement of Greek dress.

Sleeves were formed by clasping the edges together in gathers at intervals along the arm, the hands passing through the space left at the *top* of the corner. This top edge was often

Girdle encircling the waist ornamented by a narrow band of embroidery.

The *clasps* or brooches used were discs of ornamented metal, with pins attached underneath. At a later date, buttons were used instead of clasps, and occasionally the two edges of the shoulder part were gathered and sewn together.

The shape of the Ionic chiton. In its simplest form it was an oblong piece of linen, varying in width according to the texture of the material. If very fine and soft, the width H–G was twice the whole distance from finger-tip to finger-tip when the arms were extended horizontally. If the material was thicker in substance, the distance was about double that from elbow

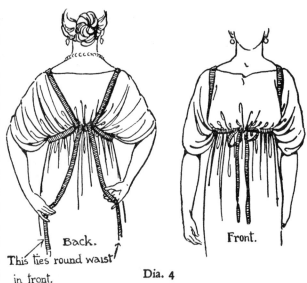

Back.

This ties round waist in front.

Front.

Dia. 4

to elbow. In either case, the length A–H, F–G from shoulder to feet was always longer than the height of the wearer, to allow for the superfluous length being drawn up through the girdle.

An ornamental band was either woven or worked along the top

edge A–F, and this edge was gathered and clasped between the distances B–C and D–E, leaving an opening for the head in the centre C–D, and openings at both ends A–B and E–F for the hands to pass through.

The girdle. The fulness was held close to the figure in **three** different ways.

Three ways of wearing it

1. By a girdle encircling the waist.

2. By a band or ribbon encircling the waist and arms, over the shoulders and tied in front (*see* Diagram 4).

3. By a band or ribbon encircling the waist and crossing the chest and back (*see* Diagram 5).

Whichever of these methods was adopted, it was necessary to draw up a certain amount of the material through the belt, to raise it from the ground, and this formed a bulge or *kolpos*, κόλπος as it was called by the Greeks.

But the material still trailed on the ground at the sides, so a larger quantity of the material was drawn through the girdle at the sides, to make the skirt level at the front, and this produced the curved line of the bulge or kolpos across the hips.

At the back, the material was not always pulled through the girdle to form the kolpos. It was allowed to trail upon the ground as a train.

Dia. 5. Front
(Back same as Dia. 4)

When less material was used in the width of the chiton, the kolpos was less pronounced, and took a more horizontal line.

Hip girdle. When the skirt part of the chiton was required to be shortened, to give freer action in walking or running, the ends of the band or ribbon, after they had been tied at the waist, were brought round the hips also, and through them the material was drawn and raised up.

The Crinkled Ionic Chiton

The top part. The crinkled Ionic chiton (*see* Fig. 15) was shaped like the original garment, but made of even thinner material, almost transparent, for the limbs could be seen through it. It was necessarily thinner, as more material was required in its width.

It is seen on statues, the top part being crinkled in some way, in zig-zag or wavy lines, to about the hip level, where it is turned under and secured by an invisible waist-belt.[1] It was fastened by buttons or clasps, or sewn as described earlier, to form sleeves.

[1] It has the appearance of a jacket. This originated the knitted jumper of to-day.

The skirt part was *not* crinkled, but, being very full, it hung in many flat folds, which gave a zig-zag effect at the bottom edge.

The whole garment was evidently cut much longer than was convenient, and was always raised by an invisible belt or cord at the waist, giving the turned-under effect just mentioned. The fold-over edge made a line just above the hips (*see* Fig. 15); in some instances horizontally, in others curving upwards at the centre, this being due to more material being pulled through the belt at the sides to make the skirt hem even.

The girdle. The pleats or folds of the skirt were regulated by means of a girdle, and often, especially when the curved lines across the hips were adopted, the folds of the skirt were concentrated in a heavy mass in the centre between the legs, forming a cascade down the front, and leaving the material at the sides to follow the contour of the limbs (*see* Fig. 16).[1]

Fig. 15 shows the crinkled chiton, girded under the arms as well as by an independent waist-belt, invisible under the crinkled part, which gives the appearance of a modern jumper. This figure is wearing the hair dressed in the fashion of the fourth and third centuries B.C.

It was the vogue to hold the centre of the skirt, *with* the end of the girdle, in the left hand, draping it across the knees (*see* Bronze Statue, British Museum, Ped. 2).

The girdle was a very important part of Greek women's attire, and is often mentioned in Classic literature. The different ways of wearing it are seen in Diagrams 4 and 5 and Figs. 15, 16, 17, 18 and 19; but, as worn with the crinkled chiton, it was either an invisible cord [2] or an elaborately ornamented belt, fastened at the waist in front, the long end descending the skirt, in the centre of the cascade, to the feet (*see* Fig. 19).

The Doric Chiton, 550 B.C. (*circa*)–A.D. 100

About the same time, or shortly after the introduction of the Ionic chiton, a variation of the peplos [3] was adapted under the name of the

[1] There is a good deal of doubt regarding the authority for the foregoing description of the crinkled chiton. Some authorities consider that the wavy or zig-zag lines were but the artist's conventional way of treating different textures on various surfaces.

[2] *See* Kylix by Euphronios, British Museum, E. 44.

[3] The peplos, a garment of the previous age (see p. 29).

Fig. 16 wears the chiton, crinkled at the top, but not to so great a depth as that shown in Fig. 15. The top edges are brooched on the upper arms to form the sleeves. The plain skirt has most of the fulness drawn to the front, and hitched up to the waist-belt, forming a cascade down the centre. A simple cord encircles the waist. The head-dress is a reproduction of that shown in Fig. 23B. She is holding a distaff and spindle.

Doric chiton. It was worn simultaneously with the Ionic chiton, even to the end of the first century A.D., as may be seen on many vase paintings and pieces of sculpture.

It was made of fine woollen *material* and woven complete in itself (*see* Diagram 6).

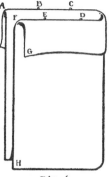

Dia. 6.

The shape of the Doric chiton. The dimensions of the Doric chiton were as follows. The width A–B–C–D–E–F was about twice the distance from elbow to elbow, when the wearer's arms were held out horizontally. The length G–F–H was about twelve to fifteen inches more than the wearer's height, taken from the point where the neck meets the shoulder. The additional inches F–G were utilised by folding over the upper edge so that the material was double from the neck to about the waist.

How to wear it. It was put on in much the same way as the old-fashioned peplos, by folding it round the body; but the garment was more ample and made of softer, thinner material than the peplos, with the result that it hung in a broken surface of folds.

The Doric chiton was fastened on the shoulders with brooches at

Girdle over Doric Chiton with deep over-fold.

the points B–E and C–D, the back portion being brought over on to the front, which made four thicknesses of stuff where the brooches were inserted. The same method of making a small pleat was adopted here as with the Ionic chiton, and similarly the front portion between the brooches was a few inches wider (*see* p. 30). It was usually girded at the waist, any superfluous material being drawn up through the girdle and falling over it in a bulge or kolpos. The amount of material so raised depended entirely on the length of the skirt required. The curved line of the kolpos, described under the Ionic chiton, became more pronounced in the Doric. At first this garment was generally left open down one side, usually the right.

It was worn precisely as described, especially in the province of Laconia (Sparta), and sculpture shows it so worn, but it was considered

Fig. 17 represents the Doric chiton, in fashion from about 500 B.C. to A.D. 300. It is girded, and shows the curved kolpos. The open side is caught at the knee. The hair and head-dress are of the fifth century, and a sunshade is carried. A thin scarf is draped over the arms—a usual accessory. The ornamental design is one of the fifth century B.C.

indecent by the rest of the inhabitants of Peloponnesus, more especially
if ungirded, and many scathing remarks about this method occur in
literature of the time. The general practice was to gird it at the waist-line
and fasten it together with brooches down the side (*see* Fig. 17). At a later
date the open side was sewn up; the garment then assumed the shape of
a cylinder, open top and bottom. It was more usual, however, to seam
up the side from the bottom edge to just below the armpits.

Another manner of wearing the Doric chiton was to make the
over-fold considerably deeper, reaching to about the thigh. The girdle
was then worn *over* it at the waist level, and this arrangement produced
some very beautiful zig-zag lines on both hips.[1]

The Doric or Ionic chiton was often the only garment worn; at other
times the Doric would be worn over an under-garment shaped like the
Ionic; and in like manner the Ionic would be worn over one or even
two under-garments shaped like the Ionic, only less ample.

The corset. Practical experiments prove beyond question, besides
sufficient evidence of the fact (*see* Cestus Fascia, στρόφιον), that in
many cases Greek women found it necessary to wear next to their skin
a fairly tight-fitting broad body-wrap, bandage, or corset, of linen,
wool or a soft skin (probably kid), from below the armpits, and level
with the breast, to about the hips. Besides supporting the figure, it gave
a foundation on which to arrange the chiton with security. Shoulder-
straps were attached to it for fixing the girdle on the shoulders.

It was evidently a habit, among extravagant women of these times,
to wear many other garments in addition to an outer one; for in the
year 594 B.C. Solon introduced a sumptuary law whereby women's
dress was limited to three garments.

The Himation, 600–146 B.C.[2]

From this time onward another garment, distinct in itself, came into
general use, and remained until the end of the Classic Greek Period.
This was the himation (*see* Fig. 18), an essential part of a Greek woman's
costume, and indispensable with the Ionic chiton. It was often worn in
the house, and always out of doors. In shape it resembled a shawl, and
was an oblong piece of woollen or linen material, twelve to fifteen
feet long, and in breadth about equal to the height of the wearer.

[1] This arrangement of the Doric chiton is often seen on statues and paintings of Greek
goddesses. The shoulders and breast part were usually surmounted by the "Ægis," a sort
of scaled cape-cuirass. Athena is generally represented wearing it (*see* Fig. 17A, page x).
[2] Used later in Rome: see "Palla."
Fig. 18 represents ladies of the fourth, third, second, and first centuries B.C., and also
the type of dress adopted by Roman ladies of the same period and the first, second, and
third centuries A.D.
The top border is of the fourth century B.C.

FIG. 16. A WOMAN OF THE PEOPLE, FIFTH CENTURY, B.C.
(*see* p. 32)

FIG. 18. THE HIMATION. A GARMENT WORN IN GREECE AND ROME
BETWEEN 550 B.C. AND 300 A.D.
(*see* p. 34)

Seven ways of wearing it

It was possible to wear it in at least seven different ways:

1. As a head-covering and cloak combined.

2. As a cloak only.

3. It was worn over the shoulders, with the ends hanging down symmetrically, one on each side of the figure.

4. Another way was to draw one end over the left shoulder, from the back towards the front, so that it hung down in a point in front; then the mass of the material was passed across the back, under the right arm, and the other end thrown over the left shoulder again, so that the second point hung down at the back.

5. Yet another way of wearing this garment was to drape it, as before, over the left shoulder, but instead of throwing the remaining part over the left shoulder a second time, this end was carried on the bent forearm, as shown in Fig. 18.

6. The fourth method described was repeated until the mass of material passed under the right arm, and the top corner of the front portion of the himation was then tucked into the girdle on the left-hand side.

7. A development of the fourth method by which the left shoulder, the left arm, and very often the entire hand was enveloped in the portion flung across the left shoulder (*see* Tanagra Statuette, 295, British Museum).

Methods five and six gave very beautiful centrifugal lines of drapery around the right hip and leg, especially when the wearer stood with her weight on the left leg.

The himation was worn, in the manner indicated in the third method, over the crinkled chiton (*see* Fig. 671, the Acropolis Museum).

The prevailing fashion of wearing the himation during the *sixth and fifth centuries* is described in No. 4; that of the *fourth, third and second centuries* in No. 7.

5th cent.

The *decoration* of the himation was very varied. At first (*sixth century*), it had a border of a different colour, being woven all in one piece with the border in it. Borders were also worked in various designs (*see* Fig. 18).

Between 500 *and* 450 B.C. an himation is met with (*see* Vase E. 140,

British Museum), elaborately embroidered all over in a series of ornamental bands, and between each band and the next is a procession of
figures of men, beasts and birds.

Other examples show the whole surface powdered diaper fashion
with spots, sprigs, squares, circles, and all manner of devices, as well as
surrounded by a border.

7th cent.   6th cent.   5th cent.

During the *fourth century* B.C., the himation became stronger in
colour, and for a while it was left plain.

The Narrow Himation, 600–468 B.C.

A curious decorative garment or drapery was worn by noble ladies
of Athens at the beginning of this period. It was of Ionic origin, and
sometimes worn over the chiton of the same name, but it was more
usual to wear it over the crinkled chiton (*see* Fig. 19). The cut or shape of
this drapery—called the narrow himation—has caused much controversy, on account of its intricate folds and arrangement as displayed
on statues of the time—the Archaic Period (*see* statues at the Acropolis). It became obsolete after 468 B.C.

7th cent.   7th cent.

7th cent.

A considered suggestion as to its possible shape is given in Diagram 7,
taking it to be a separate garment—*not*, as some authorities suggest,
in one piece with the part of the dress that envelops the legs.

Fig. 19. An Athenian Lady of Fashion during the period between 600–468 B.C. She
wears the narrow himation over the crinkled chiton. The folds of the skirt part are gathered
together at the centre of the waist, from thence forming a cascade to the feet, the end of the
girdle hanging in the middle. The hair is dressed in the style of the Archaic Age, and the
stephane in its primitive form is worn over it.

How it was made. In Diagram 7, A–B–C–D–E–L–K–J represents the front portion. This is duplicated at the back, A–I–H–G–F–L–K–J. The edges of E–L—L–F are folded over, and the double material pleated into a band which passes from the left hip, or waist, over the bust and on to the right shoulder. From thence it passes across the back and on to the left hip again.

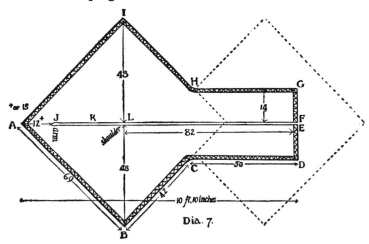

Dia. 7.

Point B hangs down at the right side in a line with the right armpit and shoulder; I hangs in the same way at the back. The portion L–K is also pleated on to the right shoulder, and K–J is buttoned to the corresponding portion at the back. This covers the upper part of the right arm; the forearm and hand passing through the loop at J.

When this is placed on the figure it will be found that the pleats or folds are formed at slightly varying angles. These should be fixed when on the figure, and pressed when the garment is taken off.

Two other ways of wearing it. The arrangement of the drapery could be reversed from the right shoulder and left hip to the left shoulder and right hip. Many examples show it so worn. Examples are also known where the long pointed part B, seen on the right side of Fig. 19, is repeated on the left side.[1]

THE VEIL OF CLASSIC GREECE

In the early Archaic Period (*circa* 1200–600 B.C.), when women's chief article of clothing was the peplos, an indispensable garment for

---

[1] Taking into consideration the very simple geometric cut of the garments of the Greeks, and costume in general of all peoples of early civilisations, I believe that this last arrangement was the first in use. My belief is that in order to achieve this particular arrangement— the point B worn on both sides of the figure—the material was cut in two squares, and joined together a little way across their two points, divided diagonally, and pleated into a neck-band as described above: see dotted line on Diagram 7.

It may have been found inconvenient to have both arms thus enveloped, so one square was dispensed with, and a small piece added, reducing it to the plan of Diagram 7.

outdoor use was the VEIL (κρήδεμνον), made usually of heavy cloth and used over the peplos. It was often folded corner-wise and some-times drawn over the head. That it was also made of linen of fine texture is proved by references to it in Homer (*Iliad*, III. 141). It was not only used as a head-covering, but was also drawn across the face when so desired.

The veil was superseded early in the Classic Period by the himation, its ampler lineal descendant; but reappears occasionally in a filmy linen version, of much smaller dimensions, as a head-covering (*see* the figure in illustration at the head of this chapter, p. 28), or as a scarf worn in the manner of the early nineteenth century (*see* Fig. 17).

The Alexandrian Age, 338–146 B.C.

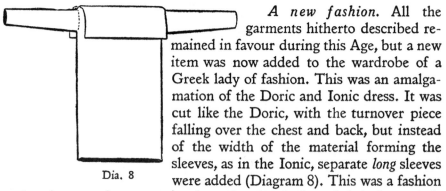

Dia. 8

A new fashion. All the garments hitherto described re-mained in favour during this Age, but a new item was now added to the wardrobe of a Greek lady of fashion. This was an amalga-mation of the Doric and Ionic dress. It was cut like the Doric, with the turnover piece falling over the chest and back, but instead of the width of the material forming the sleeves, as in the Ionic, separate *long* sleeves were added (Diagram 8). This was a fashion set by the men (an exceptional case), who had copied it from their Persian adversaries (*see* p. 44), but it does not seem to have enjoyed a very great or lasting vogue.

Hairdressing and Head-dresses, 600–146 B.C.

The Archaic Age, 600–468 B.C.

Hair dressed with a wave on the temples was the most important feature of hairdressing at the beginning of this period, and during the first two centuries the elaborate stiff waving had the effect of a scalloped edge (*see* Fig. 20).

On top of these waves, a series of stiff curls, pointing downwards, was often arranged.

Another style in vogue at the same time was the dressing of the front hair to form a coronet of circular curls, all round the head from ear to ear (*see* Fig. 21). The side ringlets, "braided tresses," were still retained, coming from behind the ears, and brought forward on to the shoulders, and the back portion (*see* Fig. 20) was allowed to hang down behind in waves or ringlets. Above this was tied a band, or fillet, of ribbon or

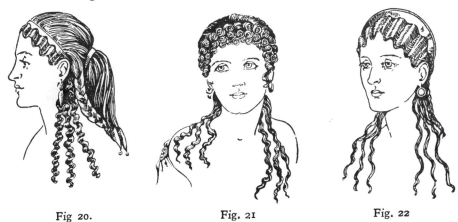

Fig 20.   Fig. 21   Fig. 22

metal, also encircling the head behind the row of waves or curls. Late in the sixth century the fillet became a little wider in the band, and was more upstanding on the head, forming a coronet that was often richly ornamented (*see* Fig. 22), and this was the early form of the stephane.

The Age of Pericles and down to the year 338 B.C.

Women's hair during this period was dressed in a great variety of ways, generally combined with a head-dress. Side ringlets were discarded altogether as being too Oriental in character, and the fashion was to bind the hair with a piece of gold or ribbon several times round the head, with the long ends of hair dressed in a knot on the crown. Strings of beads or pearls were used in the same way (*see* Fig. 23C). The hair being dressed in a knot (Fig. 23E) it was usual to tie a small kerchief, folded corner-wise, the wide part round the back of the head *underneath* the knot, with the narrowing points tied in front above the forehead.

Fig. 23D shows another arrangement of the kerchief. It is encircled by a small wreath.

The stephane. The upstanding head-band worn in the previous period now took the shape of an inverted crescent, the wide part standing up in front and the two points tied or fastened together at the nape of the neck. This coronet was called the stephane, and was beautifully decorated (*see* Figs. 17 and 23B, and section Jewellery, p. 61).

It is frequently seen on statues of this and later periods. It continued in favour with noble ladies, both Greek and Roman, throughout the pre-Christian centuries, and up to the end of the Roman Empire in the West.

In Fig. 15 the hair is worn dressed in the special and characteristic style of the late fifth, fourth and third centuries; that is, *far back on the head*. This figure has a head-dress of two shaped pieces of embroidered material, the front piece forming the stephane, and the shaped piece at the back being a development of the kerchief. A

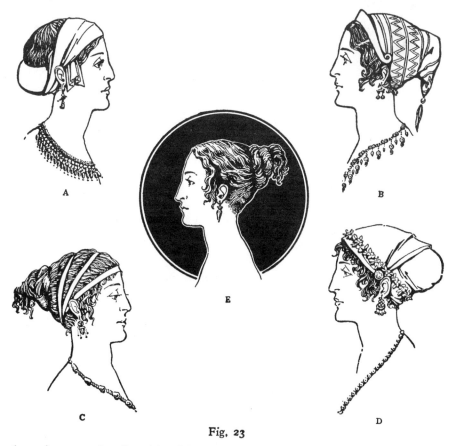

Fig. 23

shaped network of gold, either plain or set with jewels, often took the place of the back portion, being worn in addition to the stephane proper.

A cap. Fig. 23B has the same line, accentuated by a head-dress in the shape of an embroidered bag, with a small stephane placed in front of it (*see also* Fig. 16).

Fig. 23A wears a *scarf* arranged to cover the back of the hair with its central portion; the scarf is then wound round the head, crossing itself on the top of the forehead; it is crossed again at the nape of the neck, and the ends are tucked through the folds and just appear in front of the ears.

Fig. 17 has the stephane, with a small scarf tied round the head behind it, the end falling on the left side.

The Alexandrian Age and down to the year 146 B.C.

After 338 B.C. the hair was usually waved off the temples, and dressed in a knot at the back, giving the head a less decided length.

Any of the head-dresses described under the previous period could be worn at this time, but Fig. 18 shows the most fashionable style.

Hairpins. It now became the custom for ladies to wear in their hair a few of the ornamental pins described under Jewellery on p. 63.

It was the general rule during all this period, from 600 to 146 B.C., for *young girls* to wear their hair flowing, and kept close to the head by a ribbon, a simple fillet, or a garland of flowers.

The fan, which was used by the Assyrians, Egyptians and Persians, was adopted by Greek ladies, and came into general use after the fifth century B.C.

At first the fans were made of leaves, then of feathers, and the wings of birds. Later, they were made of linen, and, after the second century B.C., of silk, over a frame modelled on the leaf shape, but always rigid with a handle (*see* Fig. 18). Large fans attached to long handles were carried by slaves in the retinue of nobles.

The sunshade was in use in Assyria, Egypt and Persia long before the idea was copied by the Greeks, after the beginning of the seventh century B.C. It was carried for the most part by women, and never by men, except dandies who sometimes used it.

In shape the sunshades were similar to those in use at the present day, not quite so concave, but more like the flat Japanese style. They were made of linen and afterwards (first century B.C.) of silk, generally green in colour, on a framework of ribs, and could be closed up (*see* Fig. 17). When out of doors, the nobility of both sexes were shaded by a sunshade on a long handle, carried by a slave.

COSTUME OF THE MEN OF THE CLASSIC PERIOD
600–146 B.C.

The Chiton

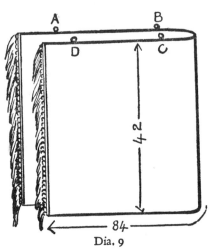

Dia. 9

The early chiton. At the beginning of the sixth century B.C. men followed the example of the women by adopting the Ionic chiton for general use. The masculine variety was a shortened version of the original worn by the women, and reached to just above the knees. In its early stage (sixth century B.C.) it was no more than a rectangular piece of linen, or wool, folded round the body and fastened on each shoulder at A, B, C and D (*see* Diagram 9) by buttons or brooches, and round the waist

by a girdle; or it could be girded under the arms, as shown in Diagram 4. It was worn open down one side, and these two edges were usually finished off with a fringe, probably the raw edges left in the weaving [1] (*see* Fig. 24).

The later chiton. Shortly after this, approximately at the beginning of the fifth century B.C., the chiton was made on the same principle as the women's Ionic chiton (*see* p. 30), using wider material; and was bound or worked at the top edge, with the portion covering the upper arms slightly gathered. This part was buttoned or clasped back to front, and later on sometimes sewn together, to form a sleeve. It was girded at the waist and under the arms, as shown in Diagram 4 and Fig. 25.

It eventually became customary to sew up the open side, thus making the garment a cylinder in shape.

Fig. 24

[1] This fringe is generally translated as " tasselled " (*Od.*, XIX. 242).

Fig. 25 represents a young man dressed in accordance with the fashion of the fifth century B.C., but his hair is of the sixth and fifth centuries. The lyre is a development of the more primitive instrument of an earlier Age.

Fig. 26 is a young man wearing a crinkled chiton under the chlamys (p. 45). His long hair is twisted up and banded. He carries his petasos (p. 50) in his hand.

The short chiton was worn for the most part by young men; older men and high dignitaries preferred the long chiton which reached to the feet.

The material used for making the chiton was woven from hemp, carded wool, and a very fine flaxen linen; often semi-transparent, and almost invariably white.

Crinkled chitons, 450 B.C., were as much in use as the plain ones— in fact more so; but the men do not appear to have crinkled their garments in zig-zag or wavy lines, but in very small straight pleats, resembling the modern accordion pleating (*see* Fig. 26).

Many instances are shown where this crinkled chiton is girded, forming a very pronounced kolpos in front, and an uneven edge at the bottom. It is rare to find them girded a second time and round the hips.

The Doric chiton, with the overfold hanging over the breast, appears on many men's figures in vase paintings, but is generally shown made of crinkled linen.

The Kolobus, 400–146 B.C.

Another form of the chiton came into use about the beginning of the fourth century B.C. In *shape* it was two pieces of material cut square and sewn together on the shoulders, leaving an opening in the middle for the head, and sewn down the sides with sufficient space left at the top for the arms to pass through (*see* Diagram 10).

Dia. 10

Difference between chiton and kolobus. When the kolobus was girded at the waist, it had very much the same appearance as the chiton, the difference being that the arms emerged at the *top* edge of the chiton and at the *side* edge of this garment, known to the Greeks as the KOLOBUS, or "short," in reference to what might be called a sleeve.

There is reason to believe that the Greeks wove the material of this garment in one piece, with the three openings for the head and arms left in the weaving: *the whole garment then would be without a seam.*

The Alexandrian Age

The styles previously described continued to be worn during this Age.

Fig. 27 represents a man of this particular epoch wearing the kolobus ornamented with bands of embroidery. It is girded at the waist, and a himation of small dimensions is draped over the left shoulder, ready for the other end to be thrown over it. He wears the pilos (p. 50), and his hair has been allowed to grow longer than heretofore, in accordance with the new fashion of this age.

If this young man had desired to be in the height of fashion, he would have had long close-fitting sleeves added to his kolobus.

The first craze. A craving for something new has always been a weakness of mankind. The desire for novelty appeared among the Greeks in the Alexandrian Age, 338–220 B.C. The history of Costume will reveal divers manifestations of the same desire, peculiar to no one country, race, or time.

A period of long sleeves. During the campaign (334–333) against Darius III. Alexander is said to have admired the costume worn by the Persian nobility. Its characteristic features were the trousers, and the long sleeves to the wrist.[1]

The trousers must have been looked upon as too barbaric to adopt, but the sleeves found great favour, and were added speedily to the kolobus of the Macedonian Greeks for military, official, and every-day use. From this time onwards, long sleeves are sparsely represented in Greek paintings and sculpture. An especially good example is to be seen in a mosaic at Pompeii (a copy of a Greek original), and another on Alexander's sarcophagus from Sidon. Long sleeves as a fashion, however, did not meet with general adoption, and during the following century they became practically obsolete. They were looked upon as barbaric.

Fig. 27 represents a young man of the Alexandrian Age and onwards.

The Himation, 600–146 B.C.

The Himation was not exclusively a feminine garment; it was also worn by men. It was an oblong piece of material, woven with a border, and in dimensions approximately eighteen feet by six feet.

During the sixth century of the Classic Period, it was often the sole garment worn.

How to wear it. It was draped over the left arm, with one end

[1] In use not only with the Persians, but in many other countries of the East.

hanging in front, the rest of the material being drawn across the back, round the body on the right side, and over the left shoulder again (*see* Fig. 28). As civilisation progressed, it was deemed necessary by ordinary men to add an under-garment—either the chiton or the kolobus.

Worn by philosophers. Philosophers, sages, and savants, who could not be considered as ordinary men, advertised the simplicity of their lives by wearing the himation without an under-garment. The statues of Sophocles (495–405 B.C.) and Demosthenes (385–322 B.C.) in the Lateran Museum, Rome, and others, show it worn in this manner.

The *arrangement* of the himation was the subject of much care and consideration, as the wearer's character and culture was judged by the way it was put on. As no pins or fastenings were used in fixing this garment, it required no little dexterity to keep the drapery steady and in its right folds, and success demanded considerable practice and some assistance. However, it accorded with the mode of the day to throw it off or on at will, or readjust it from time to time.

Fig. 28

To envelop entirely the left arm, and even the hand also, was considered a mark of good breeding. To reverse this method, that is, to envelop the *right* arm, was distinctly bad form.

The Chlamys

THE CHLAMYS now makes its appearance (500 B.C.). It was a cloak, generally worn over the Ionic chiton, but sometimes would be the only garment worn, especially for riding. In *shape* it differed very slightly from the himation, but it was considerably smaller. When folded in two, it formed a square, and when open measured about seven feet by three and a half.

It was worn enveloping the left arm and side, and its top edges were fastened together with a brooch on the right side of the neck, from whence the remaining portion hung in folds down the right side, leaving the right arm free (*see* Fig. 26).

The chlamys was much used as a military cloak.

PEASANTS, 600–146 B.C.

The following excerpt from Homer's *Odyssey*, XXIV. 225, gives details of the costume worn by peasants of an earlier period, and this description applies equally to the dress of peasants between the years 600 and 146 B.C.

He was clothed in a filthy chiton, patched and unseemly, with clouted leggings of ox-hide bound about his legs, against the scratches of the thorns, and long *sleeves* over his hands by reason of the brambles, and on his head he wore a goatskin cap (*see* Fig. 29).

Fig. 29   Fig. 30

Shape, material, colour. The chiton was of the shape seen in Fig. 24, made of a coarse cloth in natural colouring, and without decoration. When engaged in any active pursuit, the wearer undid the fastening or button on the right shoulder, leaving the shoulder and arm free.

The binding of ox- or any hide is the most primitive method of protecting bare legs—the origin of the GAITER.

"Sleeves" did not mean arm-coverings in the way the term is generally understood, but were pieces of hide tied or laced round the forearm, wrist and hand, leaving the fingers free, with possibly a hole for the thumb. This was the first GLOVE.

"Sleeve"

The goatskin *cap* was merely a shaped piece. When necessary a small circular cloak of felt, or coarse cloth, often with a hood attached, would be worn (*see* "Paenula," Rome, p. 71).

Loin-cloth. Working-men and slaves wore nothing else but a piece of hide, cloth or linen, wrapped round their waists as an apron or loin-cloth. This was a method borrowed in very early times from the Egyptians and Cretans (*see* Fig. 30).

Footgear. As a rule the feet were bare, but for protection they either tied a piece of stout hide around the foot, or wore primitive sandals.

Fig. 13A, on p. 28, is a drawing made from the Pandora Vase, dated 460 B.C., in the Ashmolean Museum, and is given as an example of the treatment adopted by Greek artists in delineating the following garments: It represents Zeus (on the left), Hermes and Hercules, wearing respectively the himation, chlamys, and kolobus. Pandora wears the Ionic crinkled chiton, and a small himation, which is nothing more than a veil, over an elaborate stephane. Eros is holding her girdle.

MEN'S HAIRDRESSING, 600–146 B.C.

The Archaic Age, 600–468 B.C.

Long hair a feature of early hairdressing. Prior to this time, the hair was worn long, and men still continued to wear it in this manner.

Methods of dressing it were as follows:

1. Having encircled the head with a band, the long hair behind was twisted into coils. The ends were turned up, and the band which encircled the head was continued to bind these coils together, after the fashion of horses' tails dressed for a fair (*see* Fig. 26).

2. Shorter hair was allowed to flop slightly in the nape; the head was then banded with a circlet and the hair passed through it, the ends of hair falling back over the edge like an inverted S (*see* Fig. 31A). This style was adopted by men on active service, as were also the following:

3. The long hair down the back was braided into two plaits, which were crossed, and brought round the head, the two ends being fastened together in front. This style is seen on many statues of Apollo.

4. The hair was dressed as described under No. 3, but when the ends in front were small, the short front hair was combed down over the ends to conceal them (*see* Figs. 25 and 31B).

5. Often the hair was worn loose with just a fillet tied round the head, the long ends being turned up and tucked round the fillet to form a pad round the back of the head. Two curls hung from each side of the head (*see* Fig. 31C).

Hair as votive offering. It was the custom to cut off these long tails of hair, which typified manly vigour, and offer them as a sacrifice to the gods (*see* Votive Altar, Fig. 25).

6. *Elderly and dignified men* wore the hair long, sometimes hanging down the back, but often plaited and rolled round the head, and fixed with a fillet or ribbon, with one or two corkscrew curls escaping from under the fillet and from behind the ears. On the forehead the hair was curled.

Beards of soft wavy curls, with or without beards on the upper lip, were worn with this hairdressing (*see* Figs. 28 and 31D).

A

B

C

D

E

F

ALEXANDER

G

Men's
Hair-dressing

Classic Greece
600 to 146 B.C

FIG. 31

The Age of Pericles down to the beginning of the Alexandrian Age
468–338 B.C.

7. *Close-cropped hair.* After the period of the Persian Wars it became the fashion for young men to wear their hair cut close to the head; in fact, almost as it is worn at the present day. It was still customary to bind the head with a ribbon, tied behind, or by a fillet of gold or bronze (*see* Figs. 24 and 31E).

Shaving. Mention has been made under various dates of the fashions in clean-shaven faces and beards.

8. *Whiskers.* From the beginning of the fifth century it became the custom for young men to wear a small patch of hair upon the cheeks, just in front of the lobe of the ear, without any moustache or beard (*see* Figs. 24, 31A, and 31F).

This fashion came again into favour early in the nineteenth century A.D., during the classic revival of the First Empire. Its climax was reached during the 1860's, under the title of " Dundreary Whiskers."

The Alexandrian Age, 338–220 B.C.

Longer hair. A revival of Greek national feeling, as opposed to encroaching Roman influence, had the effect of bringing long hair back again into fashion during this Age; *but it was never worn so long* as it had been before, in the first part of the fifth century, namely the Archaic Age.

9. It was still short, but the head presented a mass of short wavy curls, some hanging over the forehead and some in front of the ears (*see* Figs. 27 and 31G).

Close-cropped again. 200 B.C. At last hair cut close to the head again became general (*see* Figs. 31E and 31F). Long hair was looked upon as effeminate and disappeared altogether.

Shaving. Alexander the Great introduced the general habit of shaving the face altogether, and this fashion spread from Macedonia throughout the whole of the Greek dominions. Beards continued to be worn only by high officials, philosophers, and professional men.

Headgear, 600–146 B.C.

It is curious that the Greeks and other civilised Western races, including the Egyptians, differed from the Oriental peoples in having no variety of useful headgear. A hat to put on when going out was almost entirely unknown.

The Greeks looked upon head-covering, in the comfortable and not the decorative sense, as degenerate, except as regards the PETASOS, which was worn only for travelling, and was originally the national head-covering of the Macedonians and Illyrians. This was made of felt, with a round crown and a fairly wide flat brim—not always circular, but cut into various shapes most convenient for practical purposes, so that parts of it could be turned up, down, sideways, and so forth—as a protection against the sun or rain. It nearly always had a cord passing through a hole in the brim on either side, tied in a knot on the top, and hanging down in a loop under the chin. When the hat was not required, it was carried on the back by means of this cord, which encircled the neck (see Fig. 26).

Kingly petasos. A petasos of purple, draped with a white scarf, was the cap of royalty of Macedonian kings.

Military petasos. The red petasos was awarded as a military honour, and used also as such by the Romans. It was the ancestor of the cardinal's hat.

A slightly different form of this hat had a pointed crown, and a brim wider in front than behind. The back part was invariably turned up.

Another hat, called a PILOS, was conical in shape, like a fez or an inverted flower-pot, and was also made of felt (see Fig. 27). This hat was much used by the labouring classes, peasants, and men living near the coast. A skull-cap of felt was worn under their helmets by warriors.

FOOTGEAR, 600–146 B.C.

A variety of fashions in footgear existed among Greek men and women, although it was quite usual for the wealthy to go barefooted, especially indoors.

Sandals, shoes and *boots* were all in use among all classes, their fineness or coarseness in make being the only distinction, except, of course, their decoration.

Sandal

The sandal was a sole of leather, wood, matting, felt or cork, cut to the shape of the foot, and made of great thickness *if* required to give additional height to the wearer. It was fastened on by means of straps or braids tied in a variety of ways round the instep and ankle. Usually, one strap was fastened to the sole, at a place between the big toe and the next, and two others to the sole near the heel; often a piece of leather was fixed at the back to cover the heel, and another piece covered the joints of the toes and was attached to both sides of the sole (see Figs. 15, 16, 17, 18, 24, 25 and 28).

In *colour,* these sandals were generally of the natural tone of the leather, or when worn by nobles they were gilded. They were also made in black, and a recipe for making boot-blacking is given by one of the Greek writers. Yellow, white, and red were also used.

Shoes were as much in use as sandals among the Greek men and women. There were several varieties, and many names are given to them in the Greek language. They fitted the shape of the foot, reaching to the ankle, where they were sometimes tied, or were bound round the foot, instep and ankle.

480 B.C. After this date shoes were not generally worn, and the sandal became the usual protection for the foot.

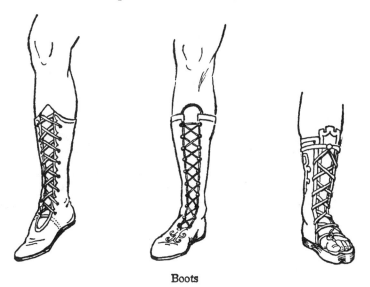

Boots

High boots were worn by hunters and horsemen, and were made of leather, fixed to a leather or wooden sole. They reached to just below the knee, and were either bound round the leg by means of braids or thongs of leather, or laced up the front, holes being pierced at the edges for that purpose (*see* Figs. 26 and 27).

Footgear an important detail. The Greeks were very particular about their footgear, and much care was bestowed upon this important detail of dress, which reflected so clearly the character of the wearer. Footgear was named after distinguished persons who started a fashion in a particular style; and people were even nicknamed after the boot or shoe usually worn by them.

It was the custom for boots and shoes to be made on lasts, and there is reason to believe that boot-trees were also used.

THE ART OF PAINTING IN CLASSIC GREECE

POLYGNOTUS, 463; APOLLODORUS, fifth century; ZEUXIS, 450; PARRHASIUS, fifth century; EUPOMPUS and PAMPHILUS, fourth century; APELLES OF COS, Court painter to Alexander the Great; LYSIPPUS, 334, a famous sculptor; PROTOGENES, an animal painter; ARISTIDES, father and son, 382, 350; ATHENION, painter of encaustics, 348—are some of the artists of this age. Those who painted on vases are far too numerous to mention.

The origin of painting is lost in antiquity. From the very earliest times it followed the course of civilisation, and was the first form of written language.

The representation of objects in colour was originally merely a method of expressing ideas,[1] and its use as decoration followed later.

No paintings of the Classic Age in Greece remain, but mention is made by classic writers of many masterpieces.

Mural painting is an art of an earlier Age—Assyrian, Egyptian, Minoan—but no record can be found of the wall-paintings or frescoes of Classic Greece until the time when Polygnotus and other contemporary artists worked in this style of art, and raised it to a high level.

Remains of Greek architecture show that painting was an allied art, and surfaces were often painted in plain colours to form an effective background for statuary and mouldings. Statues also were painted in parts, especially to accentuate certain details of dress.

The art of portrait painting was not practised in Classic Greece before the fourth century B.C. It was Zeuxis and Parrhasius who inaugurated its popularity, being expert artists in portraiture. Their paintings were executed in water-colours, pigments ground in a mortar with a pestle, and applied with a brush to a thin piece of wood especially prepared for the purpose.

Another process of painting upon small framed boards, with colours ground into wax and burnt in, was known, and called the "Encaustic" style. When the painting was finished, a polish was applied which is supposed to have acted as a preservative. Encaustic painting was used for portraits, for the decoration of ivory, and the colouring of statuary.

Mosaic work was known to the artist of antiquity, and came to Greece from the East in the third century B.C. At first the designs were carried out by the use of squares of marble of different colours; for glass, although known, was of very primitive make and was little used until late in pre-Christian times.

Vase painting. The practice of painting designs, objects and figures upon vases is also of great antiquity, and, from the eighth

[1] Compare methods used in Heraldry.

century B.C., the art developed to a large extent, as indicated by the number of vases still extant. At first, these vases were turned in a clay, which, when burnt, became a rich red or orange in colour. Upon this background were painted figures executed in a black pigment; a little white was introduced, and in baking this became lustrous.

The later, or red-figured, vases had the background painted in black, leaving the figures red, and to their decoration a little purple and white were added. Both black-figure and red-figure vases, although very difficult to decipher, are full of information regarding costume of their time.

WEAVING AND TEXTILES
600–146 B.C.

The art of weaving is one of the most ancient of all human industries.

Egyptians the earliest weavers. In the earliest period of their civilisation (3000 B.C.) the Egyptians were famous for the weaving of fine linen. This they exported to the nations with whom they had commercial relations, and no doubt much of the linen used by the early Greeks came from Egypt.

The Greeks themselves became expert weavers and, centuries before the Classic Era, thoroughly understood the art.

Fifth century B.C. It is uncertain if the Greeks used the horizontal as well as the upright loom. A few representations of the latter type are seen in sculpture and paintings. These give a fair idea of what the looms were like, but in drawing they are not complete, or even correct in detail. The weaver stood at her work, beginning the web at the top and working downwards. In striking the weft with the spatha, or batten, the shuttle was always thrown upwards.

During the *first century* B.C., the Egyptian method of weaving in the upright loom was adopted, beginning the web at the bottom and working upwards. This enabled the weaver to work in a sitting posture.

In the earliest times flax was used in preference to all other fibres. Later, the use of wool became very general.

The *distaff* was the stick, held in the left hand, on which the flax or wool was loosely mounted, the threads being drawn out with the right hand, the spinner at the same time giving them a spiral twist with the forefinger and thumb. When sufficient thread was spun into yarn, the end was attached to the spindle (a stick with a disc and a weight at the end) and wound round it, the weight augmenting the rotation (*see* Fig. 16). This method ensured the strongest and most durable yarn.

The distaff was often an elaborate article, and sometimes very richly ornamented. Ivory distaffs are mentioned (Theocritus, Idyll XXVIII.), and ladies of high rank received gifts of a distaff and spindle wrought in gold. It was usual for a woman to present her distaff and spindle with the wool or flax on it, to the temple, as a votive offering.

The weaving was all done by the women of the household. In the establishment of a great lord, these women would consist of handmaids (to the number of fifty; *Odyssey*, VII. 107), servants and slaves, under the supervision of the lady of the house. The weaving of the plain stuff was generally undertaken by servants and slaves, while the handmaids and the lady herself passed their time in decorating the material with beautiful designs, either with the shuttle or the needle.

Flax and wool were the raw materials most used.

Textiles used by upper classes. The better classes wore wool and linen of a very fine make. Fine linen was considered a very great luxury, and very transparent linen, manufactured at Amorgos, approaching a muslin in its fineness, was among the materials used chiefly by the wealthy and upper classes.

Flax woven in oil. A method of weaving the flax in olive oil was widely practised. It produced a glossy effect, very much like silk or satin, and could be described as "shining brilliantly" (*Odyssey*, XIX. 232); "like the gleam over the skin of a dried onion, so smooth it was and glistening as the sun" (*Odyssey*, XIX. 242). The oil also made the fabric soft, and helped the drapery to hang in smaller folds.

Textiles used by peasants. The commonest materials were woollen stuffs of various textures, some loosely and some closely woven. The garments of the lower orders and peasants were made of these textiles.

With regard to the plain woven stuffs, some linen of Egyptian make, recently discovered, and dating about 2000 B.C., presents the same technique when compared with Greek linen of the fifth century B.C.; also Egyptian linens, found in Coptic graves of the second and third centuries A.D., prove that the art of weaving in the earliest times was little, if at all, inferior in skill and workmanship to that of the first century of the Christian Era.

After the fourth century B.C., Alexandria was a very important and much renowned centre of the linen-weaving industry. Akhmim was another of the cities of Egypt famous throughout the world for its linen manufacture.

The chiton, himation, and chlamys were of very fine wool or linen, woven complete in themselves *with the selvedge all round*, so that it was unnecessary to hem them. This fact accounts for the very beautiful folds of the drapery seen in Greek sculpture.

Chitons were made of very soft crinkled material, very like crepe, in wool or linen. Whether the crinkle was woven in it, or obtained by some process, is not quite certain.

A very simple method of fixing a crinkle was to soak the material in water, then wring it up tight, and leave it so twisted until dry. How the zig-zag or wavy effect was obtained is a mystery, unless the Greeks had special irons made for the purpose.

PATTERNED TEXTILES

The art of weaving a fabric with a pattern upon it was unknown to the Early Egyptians and Greeks. Nothing of this nature dating from before the fifteenth century B.C. has yet been discovered in Egypt. After this date, a method of ornamenting the surface was adopted, by which a pattern was applied by painting or dyeing; but the more usual way was to embroider it, either during the process of weaving or after the fabric was finished.

Patterns. In the East, the earliest effects in decorated materials were produced by weaving them with a weft of different colours, in a series of stripes.

The Greeks were acquainted with various methods of decoration long before the opening of this period, and the patterns employed by them can be grouped into three divisions:

1. Sprigs, flowers and leaves were dotted, diaper fashion, over the surface. This style of design is mentioned in Homer, which dates it before the ninth century B.C.

2. Scenes from history and mythology were favourite subjects, also mentioned by Homer. Although of a much earlier date than the period with which we are dealing, these subjects are seen on vase paintings of the fifth century.

And in the hall she found Helen weaving a great purple web of double woof, and embroidering thereon many battles of horse-taming Trojans and mail-clad Achaeans. —*Iliad,* III. 124.

Iliad, III. 124   The Peplos

3. Animals, and wild beast hunting, originally copied from Persian ornamentation. The Persians themselves had copied this style of animal design from India. The Egyptians and Phœnicians had commercial intercourse with India in early times, so Indian art may have drifted into Persia and even Greece, through Egyptian and Phœnician channels.

Darius I. of Persia was in India in the year 509 B.C., conducting his campaign, and had opportunities of seeing the arts and industries of that country.

Probably the earliest woven patterned fabric known to exist was found on the site of a Greek colony in the Crimea. It dates from the fifth century B.C., and represents ducks statant, arranged in diaper.[1]

5th cent. B.C.

Much more variety in design was introduced after Alexander the Great had had direct contact with India in 327 B.C. The absence of any mechanical means for the weaving of these patterned materials resulted in a delightful freedom of treatment and design—an artistic touch sadly lacking in the machine-made fabrics of the present day. Another feature of this early weaving was that the pattern was perfect on both sides.

New stuffs introduced. During the fourth century B.C. many new stuffs were introduced into the world of dress. The expeditions and conquests of Alexander the Great opened new centres from whence different materials were introduced.

Cotton, from which muslins and gauzes were woven, came from India; and a wonderful stuff called " *silk* " ($\sigma\eta\rho\iota\kappa\acuteo\nu$) was brought from the far-off East (the land of the Seres, $\Sigma\hat\eta\rho\epsilon\varsigma$, now known as China) by Persian traders who charged a prohibitive price for it.

[1] Now (ç) in the Hermitage, Petrograd.

Satin or *samit* was also known, but was of very great rarity. It was much coveted by the Greeks, and later by the Romans, and for it they paid fabulous sums.

Felt. The art of making felt is as old as the art of weaving, and was practised extensively by the ancient Greeks. It was made by matting hair, or flocks of wool, together while moist. Felt was used for making cloaks, hats (the petasos and pilos), shoes, and for covering many things.

COLOURS AND DECORATION, 600–146 B.C.

If Greek costume was simple in its make, it certainly was not so where colour and decoration were concerned, according to the descriptions that have come down to us from Greek and Roman writers; but it must be remembered that these early writers used colour names in an unfamiliar manner, and many words used in the original text are untranslatable.

Coloured borders. Many garments were woven with bright-coloured borders, and the patterns which decorated the edges, or were scattered over the garments, were either embroidered or woven in the most vivid hues, interspersed with gold threads.

Articles of wearing apparel were often sent to the goldsmith to be embellished with intricate designs in gold and silver. Thin strips of narrow gold plate, and pliable wire, were worked upon and into the material, in the manner of Oriental embroidery to-day. This gave weight and helped the drapery to hang well.

List of Colours

The Greek word πορφυρέη did not always apply to the colour purple, but very often occurs in an enhanced descriptive sense.

Purple of Tyre as a colour was appropriated by the aristocracy, and was obtained from the Tyrians, whose skilled and expert knowledge of its preparation secured their wares pre-eminence over all other purples. It was compounded from a species of shell-fish—the murex—which abounded on the eastern shores of the Mediterranean. Both the blue-purple and the red-purple were obtained from this source.

Purple of Cassius was also a red-purple, or wine colour.

True purple is a name often used in writing, and must apply to Tyrian purple.

Colours mentioned as those in general use are: *Red, dark red, scarlet, vermilion, yellow, saffron, yellow ochre, sulphur, emerald, veridian, apple-green,* and a colour spoken of as "*like an unripe grape.*"

Black and *grey* were reserved for mourning habits.

Blue. There is a suggestion that blue dye was entirely unknown to the Greeks; and if so, materials of a blue colour could never have been used by them for their costumes.

Blue as a paint or pigment was certainly known before 1400 B.C., as the frescoes at Knossos prove. Homer also mentions a frieze of blue (*Odyssey*, VII. 85).

One of the statues in the Acropolis Museum, No. 681, date about 480 B.C., is wearing a chiton *painted* blue, and a Tanagra statuette in the British Museum, No. 295, of the fourth and third centuries B.C., is wearing a chiton of cerulean, showing beneath the himation of cyclamen-pink; but *painted* statues do not provide convincing argument that clothes were dyed blue.

Indigo was obtained from Egypt and, after the fourth century B.C., from India.

The people. The colours in common use were *greens* and *greys*, and peasants usually wore *greys* and *browns*.

The aristocracy preferred a pure white for their linen robes, especially during the period 480–350 B.C., and their spotlessness was a test of good breeding.

The great variety of patterns which decorated the costume of the

5th cent.

Greeks is too extensive to discuss in detail, but some particulars will be found in the drawings of the dresses, and under "Weaving."

During the fifth century B.C. there appears to have been less ornamentation used. Clothes depended more upon the beauty and graceful lines of the drapery, which were enhanced by the plain material; but in the reign of Alexander the Great, lavish display and a richness of material and decoration returned into fashion in full splendour.

GREEK JEWELLERY AND ORNAMENTS OF THE
CLASSIC PERIOD, 600–146 B.C.

INTRODUCTION

The treasures of Alexander and Mithridates. Crowns of Honour. Garlands. Head-dresses. The Stephane. Bands. Ear-rings. Necklaces. Bracelets. Finger-rings. Pins. Fibulæ. Hairpins. The Intaglio. The Cameo.

Jewellery came into use gradually and did not assume widespread popularity in Grecian society until the increasing skill of craftsmen, and the discovery and mastery of new processes, began the succession of fashions in personal ornaments which spread, in the course of centuries, over the Western world. The ornament that was primarily a frank piece of decoration was produced in time; but for a considerable period such things were rare. Articles which had a definite function, such as pins and the stephane, were embellished with decorative work and the addition of jewels; but it was only after a measure of perfection in the finish of such objects had been attained that we find a growing appreciation of the adornment devoid of utility.

The work of Greek goldsmiths attained perfection during the fourth century B.C., and ornaments worn by men and women of distinction were magnificent examples of metal work.

Ornaments for personal adornment were made of gold, silver and bronze, but prior to the third century B.C., gems or jewels were rarely used in them. Patterns were worked on ornaments of thin metal plate by embossing or beating the plate into stone moulds. These designs were outlined by a series of small points or dots. A similar result was obtained by the use of fine gold wire twisted together to form lines and curves.

Fine gold wire was worked into intricate and delicate network designs, some containing beads or globules, a style since called filigree.

The epoch of Alexander (338–220 B.C.) was an age of great splendour. In the course of their travels, Alexander the Great and his attendant nobles collected large numbers of the precious stones and gems which abounded in Asia, and these were used later to decorate their jewellery.

63 B.C. *Mithridates: his wealth and treasure.* The personal ornaments of Alexander descended to Mithridates, King of Macedon

(120–63 B.C.), who was a great patron of the arts, besides being a very wealthy monarch. He was a serious opponent to Rome, and when his treasury became the spoil of his Roman conquerors, it contained immense stores of goldsmiths' work—a golden throne, crown, sceptre, sword, and a chariot of gold set with precious stones; royal mantles of purple encrusted with gold and jewels; a collection of precious stones, among which are mentioned: rubies, topazes, emeralds, carbuncles, opals, onyx, pearls and diamonds. The last-named jewel was held in high esteem because of its great rarity.

The practice of *cutting the diamond* is of considerable antiquity, but the art of faceting this gem was not discovered until the middle of the fifteenth century A.D.

Crowns were ornaments for the head and originally were merely garlands of leaves or flowers. They were used by the Greeks of the Early Period as symbols of honour, and bestowed upon victors, athletes, poets, and distinguished citizens, as rewards for valour, prowess, genius and public service.

Victors, both military and naval, received crowns composed of laurel or bay leaves:

Athletes—the olive or palm:

Divinities were crowned with garlands; Aphrodite with myrtle, Apollo with laurel, Athene with olive, Dionysius with ivy or the vine, Zeus with oak leaves:

A crown of oak leaves was also worn at *religious festivals*:

Bards, poets, orators—laurel or parsley.

On occasions of rejoicing, crowns of leaves and flowers were the fashion; and, in early times, guests attending a *banquet* or entertainment brought their own, made of flowers or leaves, especially of myrtle or the rose. Later in this period it became the custom for the host to supply one for each of his guests.

At *funerals* the wild celery was chiefly used; but other kinds of foliage were employed. Garlands were placed upon the tombs of the departed, a custom which has continued until the present day.

Greek kings or overlords before the ninth century B.C. wore only a plain white band or ribbon round the head, with the ends tied behind. Divinities are also represented as wearing such bands.

The Greek name for "crown" was στέφανος, but this was applied to a particular kind.

Homer makes no mention of crowns being worn by kings, though he does record that they carried *sceptres*.

The garland in gold. At the beginning of the Classic Period (600 B.C.), garlands of flowers were modelled in gold, and it became general for all crowns of honour to be made of this metal. Wreaths of laurel, bay, myrtle and oak, however, in their natural state, still continued to be popular.

Circlet of royalty. The gold circlet became the distinct badge of royalty about the fourth century B.C.

HEAD-DRESS: THE STEPHANE

A head-dress was worn by ladies at the commencement of this period, and consisted of a band of metal, gold or bronze, fitting the head. These bands later were slightly decorated and became considerably wider, and, instead of fitting the head like a circlet, stood away from it (*see* Figs. 19 and 22). This and later forms were known as the "stephane." In its simplest form, the ground-work was of gold plate, edged in most cases with twisted gold wire to suggest a cord; but, as time went on, more elaborate decoration was desired, and human figures, and figures of beasts, birds and fishes, were added in repoussé work or coloured enamel.

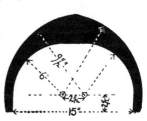

During the Age of Pericles (468–404 B.C.), this coronet took the shape of an inverted crescent, its widest part standing up in front, and the two points fastened at the nape of the neck (*see* Fig. 18).

Bands for the head became very ornate. Often a *motif* in gold was worn on the forehead, and attached by chains or jointed pieces

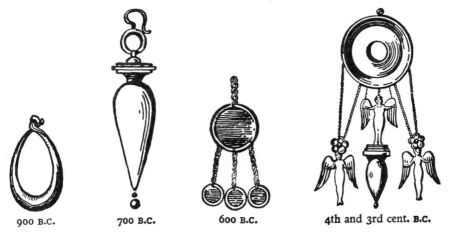

| 900 B.C. | 700 B.C. | 600 B.C. | 4th and 3rd cent. B.C. |

encircling the head. At a later period these bands were set with jewels or enamels, sometimes both.

Ear-rings. The very earliest shape (*circa* 900 B.C.) was a swelling loop of gold or bronze. Later, a simple drop—a gold ball, or a vase-shaped pendant—was used, which in course of time became three or four inches in length (*Odyssey*, XVIII. 291). Although precious stones were rarely used, single pearls, especially those of pear-shape, were most popular.

Ear-rings composed of many pieces were worn about 600 B.C., chiefly coin-shaped, and suspended by small rings from the main ornament; and the much-desired tinkling sound was produced by contact between these as they swung.

Filigree and repoussé. A characteristic ear-ring of the Alexandrian Age had an ornamental disc—of filigree or repoussé work—attached to the ring which pierced the lobe of the ear, and from it were hung little chains with ornaments at the ends. Others were more elaborate, having tiny winged figures, vases, and baskets of flowers suspended by small chains.

A fashion for youths and children. It was a custom among Greek youths of fashion to wear a single ear-ring. Children sometimes wore a ring in the right ear only, but this was not general.

Necklaces (ninth century B.C.). In the *Odyssey*, XVIII. 291, a necklace is mentioned—"a golden chain of curious work strung with amber beads shining like the sun"—"a necklet, a very lovely jewel" (*see* Fig. 23C). Pearls were worn, strung on thread, and wound round the neck (*see* Fig. 23D). There are many Greek necklaces of the third century B.C. in the British Museum, and for the most part these are composed of gold ornaments—discs, balls, plaques—and natural objects linked together. Other ornaments are hung from these by small rings or chains, to a depth of two or three inches (*see* Figs. 15, 23A, 23B).

Bracelets. The most familiar design of the early part of this period was made of gold, silver, or bronze wire, twisted round the arm in imitation of a snake, with the ends of the wire flattened out to represent the head and tail (*see* Figs. 15 and 16).

One, two, or three large rings or bands of gold, and rings of carved precious stone, were worn on the upper arm, as well as on the wrists (*see* Figs. 17 and 19).

Rings were worn on the fingers from early times, either bands of plain gold, or decorated with gems arranged singly or in clusters.

Signet rings. Engraved gems set in a finger-ring to form a seal were frequently used.

Pins of gold, silver, or other metal were used in an earlier period (the Archaic) for fastening clothes, and were simple in shape, straight, and with small heads. The straight parts were often pierced with eyes in which chains were fastened, to secure the pins to the dress or each other. In course of time the head

900 B.C.

600 B.C.

of the pin developed, and in the sixth century B.C. it became a distinctive ornament.

The *fibula* (earliest form 1000 B.C.) was a brooch on the safety-pin principle, and, in its earliest form, had an arch or bow, furnished

1000 B.C.   Fibulæ

with a pin attached to a spiral spring at one end, and a catch to secure the point at the other. The catch, or plate, and the arch were the first to receive the goldsmith's attention. All sorts of quaint designs were worked on to them, and beads, pebbles, etc. were added to the arch. These fibulæ were used to fasten the edges of the Ionic and Doric chiton.

Brooch

Fibulæ with circular disc tops had the pins fixed underneath, with a sheath to protect the points. These were used to fasten the chiton on the shoulders and upper arms (*see* Fig. 19) and the chlamys (*see* Fig. 26).

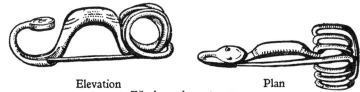

Elevation   Plan
Fibulæ, 4th cent. B.C.

The designs worked on the disc were sometimes very elaborate (*see Odyssey*, XIX. 242).

In the fourth century B.C. the pin was placed in the centre of the spiral spring. In plan this fibula took the shape of a T, and this was the basis of many later designs.

Hairpins and ornaments for the hair were made in the third century B.C. of metal and ivory, and occasionally took the form of figures in gold, embellished with enamels or jewels.

Engraved Gems

The art of engraving on precious stones was known to the Early Assyrians and Egyptians, but it was not practised in Greece until after the commencement of the sixth century B.C.

The *stones* commonly used for this purpose were the onyx, sardonyx, agate, cornelian, sard, chalcedony, jasper, and

Hairpin, 3rd cent. B.C.

lapis lazuli; for special objects, the emerald, sapphire, ruby and garnet were used.

The intaglio. The oldest method was that of cutting a design sunk below the surface of the stone, and *polished*—an art now lost. It is called the "intaglio" and was employed chiefly on stones of small size, which were used as signets, and cut from the cornelian, quartz, sard, chalcedony and jasper.

The cameo. The engraver of gems became most proficient about the middle of the fourth century B.C. (the Alexandrian Age), and at this time a new feature was introduced, namely the "cameo." This was a method of cutting various objects in relief upon stones such as sardonyx or chalcedony; but the greatest achievement was the engraving of portraits upon different layers of the gems. These were of large size and used for personal adornment.

LIST OF AUTHORITIES CONSULTED FOR CHAPTER II

Homer	Lady Evans
Ethel V. Abrahams	Luther Hooper
Prof. Baldwin Brown	Joseph Clark Hoppin
Ernst Buschor	John Penoyra, Hellenic Society
F. Warre Cornish	A. H. Smith, British Museum
Daremberg and Saglio	William Smith, Wayte and
Guy Dickins	Marindin

CHAPTER III

ROME

Section I.—MONARCHIC AND REPUBLICAN ROME
753-27 B.C.

HISTORICAL DATA

B.C.

753. Many legends concerning the foundation of Rome have been preserved, but April 21st, 753 B.C., is officially accepted as the date. "Rome was not built in a day." Its first walls were not erected until nearly two hundred years after its foundation. Its government was monarchic until the ejection of the Tarquins in 510 B.C. The appointment of the first consul occurred in the following year, and this (509) marks The Beginning of the Republic.

396. The first war of importance was waged against the Veii, and the fall of the Etruscan city took place in 396. During this campaign the Roman soldiers received pay for the first time, and a standing army was formed on this basis.

390. The Gauls under Brennus defeated the Romans at the River Allia, but were afterwards routed by Camillus (389).

387. The Gauls took Rome and besieged the Capitol, but it was saved by the cackling of Juno's geese. The Gauls retired in 361 and were defeated in 358.

340. War with the Latins and Samites.

311. War with the Etruscans.

266. Rome supreme in Italy.

264. The First Punic War. Gladiators were introduced from Etruria and gave their first performance in Rome.

238. War with the Gauls.

235. Nævius (d. 204) produced his first comedy.

B.C.

218. The Second Punic War. Hannibal (247-184).

215. The First Macedonian War.

200. The Second Macedonian War.

174. The expense of stage plays taken over by the State.

171. The Third Macedonian War.

167. Polybius, the Greek statesman and historian (204-122), brought a prisoner to Rome.

156. The Third Punic War.

146. Destruction of Corinth by Lucius Mummius. End of Greek independence.

133. The Age of Gracchi.

104. General Caius Marius (157-87) became a ruler of Rome; a great reformer and organiser of the army.

88. War against Mithridates, King of Macedon.

66. He is defeated and becomes a fugitive.

62. Praetorship of Caius Julius Cæsar. First expedition (55) into Britain.

54. Second expedition into Britain.

51. The conquest of Gaul complete; it becomes a province of Rome.

48. Caius Julius Cæsar (100-44) the first to become sole and perpetual dictator. Assassinated in 44.

37. Jerusalem captured, and Herod nominated king.

31. Octavius succeeds to the dictatorship. Battle of Actium.

30. End of Antony and Cleopatra's rule, and of Egyptian independence.

29. The title of "Augustus" (Honourable) given to Octavius Imperator.

End of the Roman Republic

INTRODUCTION

During the course of centuries the flame of Roman civilisation, fanned by increasing prosperity, a growing commerce, and an efficient and victorious military organisation, grew to a great blazing light that eclipsed the civilisations that had gone before.

Greek civilisation waned politically, although the intellectual domination of Grecian culture remained intact and swayed the thought of the world and moulded its culture. But Rome grew in power and enterprise, and the early days of its power as a State were its true days of greatness, for later it became vulgarised, commercial and debased. The Romans were essentially men of action, and they did not develop an individual art; their art was based on Greek models, which they copied without much discernment, bringing to the purity of Greek design a harsh, mathematical touch; the artistic ineptitude of sternly practical and essentially unappreciative men. Laws, customs, art and literature all had something of Grecian influence in their fabric, so it is not surprising to find a marked similarity between Greek and Roman costume.

PLAUTUS, *d.* 184 B.C.; CATO THE ELDER, *d.* 149 B.C.; CICERO, *d.* 43 B.C.; VIRGIL, *d.* 19 B.C.; HORACE, *d.* 8 B.C., are a few of the literary men of the Republican Age.

COSTUME OF THE ROMANS

UNDER THE KINGDOM AND THE REPUBLIC, 753–27 B.C.

THE MEN

Centre of fashion. Athens was the chief centre of fashion during this period, and all Romans of importance adopted Greek dress, tempered by a strain of Etruscan influence.

The description of clothes given in the last chapter applies to the Roman as well as to the Greek, with the sole addition of one garment— THE TOGA—which was the most distinctive feature of Roman costume.

THE TOGA

During the early years of Rome's existence (that is, the seventh and sixth centuries B.C.), it appears to have been the only garment worn alike by men and women of the highest and lowest orders, the only difference being in the material used. For the highest it was made of the finest wool in its natural colour, and by the lowest of a coarse cloth or felt, in various colouring (*see* Greek Peasants, p. 46). As time went on the toga was discarded altogether by women of all ranks, and by men of the lowest class. The lower orders adopted in place of it a short cloak, with a hood invariably attached, in use among the Greeks, but called by the Romans *The Paenula* (*see* p. 71).

The toga the national dress. The toga remained a costume of distinction during the whole Roman period, and became the character-istic national dress of the Roman aristocracy and freemen. Its use was denied to all peasants, foreigners and outlawed subjects.

It was used, with variations, for all ceremonial and official purposes until the fifth century A.D., and, with alterations and additions, became the Court dress of emperors, kings, and princes throughout the various phases and periods of European history.

Its shape. The Roman toga in its numerous variations received different names, but retained its original shape throughout (*see* Fig. 32). In shape it was a segment of a circle, measuring about eighteen or fifteen feet long, and from five to six feet at its widest.

Diagram 11 gives the shape of the toga, showing its approximate dimensions. When a band was added (*toga praetexta*), it was placed along the straight side A–F at a distance of an inch or so from the edge. The band itself was three inches in width, and purple in colour (for shades, *see* Clavus, p. 106). The question of the use of a border all round the toga (on the curved side as well as the straight) is a matter of conflicting views among certain authorities; it is to be regretted that an authentic ruling on the point is lacking, for unfortunately the band or border is not distinctly shown on sculpture. As a solution it is suggested that the toga praetexta had only a band, and the toga trabea and toga picta had both a band and border.

How to wear the toga. The toga was draped on the figure by starting with point A at the left foot; the straight edge was taken over the left shoulder and arm, B. It was then passed across the back, and hung loose under the right arm, D, across the chest, over the left shoulder and arm again, E, with the remaining portion hanging down the back, finishing at point F.

Having arranged the toga as described, it will be found that the straight edge at D under the right arm can be made, by turning it over, to form a second piece of curved drapery over the right upper leg. This is called the "sinus." Also, if the straight edge of the first portion (which passes over the left shoulder at B) is pulled out, and pouched over the top part which also crosses the left shoulder, the draped effect is obtained. This part, called the "umbo," was often used to envelop the right hand. The loose portion C at the back of the right shoulder was often drawn up over the shoulder, and attached to the belt at the waist, so as to form a sort of sleeve. It was also the custom to utilise this loose portion C alternatively as a head-covering; and it was in use for this purpose during all religious ceremonies—it also served as a protection from bad weather.

1. *The toga pura.* Dating from the third century B.C., the toga pura became the characteristic dress of the Roman citizen, and denoted his enfranchisement. It was of wool, in its natural colour, without a band.

2. *The toga virilis.* This was the same garment, assumed by a young Roman between his fourteenth and sixteenth year; and its adoption was celebrated at the feast of the Liberalia, held on the 17th of March.

3. *The toga praetexta* was used for the same purpose by noble youths. It had a straight band of purple or scarlet on the white toga. This toga praetexta, according to tradition, was also worn exclusively by kings at an earlier period. In later Republican times it was the distinctive garment worn by the higher magistrates (curule) and senators. It was awarded as a badge of rank, under the name of:

4. *The toga ornamentum.*

5. *The toga candida* was worn plain by candidates for public offices. The wool was bleached a pure white. Clients also wore this toga candida when visiting their patrons.

6. *The toga trabea* was worn by a sect of priests—the Salii—and augurs. In shape it was somewhat narrower, of white striped with scarlet, with a purple border all round.

7. *The toga pulla* was of black, and worn as a mourning robe.

8. *The toga picta.* The Latin word "picta" means to paint or to picture, and applies to the rich embellishments of this garment. Originally it was worn by Etruscan priests and magistrates on State occasions. It was profusely embroidered, or probably painted, with all sorts of subjects, especially conventional figures of men and beasts, with an ornamental border. The toga picta was adopted by the Romans about the third century B.C. The Roman version was *at first* much less ornate, having an embroidered border, usually of gold laurel leaves, as its decoration. It superseded the natural-hued home-spun

Fig. 32. A patrician of the third, second and first centuries B.C., and the first and second centuries A.D., wearing the toga praetexta over the colobium with latus clavus. The "sinus" is marked with a D, and the "umbo" with a B. The portion marked C can be drawn over the head if required.

Fig. 32. THE TOGA PRAETEXTA

woollen toga, but was of a much finer make of wool, and dyed a rich Tyrian purple. During the first century B.C. it was made of silk of the same colour.

It was worn by generals when making triumphal entries into Rome; by magistrates when conducting the statues of the deities in solemn pomp to the Circensian Games; and by praetors and governors of provinces — afterwards called "consuls" — while in office. The privilege of always wearing the toga picta was first conferred upon Caius Julius Cæsar.

The further developments of this garment are traced in the section dealing with Imperial Rome, on p. 93.

Various Cloaks

THE ABOLLA was a cloak used by officers of the Roman army; it was of the same shape as its prototype, the Greek chlamys (see p. 45), of thicker material, and usually red.

THE PALUDAMENTUM was another name for a military cloak, identical in shape with the chlamys, and worn clasped on the right shoulder. It was usually purple, but sometimes of a "dark colour." It was regularly worn by generals, when on active service, and by magistrates and lictors.

THE LAENA was the same shape as the chlamys, namely, an oblong. It was made of thick *soft* shaggy woollen stuff, like a blanket, and used as a covering to be thrown round the figure for protection and convenience.

THE PAENULA. A cloak of cloth copied from the Greek peasants (see p. 46). It was in common use among all classes, both men and women, as a travelling or rain cloak, and was an important garment with the peasantry. In colour it was dark, and in shape a semicircle with the straight edges fastened down the centre-front, converting it into a bell or funnel. Alternatively, the edges were sewn together down the front; but in either case it fitted close round the figure. A hole was left for the head, which was usually encircled with a hood (see Fig. 33 and Diagram 12 overleaf).

Fig. 33

THE LACERNA was a cloak like the chlamys, but the corners were

rounded off. It was worn fastened on the right shoulder by a fibula.[1]
It was made of fine wool, sometimes with a hood attached, and used
by fashionable people as a light wrap for summer wear.

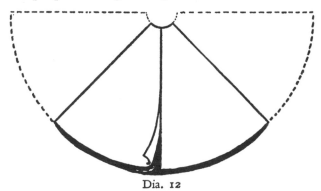

Dia. 12

THE BIRRUS. A cape-like cloak, with a hood like the paenula,
and resembling a smaller edition of the lacerna, but made of much
thicker stuff and used as a winter wrap.

The further development of these cloaks is given on p. 110.

THE SUBLIGACULUM. It has been noted (p. 66) that the
toga was at first the only garment worn; but in these early years a small
garment or piece of cloth called a "subligaculum" was worn bound
round the hips as a loin-cloth (see p. 46). This was worn under the toga,
or frequently without any other covering. It was but a fashion copied
from the Greeks, who themselves derived it from the Egyptians and
Assyrians. The subligaculum was superseded by the tunica, soon after
what is called "Society" was established on the Palatine Hill. It afterwards became the general garb of hunters, wrestlers, craftsmen, labourers
and peasants (continued on p. 112).

The Tunica and Colobium

Origin of the tunica. The tunica was introduced at a later date
and worn under the toga, by which it was covered when out of doors:
it was a copy of the Greek chiton (see Figs. 24 and 25). At first it was
left open down the side, but later sewn up. It reached half-way down the
thigh, sometimes just below the knee. A longer garment—the "tunica
talaris"—was worn officially by high dignitaries, by women and old
men. For ordinary use it was considered effeminate. It was girded at
the waist, and the length of the skirt part was regulated by pulling the
material through the girdle. For vigorous exercise, or riding, the tunica
would be girded higher than for normal use.

[1] *See* Jewellery, p. 131.

The kolobus of the Greeks (*see* p. 43 and Diagram 10) was also worn by the Etruscans, and, at some time after the fourth century B.C. or even later, was adopted by the Romans and Latinised by them into the

Colobium

Shape. This garment varied in width across the shoulders. The greater the distance between the neck-hole and the edge of the top corner (*see* A B, Diagrams 10 and 13), the more the upper arm was hidden. This has the misleading effect of a sleeve to the elbow.

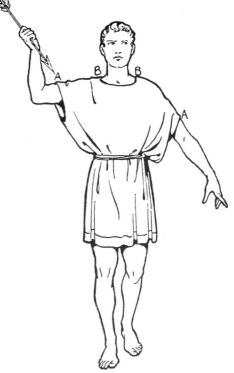

The Romans had a great aversion to anything in the nature of a close arm covering, so the fashion of wearing long shaped separate sleeves, set by Alexander the Great (*see* p. 44), was not followed at Rome, as it was considered unmanly; besides, such sleeves were worn by foreigners and barbarians, so naturally this mode was distasteful to the patriotic intolerance of a Roman citizen.

Materials, decoration and colour. The materials used were wool and linen, for cotton was little known till after the year 180 B.C. The wealthy used a material of very fine make; the decoration was simple, following the designs set by Greek fashions. In colour the tunica followed the same traditions. During the

Diagram 13. The Greek "kolobus," called by the Romans the "colobium." Another name for this garment was the "tunica." When more than one was worn, the under ones were called the "tunica interior," or "subucula." A long tunica was called "tunica talaris."

third, second and first centuries B.C., the tunica was an indispensable article of men's attire.

The tunica palmata was a ceremonial garment of great dignity, and consequently long (tunica talaris), reaching to the ankles. It was worn during the Republic by generals making their progress to the Capitol, to pay their vows and offer sacrifice to Jupiter, before a campaign, or their triumph after return from important victories. The dress of a general on this occasion was the "Ornamenta Triumphalia"—the tunica palmata and the toga picta, both of purple. He was crowned with a wreath of laurel, carried a laurel bough in his right hand, and an ivory sceptre surmounted by an eagle in his left. It was the custom, from early times until the fourth century B.C. (when it was abandoned), for the general to ride in a circular chariot, drawn by four white horses also wreathed in laurel. The lictors attending him wore red tunicas, and wreaths of laurel about their heads, and carried "fasces" (see p. 76), the attribute of superior magistrateship (*continued on p. 105*).

HAIRDRESSING—MEN

The Romans of the Kingdom and the Republic followed closely the fashions in hairdressing set by the Greeks. The manner of wearing beards and moustaches also changed at different periods, in accordance with the dictates of the Greek mode (*see pp. 47 and 49*).

From about the third century B.C., the hair was worn short, without any parting, and brushed forward over the forehead. It either lay flat or was crisped with curling-tongs into small curls.

Only in times of grief, misfortune or national calamity was the hair allowed to grow long.

Pliny (VII. 211) informs us that shaving was first introduced to the Romans in the fourth century B.C. The fashion set by Alexander the Great (*see p. 49*) was followed at Rome, and remained supreme throughout a period of 426 years (*see p. 112*).

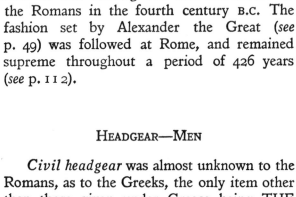

Dia. 14

HEADGEAR—MEN

Civil headgear was almost unknown to the Romans, as to the Greeks, the only item other than those given under Greece being THE CUCULLUS: a hood, a covering for the head, used principally as a protection. It was worn by travellers and countrymen, also by people in general when wishing to remain unobserved and unrecognised. It was in use among the common soldiers when on service in cold climates. Diagram 14 shows one. The long ends could be wound round the neck to keep it in its place, and for further protection.

Footgear—Men and Women

The Romans did not adhere rigidly to Greek fashions in footgear, particularly as regards the sandal. Patriotic instinct would not sanction the general use of the sandal, as it was essentially Greek. Instead, they copied the Etruscan method of covering the feet. Nor was the custom of being barefooted in the house considered quite good form.

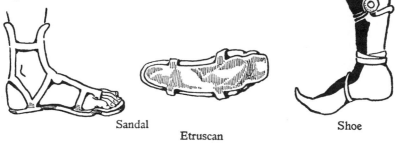

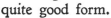

Sandal   Shoe

Etruscan

Slippers, after the modern pattern, made of leather and often coloured and ornamented with cut-work, were used for indoor wear. Slippers of felt, like the present-day bedroom slipper and named "Udo," were often nothing more than a low shoe, but frequently they were made to reach higher up the leg, and assumed the shape of a sock. These were worn for comfort and warmth, and were much used by the peasantry (*see* Fig. 34).

The boot, "Calceus," was the most important of Roman footgear. It had a sole following the shape of the foot, with an upper

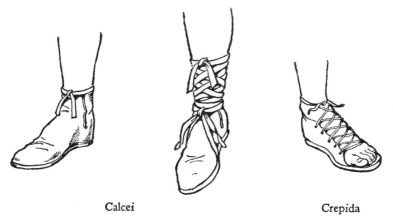

Calcei   Crepida

part of leather sewn on to the sole, and covering the foot in the same manner as a nineteenth-century elastic-side boot without the elastic. A pair of straps was fastened to the back part of the uppers.

These were wound round the ankle two or three times, to a distance of about half-way below the calf, and tied in front with a knot and ends. A second pair of straps was attached on each side of the sole, at the widest part of the foot, and crossed over the instep, fastened round the ankle on top of the first pair of straps, and tied in a knot in front below the first one.

Official boots. Boots of red leather were the distinguishing mark of senators and higher magistrates (curule). Patricians wore the shoe part in untanned leather and the four straps in black.

Ladies' boots. Ladies used this same shaped boot, but in various colours, and often in white. Sometimes, in place of straps, narrow bands of coloured silk were used to tie on the boots.

Half-shoes, "Crepida," were soles to which a piece of leather or stuff was attached, enclosing the heel and the sides of the foot. They were fastened across the instep by straps or bands laced through eyelet holes set in the side pieces.

CONSULS

Prologue to the Pallium

A consul was one of the two highest magistrates who conducted the government of Republican Rome. One consul held the office of chief magistrate, civil authority and dictator. The other held the supreme control of the army. At the end of the Republic the consulship lost its power and importance, and under the Early Empire its office became vested in that of the Imperial Dignity.

The insignia of the consul was the toga praetexta, later the toga picta, worn over the tunica talaris. When in exercise of his office, he was seated upon a square folding-stool—"sella curulis"—having curved legs, but without arms; and he was always attended in procession by twelve *lictors* carrying the "fasces," who preceded him walking in a line one behind the other (continued on p. 158).

The fasces were bundles of rods, usually twelve in number, made of birch or elm wood, bound together by a red thong round the handle of an axe, the blade projecting from them. This insignia denoted that the magistrate had the power of Life and Death.

Fasces

Peasants, Labourers and Slaves of the Republic

The peasant class wore the chiton in its original shape (*see* Fig. 24 and Diagram 9), but of the coarsest materials. The very poorest of them had garments without any pretension to shape, made up of pieces of old materials and the cast-off clothing of their superiors. With a minimum of skill, such garments could be shaped as the colobium or the tunica, but it was still the prevailing habit among the working-class to have the right arm and shoulder bare when at work.

Materials. The tunica, made of thick woollen material, was worn by the more affluent. In all cases the garments were short, reaching to just above the knee (*see also* the Subligaculum). Coats of fur—two pieces of skin with the hair outside and sewn together— and shoulder-capes of fur were worn for additional warmth. The paenula and the cucullus (*see* p. 74) were used as coverings in rough weather.

Fig. 34

On the legs, when required, they bound pieces of hide, after the fashion of the Greek peasants, and the better class peasant had stout ankle boots, of untanned leather fixed to wooden soles. The meanest slave was shod in shoes made from a solid piece of hollowed-out wood.

Fig. 34 is a young shepherd wearing the chiton or tunica, paenula and ankle boots. He carries a crook, and a wooden receptacle is slung across his shoulder.

THE ROMAN ARMY

[As the Roman Army played a very important part during the latter part of the Republic, as well as in Imperial times, a description of the armour and other accoutrements is given.]

THE ARMOUR, ETC. OF THE ROMANS

This was copied in a great measure from the Greeks.

Outfit of a Roman General

Having first vested himself with the tunica, usually white, but sometimes coloured, he placed over it the LORICA. This was a cuirass of brass or bronze moulded to the shape of the body with perfect fit,

Lorica

and following the outline of the abdomen. It was frequently enriched with reliefs and ornaments in metal work. On the breast, a gorgon's head was sometimes embossed, as a charm against evil, and on the shoulders and shoulder-straps scrolls and thunder-bolts. Underneath the cuirass, and often riveted to it, was worn a tight-fitting jacket of leather, its skirt consisting of a row (frequently two) of straps hanging below the cuirass. A single row of similar straps outlined the armholes. These leather straps were often gilded or coloured, and were highly decorated with bronze and other metals, and fringed at the ends. The cuirass was hinged on the right side, and fastened by means of straps and buckles on the left. Frequently a narrow scarf of material was tied round the waist, with one loop and two ends in front, to keep the breast- and back-plates together with more certainty.

Attached to the back-plate were straps which, being brought over

FIG. 19. AN ATHENIAN WOMAN OF FASHION (B.C. 600–468)
(*see* p. 36)

FIG. 35. A ROMAN GENERAL
(see p. 79)

the shoulders, were fastened to the breastplate for further security. Over this would be draped the abolla, paludamentum, or the birrus, according to rank.

The *helmet*, of brass or bronze, had a movable piece which descended on to the forehead, and flanges on either side protected the cheeks. These were often tied together under the chin to make the helmet more secure. On the crown of the helmet was an ornamental ridge, supporting the crest of horsehair, generally dyed a brilliant scarlet.

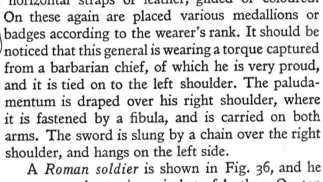

Helmet

On the feet, high boots, or sandals with straps bound round the ankle and lower leg, were worn.

Scaled lorica. Fig. 35 shows a *General,* but he is wearing a cuirass of a different character. The foundation is of leather covered with metal scales, and over it vertical and horizontal straps of leather, gilded or coloured.

On these again are placed various medallions or badges according to the wearer's rank. It should be noticed that this general is wearing a torque captured from a barbarian chief, of which he is very proud, and it is tied on to the left shoulder. The paludamentum is draped over his right shoulder, where it is fastened by a fibula, and is carried on both arms. The sword is slung by a chain over the right shoulder, and hangs on the left side.

A *Roman soldier* is shown in Fig. 36, and he wears over the tunica a jacket of leather. On top of this is a breastplate and back-piece all in one, with shoulder-pieces made of a series of bronze or iron hoops, sliding over each other and attached by straps underneath.

The *helmet* is basin-shaped, with a projecting piece over the nape of the neck, and has cheek-flanges.

On the feet are sandals of leather, attached to strong soles studded with hobnails.

Fig. 36

He is armed with a spear and a sword, and carries a shield on which is the device of the winged thunderbolt of Jupiter—a very common one.

Fig. 35. A General, wearing a cuirass of leather covered with metal scales and various medallions, and a torque tied on the left shoulder. The standard shown is that referred to on p. 80.

This soldier, being on active service in a cold climate, wears the bracco.

Another kind of body armour or cuirass worn by soldiers was composed of metal scales, usually iron, fixed by wire or thread on to a garment of leather or coarse linen. It was without sleeves, and descended to a little below the waist. As usual it was worn over a tunica.

Shields were of various shapes—square, oblong, oval, hexagon, or octagon. The circular shield, which was of a small size, was used only by mounted soldiers. Devices of different sorts were embossed or painted on the shield, but the common soldier usually had his name and the number of his legion, cohort and century painted on it.

The best shields were made of embossed metal, brass, bronze or iron, reinforced with wood. Those carried by the rank and file were of wood or wicker-work covered with leather and strengthened with iron bolts, bosses and rims. They were carried by a strap passing over the right shoulder and held by a handle.

Spears were of various kinds, long and short. The latter—javelins —were about six feet in length and the method of use was hurling.

Military Standards

"Signa"—were of great variety. In the early days of the Republic they were only bunches of herbs, grasses, or hay, bound to the point of a staff.

The Eagle. The most important kind is shown in Fig. 35. It has an eagle, grasping the lightnings and thunderbolts of Jupiter, mounted upon a castle or globe, above several plaques or medallions and wreaths. It was adopted during the second consulship of Caius Marius, 104 B.C., and continued in use during the Empire. The eagle thus became the insignia of Imperial power.

The *Vexillum* is the oldest standard of the Roman Army. It was a white banner, edged at the bottom with a gold fringe, hung from a transverse rod at the top of a pole. When used by superior officers it was red; by the chief consuls and, later, the emperor, of purple. In the two last cases it was surmounted by the figure of Victory.

Vexillum

Signum

The Signum of a Legion is shown here. It was carried in front of the column on the march by a soldier whose armour was that of an ordinary soldier, with the addition of a bearskin tied round the neck by the two front legs, the bear's head worn on the soldier's head, and the remainder of the animal's skin hanging down his back. In camp, or when it was required to erect the standard, its pole was stuck in the ground.

ROMAN WOMEN UNDER THE KINGDOM AND REPUBLIC

The stola. The women of Rome wore a long garment of fine linen or wool descending to the feet like its prototype the Ionic chiton, but now called in the Latin language the "stola." It was fastened on the shoulders and upper arms, and girded in the same way as described on p. 31.

The Doric chiton held second place in popularity as a general garment among women of the upper classes of Republican Rome. It was worn in the same way as described on p. 33.

The Roman name of stola was synonymous with the Ionic and Doric chiton. When the word "tunica" came to be used for the same garment, it applied, as a rule, to the chiton of the men.

Under the stola the women wore a garment cut as a rectangle, and sewn up to form a cylinder. It was fastened on the shoulders in the same manner as the Greek chiton (p. 30, Greece). This garment was called the CAMISIA and was synonymous with the subucula of the men.

The palla and how it was worn. Over the stola was draped the himation of the Greeks, now re-named the "palla." In accordance with the individual taste of the wearer, it was so arranged over the shoulders, and, if necessary, the head, as to prevent it falling off, as it was not usual to secure it by clasps or pins.

For the various ways of wearing it, *see* under the Himation, p. 34.

Fig. 37

HAIRDRESSING—WOMEN OF THE REPUBLIC

The various styles of hairdressing described under Classic Greece, p. 39, were adopted by the fashionable ladies of Republican Rome. Fig. 37 shows the simple method of dressing the hair used by women in general. It is parted in the centre, waved over the temples, and the ends twisted or braided into a coil at the nape of the neck.

Materials used under the Republic

The materials in use among the Romans were the same as those known to the Greeks, but time had very much improved the weaving industry.

Fine linen and soft woollen stuffs were employed in making the garments worn during the period of the Republic, and there is no doubt that the Romans adopted the Greek method of weaving their dress lengths in one piece, with the selvedge all round.

Later conquests by the Republican armies in the East were responsible for the introduction of new materials—*cotton*, first known in Rome about the year 180 B.C., and *silk*, called by the Romans "sericum," but very little known before the first century B.C. It was scarce, owing to the cost, difficulty, and labour of transit, and this considerably enhanced its value.

JEWELLERY

The Romans copied, as in everything else, the art of the Greek goldsmiths; and in addition they stole the ideas of their neighbours, the Etruscans, as regards jewellery.

Roman luxury, and the taste for jewellery, dates from the conquest of Macedon, 168 B.C., when Pompey the Great lodged the spoils of Mithridates with great ceremony in the Capitol. The wonderful collection of jewels, gold ornaments, and accessories of the conquered king [1] was exhibited to the Roman populace, and greatly stimulated their passion for extravagant display.

Crowns. As regards crowns they followed the Greek fashions, as set out on p. 60, but they also adopted crowns of their own, as rewards for various services—military, naval, civil and artistic.

The corona etrusca was a wreath of gold leaves, set with jewels, and tied behind with ribbons. It was held by a public officer over the head of a general when making his triumph.

The corona navalis was a gold band, decorated with the prows of ships, awarded for naval services.

The corona muralis was a band of gold, finishing in turrets or embattlements, and awarded for bravery in the case of siege. Another type was decorated with miniature palisades, and was awarded to the man who first entered the enemy's camp.

Tiaras in shape almost identical with the Greek stephane were of ornamental goldsmith's work. Bands of gold set with gems and jewels, and fillets, all more or less after the Greek fashion, were worn by ladies of the patrician class.

Necklaces of Greek and Etruscan design were much used. The decoration of the latter was extremely beautiful. Motifs worked in plate or filigree gold were often set with gems and jewels, and strung together by chains and smaller motifs. From larger motifs ornaments of all shapes were suspended, the whole necklace being fastened round the neck by an ornament clasp. Pearls, emeralds, and rubies were the precious stones mostly used.

Necklaces were also composed of beads made from glass, crystal, amber, pebbles, and gold.

Bracelets. It was the custom for the men of Etruria, as well as the women, to wear bracelets, and in the earlier times of the Republic the

[1] *See* p. 59, Greek Jewellery.

Roman men followed suit. Towards the end of this period, however, the custom was abandoned.

Bracelets described on p. 62 were also worn by the Roman ladies.

For hairpins, fibulæ, etc., *see* p. 63.

Rings. Those worn by the Romans in the early days of the Republic were generally made of iron, on which was engraved a seal. These iron rings were worn by men only, the women being content with one, and that the wedding-ring, also of iron. This custom continued in use right down to the end of the Republic, and was retained by many of the good old families well into the Empire.

Gold rings were a military decoration awarded for military service. Many Government officials had the right to wear a gold ring, which was handed down to their descendants as an heirloom. In the second century B.C. it was the distinguishing badge of cavalry officers or knights, "Equites." A gold ring was given to a man on attaining knighthood.

SECTION II.—ROMAN BRITAIN

A.D. 78–428 [1]

For Historical Data, *see under* IMPERIAL ROME.

INTRODUCTION

During the course of the first century A.D., a large proportion of Britons, notably the upper and official classes, were entirely Romanised. Thus, as previously in Gaul and elsewhere, the universal rule of history repeated itself.

Some of the old Celtic families of very conservative and patriotic ideas were not so eager to avail themselves of the doubtful advantages of Roman civilisation, and preferred the culture, costume, and traditions of their native land, which had been handed down to them from generation to generation. Therefore, for a considerable time, the good old habits of life and dress continued to exist side by side with the new customs and costume introduced by the conquerors.

The Latin or Roman element retained in our constitution, laws, language and customs has descended to us from the time of the Roman occupation of Britain.

COSTUME OF THE ROMANISED BRITONS

High officials. For the costume of Britons of high official rank under the Roman Government, reference must be made to the description of costume given under Republican Rome.

It must be taken into account that fashions took time to filter through Europe to the Far West: in the ordinary way, perhaps twenty-five to thirty years, but if a British official and his wife happened to be returning from their first visit to Rome, bringing with them clothes of the latest Roman cut, six months would be ample time to allow.

The tunica. With the middle classes the tunica remained the chief body garment of the men. This body garment has been spoken of in the Celtic Age, Chapter I., p. 10, as the crys. It was renamed

[1] See footnote, p. 220.

about this time by the Roman-Briton the "tunica," and as such will be referred to henceforth in these pages.

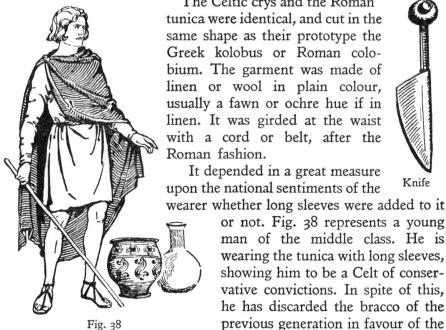

Fig. 38

Knife

The Celtic crys and the Roman tunica were identical, and cut in the same shape as their prototype the Greek kolobus or Roman colobium. The garment was made of linen or wool in plain colour, usually a fawn or ochre hue if in linen. It was girded at the waist with a cord or belt, after the Roman fashion.

It depended in a great measure upon the national sentiments of the wearer whether long sleeves were added to it or not. Fig. 38 represents a young man of the middle class. He is wearing the tunica with long sleeves, showing him to be a Celt of conservative convictions. In spite of this, he has discarded the bracco of the previous generation in favour of the Roman fashion of bare legs, his feet being shod with Roman sandals. His hair also is worn short. (By degrees it was cropped closer and closer to the head, until at last there was scarcely any difference between Celt and Roman.) On the shoulders he wears one of the cloaks described under Republican Rome, p. 71.

ARMOUR

The *armour*, etc. of the Roman-British soldiers closely resembled that of the Roman. It is recorded that the native warriors frequently wore the *lorica*, and a tunica made of leather or hide, cut in strips round the armholes and waist. The *breastplate* was composed of scales of brass, bronze or iron (*see* Fig. 39).

The *helmets* were of the inverted basin

Fig. 39

shape, with or without brims, and in many cases with side-flaps which were tied under the chin. These helmets were decorated with flanges of metal, bosses, horns, and other appendages. Their *shields* were circular or oval, made of wood covered with hide and strengthened with metal.

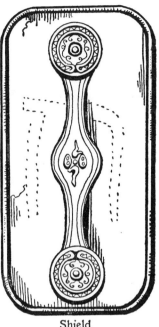

Shield

A more substantial shield of this period was found in the bed of the River Witham in Lincolnshire. It had been constructed evidently by British metal workers, who at that time were being induced to imitate the Roman fashions in the making of armour. Oblong in shape, with rounded corners, it was intended to be held at arm's length by a handle fitted into the groove made by the ornament, the grip being guarded by a convex boss. This shield appears to have been originally gilt, and the boss ornamented with pieces of red cornelian fastened by brass pins. At the same time was discovered a bronze sword, and a bronze-mounted scabbard of this period.

Spears, swords and daggers, when not actually imported from Rome, were modelled after the Roman fashion.

PEASANTS

The peasants still continued to use the skins of animals a good deal, over a coarse tunica, and sometimes a cloak of coarse cloth with a hood attached.

THE WOMEN OF ROMAN BRITAIN

Ladies of high rank adopted the Roman dress in every particular, wearing a straight garment—the gwn, now renamed the stola—fastened on the shoulders with brooches or fibulæ and confined at the waist with a belt; or the Classic method of girding (*see* Diagrams 4 and 5) might be adopted. The stola was made of imported material in preference to the coarser British-made stuff. Over it was draped the cloak or palla.

The *hair* was mostly parted in the centre, waved over the temples and twisted into a knot at the back (*see* Fig. 37). Ornaments would be hairpins, diadems, bracelets, necklaces, etc., all chosen from the catalogue of jewellery given on p. 83, together with a few precious heirlooms of Celtic workmanship.

Fibula Hairpins Bracelet

Shoes. About the house ladies would walk barefooted, or they would slip their feet into embroidered slippers; but out in the street they would wear sandals or shoes.

The *women of the middle classes* wore the gwn of the Celts (*see* p. 18) almost to the feet, with or without fairly tight sleeves, and sometimes over it a shorter tunic, with long sleeves, or sleeveless, and confined in either case with a girdle. To this, if required in stormy weather, would be added the laena (*see* p. 71), the cloak of soft material worn by the common people of Rome, but with this difference: by the Roman-British women it was wrapped round the whole figure, and obviously put on by first lying down in it, so that the top part extended beyond the top of the head and the bottom edge reached to about the calf. A belt was then fastened round over all to keep it in its place at waist level. When the wearer rose to her feet the top half naturally fell down, so that a double thickness was obtained round the skirt. The back part of this turned-over piece was then taken and drawn over the head (*see* Fig. 40).[1]

Fig. 40

The hair. The Roman-British woman was now beginning to dress her hair by parting it in the middle and twisting it into a coil at the back of the head, in imitation of the Romanised women of the superior class.

[1] This method of wrapping oneself up continued among the Celtic population, both men and women, in North Britain right through the Middle Ages. It was also the way the plaid— the belted plaid—was worn by the Highlanders from the late seventeenth century down to the middle of the eighteenth. At that time the plaid (the original laena) was divided at the waist line; the upper part remained the plaid; the lower part became the kilt.

North British women to-day wear the shawl in the same way as the Roman-British women wore the laena.

The legs and feet were bare, unless a pair of Roman sandals or shoes could be procured. The shoemakers of these times began to improve in their work, and, with the imported footwear as their model, the primitive Celtic shoes (*see* p. 12) assumed a better shape, and had a sole attached.

Peasant class. A woman of the poorest class wore a simple garment without sleeves, with or without a skin of some sort wrapped round her body, held in place with a belt. She adorned her throat with a necklace of stones, perhaps selected for their colour, or the teeth of some animal, and her hair was worn flowing. In fact, the dress worn by this class in the early part of this period did not differ much from that worn by their ancestors in the latter part of the Bronze Age.

Personal *ornaments* of this period were chiefly of bronze, and sometimes jet. Very little gold or silver was used, except by those who were in close contact with the high officials at Rome. The Roman-British seem to have excelled in the art of enamelling, and some very beautiful pieces have been discovered, which are now in the British Museum.

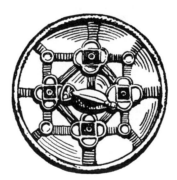

Enamel Ornaments

Section III.—IMPERIAL ROME, 27 B.C.–A.D. 400 [1]

HISTORICAL DATA, SAME PERIOD, AND CONTINUED TO THE FALL OF ROME, A.D. 476

B.C.

27. Peace to the Empire. Temple of Janus closed.

19. All Spain subject to Rome.

Anno Domini.   A.D.

B.C.

4. Jesus Christ, the Messiah, born.

Four years before the Common Era.

The Year of Our Lord.

Note.—The Christian Era commenced January 1st in the middle of the fourth year of the 194th Olympiad, the 753rd year of the foundation of Rome, and the 4714th year of the Julian calendar. Modern opinion places the birth of Christ four years previous to this date (*see* St. Luke, chap. ii.). The Julian calendar was an improved version of the old Roman record made by Julius Cæsar, and it remained in use until Pope Gregory XIII. (1572) produced a reformed calendar, called the Gregorian.

A.D.

9. Varus defeated by Herman, the Germanic chief.

14. Death of Octavius Imperator. Tiberius Emperor.

33.

37. Caius Germanicus Emperor, known as Caligula, a name given to him when a child from his habit of wearing "little" or half-boots, usually worn by the common soldiers.

41. Claudius I. Emperor.

43. The third invasion of Britain.

51. Caractacus brought prisoner to Rome.

54. Claudius Nero Emperor. The first persecution of the Christians.

62. Boadicea vanquished. Complete subjugation of Britain. The same year S. Paul brought a prisoner to Rome.

64. The Emperor Nero burns Rome, and accuses the Christians of the crime.

67. S. Peter and S. Paul martyred.

70. Jerusalem taken by Titus.

114. The Emperor Trajan. His column erected at Rome.

117. The Emperor Hadrian.

119. He made his tour in Gaul, Germany and Britain.

122. He built his wall in North Britain.

161. The Emperor Marcus Aurelius.

180. This year ends the period (96–180) of Rome's supreme happiness and prosperity. The Emperor Commodus.

A.D.

218. The Emperor Heliogabalus.

222. The Barbarians, Goths and Vandals attack the Empire.

237. Gordianus the Elder Emperor.

253. Valerian elected as Emperor "in right of his merits, and by the unanimous voice of the whole world."

269. Emperor Claudius II. gains a great victory over the Goths.

273. Conquest of Palmyra by the Emperor Aurelian. Zenobia brought captive to Rome.

284. The era of Martyrs under the Emperor Diocletian. He made great changes in the government, social life and costume.

285. Martyrdom of S. Alban, the protomartyr of Britain.

287. The Franks crushed by Maximian, and Carausius revolts in Britain.

290. Martyrdom of S. George, a noble Greek. Beheaded, April 23rd.

303. Edict of Diocletian forbidding the cult of Christianity under severe penalties.

305. He abdicated and retired to his beautiful palace (including a kitchen garden) built by him at Spalato. After his death (313) no other emperor resided there and it eventually became a cloth factory.

305. Beginning of Civil War.

306. Constantine Chlorus dies at York and accession as Emperor of Rome of his son Constantine the Great, who was with his father in Britain.

---

[1] The date A.D. 400 is given as a convenient one at which to end the history of Costume of Imperial Rome, and to begin the history of Byzantine Dress. For a period of about 150 years, however, the two styles of dress overlapped, and are practically identical. Byzantium before that date followed the lead of Rome, and after that date Roman dress was entirely overruled by Byzantine fashions.

A.D.

312. Constantine converted to Christianity.

313. Edict of Toleration published by Galerius, and Edict of Milan by Constantine.

323. End of Civil War. Constantine supreme Emperor and makes Christianity the religion of the State.

325. First Ecumenical Council of the Christian Church at Nicæa.

328. S. Helena, the Empress Dowager, makes a pilgrimage to the Holy Land. Constantine finds the Holy Sepulchre and builds a church over it.

330. Foundation of the New Byzantium, named after the founder, Constantinople.

337. Constantine the Great dies and is succeeded by his three sons, Constantine II., Constans, and Constantinus II.

343. The Basilica of Sancta Sophia built at Constantinople.

361. Julian the Apostate. He attempts to repress Christianity.

363. Jovianus Emperor for 8 months. The Persian War brought about the ignoble Peace of Dura, a memorable event in the decline of Rome.

364. Valentinian I. elected Emperor of Rome or Western Empire. His brother Valens becomes Emperor of the East at Constantinople. They execute the solemn division of the Roman Empire into West and East, June 364.

383. Maximus, a Spaniard, revolts and becomes Emperor of Britain, Spain, and Gaul.

384. Stilicho, a Pannonian Vandal, becomes commander-in-chief. A great Roman general. Married Serena, the Emperor's niece.

388. Defeat of Maximus. Full empire restored to Valentinian II., Emperor of the West.

391. Decree against Paganism.

392. Theodosius I. the Great, Emperor of the West as well as the East. Married a Spanish lady, Ælia Flacilla, who is canonised in the Greek Church, of which she was a great benefactress. The Roman Empire terminates as a single dominion.

394. Honorius becomes Emperor of the West at Rome, but Stilicho is practically ruler of the Western Empire. Arcadius, Emperor of the East at Constantinople.

396. The Goths under Alaric descend on Thrace but are met by Stilicho in Arcadia, who turns them back.

401. They invade Italy, and Stilicho defeats Alaric at Pollentia.

A.D.

403. Alaric again enters Italy, and again Stilicho repulses him at Verona. The last triumph over the Goths.

405. Radagaisus, a Slavonic barbarian, marches from the plains of the Vistula into Italy. Stilicho enlists Uldig, Chief of the Huns, as an auxiliary, meets Radagaisus at Florence and vanquishes him.

408. Stilicho put to death at Ravenna. First siege of Rome by Alaric. Edicts against Arianism, Paganism, and the wearing of trousers.

409. Second siege of Rome by Alaric.

410. Third siege of Rome by Alaric. Although he was a man of some culture, his army ruthlessly sacked the city. These hordes of Barbarians were destitute of any taste and appreciation of elegant arts and refinements. They looted the richest city in the world during their six days' sojourn, piling their baggage-wagons with everything they could lay hands on—gold and jewels, costly furniture, clothes, works of art, and the sister of the Emperor Honorius, Ælia Galla Placidia. The Goths destroyed all that they could not carry away. Although of the Arian Faith, Alaric spared all the churches, and his death the same year put an end to the campaign.

412. Ælia Galla Placidia married first Athaulf, the successor of Alaric, and secondly in

417. Constantius III., co-Regent of Honorius. She was Regent for their

425. son, who became the Emperor Valentinian III. of Rome. Ætius, the last champion and bulwark of the Western Empire (395–454).

446. The Huns on the war-path. Attila destroyed two Roman armies, and took and sacked seventy towns. He sent an embassy to Rome to intimidate the government, and made extravagant demands.

450. Death of the Empress Ælia Galla Placidia. Her body was embalmed after the Egyptian fashion and sealed up in a chapel built by her at Ravenna, where it remained, seated in state upon a throne of cedar-wood, until the year 1577, when it was accidentally set alight and burnt to ashes.

451. Ætius makes an alliance with the Ostrogoths against the Huns, and Genseric, King of the Vandals, enters into an agreement with Attila, whereby the former was to invade Italy from Africa, and the latter to attack Gaul. Attila assembled

A.D.

an enormous host of every kind of barbarian on the south side of the Danube for the invasion of the empire in the West, on the grounds, ostensibly, of the Princess Honoria, Galla Placidia's daughter and the Emperor Valentinian III.'s sister, being withheld as his affianced bride. This expedition culminated in the defeat of Attila by Ætius at Châlons-sur-Marne.

452. In the following year he made another attack on the empire of the West; this time on Northern Italy. He was met by Pope Leo the Great, near Mantua, who entreated him to return. This Attila consented to do, and a treaty of peace was made: an ignominious one, but it saved Rome!

454. Death of Attila, " the Scourge of God," and murder of Ætius, the great general.

455 (June). Rome besieged by the Vandals and the Moors under Genseric,

A.D.

and pillaged. They retired after fourteen days, taking with them large quantities of spoil, and even the Empress Eudoxia and the two daughters of Valentinian III.

455 (August). Avitus, a native of Auvergne, elected Emperor by the Goths. Ricimer, a chief of the Suevi, destroys the Vandal fleet off Corsica, and is hailed the deliverer of Italy. He deposes the Emperor.

456. Avitus is murdered in October.

472. Rome taken by assault by Ricimer.

475. Romulus Augustulus acknowledged Emperor of the West. Son of Orestes. He was deposed by Odoacer son of Edecon, a barbarian (see p.137), and a Teuton.

476. Odoacer takes Rome, and forces the Senate to abolish the Imperial Sovereignty in the West. He assumed the title of King of Italy (476–490) and completed *The Fall of the Roman or Western Empire.*

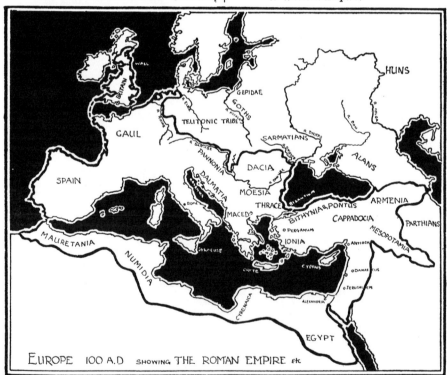

EUROPE 100 A.D SHOWING THE ROMAN EMPIRE etc

HISTORICAL INTRODUCTION

Until the fall of Rome, its history, with but little relief, is one of superlative luxury, debauchery, brutality and crime. Manners and customs became more and more decadent, and costume more luxurious. All the available arts and crafts of the time, and the accumulated wealth of conquered races—literally the loot of nations, drawn from barbarians in the north and west, from Asiatics, Egyptians, and the massacred Carthaginians—were employed to make Court life, and incidentally, costume, as ornate, costly and voluptuous as possible. The traditions of the State were insecure foundations—a system of slavery.

LIVY and OVID, *d.* A.D. 18; SENECA, *d.* A.D. 65; PLINY THE ELDER, A.D. 79; QUINTILIAN, A.D. 80; JOSEPHUS, the Jewish historian, A.D. 37–100; PLINY THE YOUNGER and TACITUS, A.D. 100; SUETONIUS, A.D. 120; JUVENAL, A.D. 128; DION CASSIUS, *b.* A.D. 155; TERTULLIANUS, A.D. 160–220; JULIUS CAPITOLINUS, A.D. 284; ÆLIUS LAMPRIDUS, TREBELLIUS POLLIO, A.D. 305, are some of the eminent men of the Imperial Epoch.

To the Western civilised world Rome was the centre of fashion from the year 146 B.C. to A.D. 400.

COSTUME OF THE MEN UNDER THE EMPIRE

27 B.C.–A.D. 400

The toga maintained its popularity during the first century, and the varieties mentioned under the Republic were still in use as described, except:

THE TOGA PICTA

Under the Empire its surface was much more ornamented, chiefly with circular and square plaques, or a sprinkling of motifs, in circles, squares, lozenges, combined with crosses, stars, crescents, suns, etc., carried out in heavy gold embroidery and surrounded by an elaborate border of gold.

The toga picta was the *official robe of the Emperor,* worn over the tunica palmata (*see* Fig. 41), and in the second century A.D. it became part of the official garb of Roman consuls.

Essentially a ceremonial dress, it constituted the correct costume of the Court during the whole of the Empire period, until the centre of government was transferred to Constantinople, when it was entirely superseded by the paludamentum.

From this toga picta all Imperial and regal robes have descended.

The wane of the toga. The popularity of the toga for general use began to wane towards the end of the first century A.D. A certain laxity of dress appears among the professional and trading classes. In

Fig. 41. An Emperor of the third century A.D. wearing the corona radiata, and the golden laurel wreath in front of it. He wears the tunica palmata, and the toga picta put on in the manner of the toga umbo (*see* Fig. 42 and description on p. 94), but with the point F (Fig. 42) draped over the left arm.

the hustle and turmoil of city and commercial life it was found that the stately toga was an encumbrance, being difficult to adjust conveniently without some degree of patience.

As early as the reign of Octavius, endeavours were made to stop the increasing inclination to dispense with it altogether, in favour of more practical garments such as the birrus, lacerna, laena and paenula. By the second century the toga was little worn outside Rome.

THE TOGA UMBO OR CONTABULATUM OF THE SECOND CENTURY A.D.

This was the ordinary toga, with a red or purple band; but it was worn in a particular manner, and came into fashion among high dignitaries toward the end of the second century A.D.[1]

How to arrange it. It was put on by folding the straight edge along its whole length to the depth of twelve or fourteen inches, and, starting with the point A at the left foot, taking it over the left shoulder and arm as before (*see* p. 67 and Diagram 11). It was then draped across the back, to a point just in front of the right armpit. Here it was given a double twist, and continued over the left shoulder again, giving a curved line to the lower band in front. The top, retaining its turnover or fold, E, crossed the breast and right shoulder, giving a collar or band (the umbo) effect, and fell down the back in panel fashion (*see* Fig. 42).

There were further developments, which will be dealt with under the Pallium.

The toga obsolete. The practical disuse of the toga as a national dress increased its importance as a ceremonial one. In the reign of Diocletian many innovations appeared. Princes and high officials of the Empire were distinguished by their sumptuous Imperial (toga picta) and military (paludamentum) mantles of purple silk and gold.

By the fourth century official costume was prescribed by law—the "Lex Vestiaria" (Jan. 12, 382) requiring magistrates and senators in exercise of public functions to wear the toga, tunica and paenula.

The toga proper (the white) as a garment was regarded in later times as the symbol of pagan denomination; and this in a measure accounts for its disappearance at the time of the establishment of Christianity.

---

[1] A portrait bust of the Emperor Gordianus (158–238), British Museum, and the Imperial Proclamation on the Arch of Constantine (315), show the toga umbo and tunica talaris.

Fig. 42. A patrician of the second, third and fourth centuries A.D., wearing the toga praetexta, arranged as a toga umbo or contabulatum, over the tunica talaris.

Fig. 42. THE TOGA UMBO

The Tunica of Imperial Rome
Including the Colobium, Subucula, Dalmatica and Albe

It became customary at this time for the men and women of Rome to wear, besides the tunica, an under-garment, usually made of woollen stuff.

Perhaps a change in the Italian climate had something to do with the addition, or the heat experienced in their Egyptian campaign made them feel the necessity for more clothing on their return to Rome. We know that the Emperor Octavius (31 B.C.–A.D. 14) was very sensitive to cold and wore as many as four tunicas at one time, and even covered his legs with barbaric braies to keep them warm. But this was an exception.

When more than one tunica was worn, the under ones were the same shape as the outer and called

The Tunica Interior or *Subucula,*

which was but another name for the colobium.

The Year ✦ *of Our Lord.*

The garments of Our Lord. It is interesting to note that the usual garments worn by Our Lord and His Apostles is identified with the colobium in its original form (*see* Fig. 27 and Diagram 10). Over this they draped the himation. Also that the kolobus (*see* p. 43, Greece), called by the Romans the colobium, was the seamless coat of Our Lord. "Now the *coat*" (*viz.* the chiton–kolobus) "was without seam, wrought" (woven) "from the top throughout" (St. John xix. 23).

A.D. 33

No change in the *colour* of the tunica took place during the first century. It was universally of white, and on that account called in Latin, "Tunica Alba."

At the beginning of the second century the two stripes of purple, the ANGUSTUS CLAVUS (*see* p. 106), now obsolete as a badge of rank, became the only decoration of the tunica. The colours in use for the tunica at this time were the more natural hues of pale ochre, yellow, fawn and brown.

The tunica and its variations, the colobium and subucula, continued in use during the first two centuries A.D., without any alteration in shape; but, towards the end of the second century, the neck part underwent a slight change. It was now sometimes gathered into a very narrow neck-band (*see* Fig. 42).

A Tunica of a New Shape

A new-shaped tunica came into use during the third century A.D., but its first appearance dates back to the year 190, when it became the custom among decadent dandies to introduce into the world of frivolity and fashion garments of foreign origin, in spite of the outrage against national feeling.

A storm of abuse was poured upon the eccentric Emperor Commodus for his audacity in appearing publicly in a costume copied from the dress in general use in Dalmatia. Long sleeves were peculiar to this garment, and hitherto unknown to the Romans; so they attracted much attention and no little scorn. Later in the year 218, even greater dissatisfaction was expressed when Heliogabalus appeared officially in a loose flowing gown with wide long sleeves of Oriental make. This garment was merely the usual type of robe worn by many Asiatic peoples for generations and centuries previously, as also in the country whence it derives its name: the DALMATICA.

The Dalmatica

One must refer to Assyrian, Persian and other Eastern paintings and sculptures, to learn what the actual dalmaticas worn by these two emperors were like. There is no doubt that they were open up the front and worn over another elaborate robe, after the Oriental fashion.

A description of Heliogabalus, as he appeared when making his triumphal entry into Rome, is worth noting. He rode in his State chariot, dressed in long loose and flowing robes of purple silk, embroidered with gold. His head was crowned with a tiara of successive radiating suns, above a debauched face made up with artificial pink and white, with eyes and eyebrows tinged with black;[1] and about his neck were collars of gems and ropes of pearls of inestimable value. His delicate arms were laden with bracelets, and his shoes were encrusted with jewels.

---

[1] Heliogabalus was the first emperor of Rome of Asiatic extraction. His father was a Syrian; and making up the eyes was a common practice among men and women of that nation. Original name Varius Avitus Bassianus: adopted Elagabalus (or Heliogabalus) as Pontiff of the Syro-Phœnician Sun-God. Known also as Marcus Aurelius Antoninus.

Dalmatica worn generally. After this sumptuous display, the dalmatica was adopted in a less ostentatious form by the luxury-loving Romans, both men and women, and, *in a simple form,* by the populace in general (*see* Fig. 43).

Description of dalmatica. Many writers of this and the following century give graphic details of the dalmatica, from which we learn that it was a *closed* garment, and that the wide sleeves were its distinctive feature. The material was shaped like a square cross, with a horizontal slit cut or left unwoven in the centre for the head to pass through. Being folded in half (*see* Diagram 15) and sewn together at the two sides, it formed sleeves of moderate length and width. These sleeves were usually cut out separately and joined to the sides. The dalmatica was ornamented by

Fig. 43

the angustus clavus, in red or purple, with one or sometimes two bands of the same colour on the sleeves.

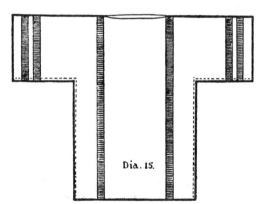

Dia. 15.

Material. It was made of wool, linen or cotton, in natural colourings, and always worn without a belt.

When worn by men, this garment reached to just below the knee, and, in the second and third centuries, sometimes showed the bottom of the tunica underneath.

The dalmatica was often the only garment worn, but, if needed, the colobium was sometimes worn under it. The two stripes which decorated the colobium and tunica were now transferred to the dalmatica when worn over them.

The Dalmatica adopted by the Early Christians

Various reasons have been suggested for the fact that the dalmatica was appropriated as a distinctive garment by the enthusiastic and faithful followers of Christ. Some affirm that in it was seen a development of the colobium worn by the Apostles (*see* p. 97); others that when the dalmatica was unsewn up the sides and opened out flat, it had the form of a cross. However that may be, dating from the middle of this century we have representations of early Christians wearing the dalmatica, with the addition of the angustus clavus in deep red or purple—the now obsolete attribute of officialdom. This, it is suggested, symbolised the Blood of Christ. S. Cyprian of Carthage (A.D. 200–258) wore the dalmatica with the paenula over it. These he removed for his execution, wearing only the colobium.

The tunica: Long sleeves first worn. About A.D. 250 long sleeves, moderately tight to the wrists, were becoming general; and a little later they were quite common. The construction of these garments still followed the lines of the original tunica or colobium (with the exception of the trifling detail of the neckband), and is shown in Diagram 16. Long sleeves could be sewn into the arm-holes, or the garment could be cut in one piece with sleeves.

Dia. 16

The *material* from which they were made was not at this time entirely limited to wool or linen, as we hear of a tunica made in semi-silk and wool, viz. an "alba subserica," mentioned in a letter from the Emperor Valerian to Zosimus, Procurator of Syria (A.D. 269 –270). The Emperor Aurelian, it is stated, made gifts of "tunicas with long sleeves" to the people in the year A.D. 270. After this we hear that *long* tunicas, the "tunica talaris," and long sleeves, were universally worn by the middle and upper classes.

The Dalmatica

Shrouds of martyrs. Eutychianus, Bishop of Rome, A.D. 275–283, and himself a martyr, issued a mandate commanding that all those who died in the cause of the True Faith were to be enshrouded for burial in the dalmatica and colobium.

The opening of the fourth century is a landmark in the history of Roman dress, especially in regard to the tunica and dalmatica.

Class distinction. The Romans, even in Republican times, had distinguished rank and grade by certain details in dress, but the increasing luxury of the people in general made it difficult to preserve these simple yet sufficient distinctions. The reign of the Emperor Diocletian [1] (A.D. 284–305) is chiefly noteworthy for the fact that he constituted himself absolute monarch (thus abolishing the last vestige of Republican institutions), and for the introduction of the Oriental magnificence of the Persian Court into social life and costume. These influences helped to create more definite distinctions between ranks and professions: sumptuary laws of a later date prescribed minutely the garments that might be worn by different classes.

Colour and decoration. A lavish display of colour, in innumerable shades, combinations and contrasts, now superseded the more delicate tones and softer hues inspired by Greek artists, and the more refined tastes of the Classic Period. Tunicas and dalmaticas, although usually of some solid, bright colour, now began to be decorated all over with patterns, embroidered or stencilled in conventional designs.

A great variety of other subjects was used in this way; processions of men and women, decorous and otherwise; mounted men, huntsmen, chariot races, and even scenes from Biblical history, were portrayed in this manner, and the practice aroused the derision of writers of the time, who referred scornfully to these "walking frescoes." The tunica, now visible at the neck, wrist, and, as it grew longer, below the dalmatica, acquired rich borders of needlework or tapestry. The tunica, as a garment to be worn without the dalmatica over it, also attained small squares, or circles [2] (segmentæ), of embroidery, [3] one on each shoulder, two in front toward the bottom corners (when the

3rd & 4th cent.

Segmentæ

tunica was slit up the sides), and the same at the back (*see* Fig. 44).

3rd & 4th cent

Segmentum

Both as regards shape and ornamentation it was the same back and front.

The segmentum. In the earliest period of this fashion the segmentum was nearly always worked or woven in one colour, chiefly the various shades of purple described on p. 106. The outline of its geometrical design was worked in with white linen thread, conventional foliage and figures being added in solid colour on a light linen background. The material used for embroidering was always wool, silk not being used until the sixth century.

These worked designs were of substantial make, and invariably

---

[1] A self-educated man and the son of two slaves.
[2] On Church vestments, the segmentæ are known as "Apparels."
[3] *See also* Fig. 67 (Byzantium): Justinian on horseback.

survived the garment on which they were placed. When the old garment was cast away, the segmentæ were transferred to a new one.

The tunica. The tunica talaris of the Republic was now much worn by men of the upper class. It conferred a special dignity upon the wearer and, being the characteristic garb of learned men, it found great favour. It was worn under the toga umbo by great personages and officials (*see* Fig. 42) at the Court of Constantine the Great, and can be regarded as part of the *Court costume.*

The short tunica, which was more convenient, was still retained by men of the people.

The dalmatica was still worn short by men, made with or without the clavus, but its general aspect changed somewhat. The long sleeves of the tunica now showed on the forearm under the wide sleeve of the dalmatica, and the skirt of the tunica talaris covered the legs to the ankles.

At this period the neck part underwent the same change as the tunica proper—its straight edge was gathered into a small neck-band.

First vestment. The Edict of Toleration and the Edict of Milan were followed in 314 by the decree of Pope Silvester, ordaining that the dalmatica should be worn over the tunica talaris by deacons when serving at the altar. His Holiness added sleeves of different lengths and widths, according to the priority in office of the deacons, and retained the angustus clavus in purple. It is sometimes represented in scarlet or crimson.

Dress of the clergy. By the middle of the fourth century, bishops [1] wore three garments—the tunica talaris, the dalmatica, and the paenula. Deacons (from the Greek διάκονος = an attendant), who were servants of the Church, wore two—the tunica talaris and the dalmatica. These garments, it must be understood, were worn simply as adequate clothing, and had no significance whatsoever *in Church ritual.*

Recognition of distinctive dress of clergy. Special dress or uniform for bishops and deacons was not an accepted practice until the middle of the sixth century, but shortly after that date:

The tunica talaris, known later as the albe, or alb, a *white* tunic
    (*see* p. 97);
the dalmatica; and
the paenula, known later as the chasuble (and, when open up the
    front, the cope),

until then the common everyday dress of the common people, became

[1] From the Greek ἐπισκοπέω = an overseer. An overseer of the Church was ordained by an Apostle in each of the First Principal Churches.

Fig. 44. The tunica talaris, showing the segmentæ and elaborately embroidered clavus, yoke and wrist-bands. Early form of Christian Cross in corner.

Fig. 44. THE TUNICA TALARIS

the recognised ecclesiastical garments of the clergy—the first vestments[1] of the Early Christian Church, throughout the East and the West.

During the seventh century the dalmatica, paenula and pallium (see p. 107) became obsolete as garments for general use among the laity.

The Tunica Palmata

Costume of emperors. Under the Empire, the tunica palmata and toga picta, which constituted part of the "Ornamenta Triumphalia," became the official costume of emperors; and the decoration on the tunica palmata was much more elaborate and rich, its surface being covered with gold embroideries of conventional foliage (*see* Fig. 41). It was also usual to have the tunica embroidered all over with the same design as that used on the toga picta, in circular, square, and lozenge-shaped motifs, with a border at the neck, wrists and bottom edge. This is seen especially in diptychs of consuls, with whom, after the second century A.D., it became the official dress (*see* Fig. 69).

THE CLAVUS

A band or stripe—and a convenient mark of office or rank.

It is said that this band was originally copied from the Etruscans by members of the Roman Senate, about the seventh century B.C., as a distinctive badge of their office. It was a scarlet or purple stripe, two fingers in width, woven or sewn down the front and back centre of the white tunica and called by them the "latus clavus" (*see* Fig. 32). The right to wear the latus clavus, but narrower in width, was granted to the sons of politicians when candidates for the Senate.

The clavus in Greece. It also appeared in Greece about the fourth century B.C., but purely as a decoration, usually down the front and sometimes the back of chitons worn by women and men (*see* Fig. 27). It was of plain material, scarlet or purple, sewn on or woven into the garment, and in many instances it was ornamented with a design in meanders, scrolls, or foliage, and often interwoven with gold thread.

A white chiton, ornamented with *two* stripes of purple over the shoulders and down the front and back, one on each side, was the official dress of the "Camilli," an association of youths and maidens employed to *minister* in religious rites and ceremonies.

The clavus in Rome. Two stripes, one on either side, back and front of the tunica, were also used as a badge, worn by members or knights of the Equestrian Order, a sort of Household Cavalry or body-

---

[1] From the Latin word "*vestimenta*"—clothing of *poor* or humble people.

guard, instituted by the Romans at an early date prior to the Christian Era; they were called *The Angustus Clavus* (*see* Figs. 43 and 44).

Colour. From the earliest times, and well into the second century A.D., the colour was invariably purple—a purple ranging through the various shades of dark carmine, red, claret, violet and dark blue.

The tunica on which it was applied was usually girded, but the punctilious Quintilianus (A.D. 35–95) advises, "that if the tunica has the latus clavus or the angustus clavus, it is better to wear it without a girdle; but it is not so convenient."

Clavi become obsolete as badges of rank. At the end of the first century both the clavi lost their significance as badges of rank, since they were used as a fashionable adjunct to the tunica in general, and also worn by women. When the dalmatica came into use, the angustus clavus became its characteristic decoration.

It was used by Early Christians, possibly because of its association as the official sign of ministration of the Camilli (*see* above); but it could hardly have been a distinctive badge, as it was in use equally among Christians and Pagans.

B

A

Repeat A, then B.

3rd & 4th cent.

4th cent.

Clavi

It was sanctified by the fact that the early martyrs wore it, and it became recognised afterwards as a detail of ecclesiastical dress.

During the third and fourth centuries A.D. the clavus was employed not only as a band of plain colour, but frequently as strips of embroidery of beautiful design, or the pattern was woven into the material.[1]

Its popularity wanes and ends. From the fourth century onward the angustus clavus was much used throughout the civilised world as an elaborate decoration for the Court and civil costumes of both men and women, and it only disappeared about the ninth century.

Its development into a shoulder-strap. In the fifth century the clavus was shortened, spanning the shoulders and reaching to a little below the breast, and terminated in a leaf-shaped ornament (*see* Figs. 67 and 72A). This form, used by men only, has its prototype in the shoulder-strap supporting the breastplate worn by Roman soldiers, also used as a sign of rank or badge of honour, and is the origin of the shoulder-strap and epaulette of the present day.

[1] *See* examples: Textiles, South Kensington Museum.

THE PALLIUM

The name given by the Romans to the himation of the Greeks, with which it was identical (*see* Fig. 28).

Its origin. The himation was the characteristic dress throughout the civilised world of Greeks and peoples affected by Greek culture and, at the beginning of the Christian Era, it had become universal among intellectual people.

It is said that Christ and His Apostles wore the himation over the colobium.

A badge of learning. As a garment associated with philosophers (*see* p. 45, Greece), it came to be regarded in Rome, during the second

Fig. 45   Fig. 46

century A.D., as the special monopoly or badge of all learned men, including the orator (*see* Fig. 45).

How to wear it. There was no deviation from the original method of wearing it (*see* Fig. 28, and description given on p. 44, Greece), and Early Christian artists invariably adopted their favourite treatment, and robed the most sacred Biblical characters in this garment.

Not until the middle of the fourth century A.D. did it undergo any change, when it ceased to be a common article of dress, remaining in use only as an official garment for certain high officers.

How it was folded and worn. For the sake of convenience it was then worn folded—contabulatum—lengthways, two or three times, reducing its width to about eighteen or fifteen inches, and carried on the person according to its original arrangement (*see* Fig. 46). The result was that it presented a great similarity to the collar or band of the toga umbo (*see* Fig. 42), and as such came to be regarded secularly as a very honourable attribute.

Methods of Wearing the Pallium

The first method of wearing the pallium has already been described (*see* Fig. 28 and p. 44, Greece), and this fashion still continued; but, when it was worn over *the paenula*, it was first placed as usual

Fig. 47

over the left shoulder, one end hanging in front, but it returned to the front, having crossed the back of the neck, *over the right shoulder* instead of under the right arm, for obvious reasons, then across the breast to the left shoulder again, falling down the back as previously (*see* Fig. 47).

In the year 382, a sumptuary law— the "Lex Vestiaria"—was passed, prescribing the pallium "discolor," in two colours, to be worn over the paenula by officers of the Senate as a badge, in order that they should be recognised and their importance duly respected.

It becomes a scarf or stole. It must have been about this time that the himation or, as it was now universally called, the pallium, ceased to be of the usual width when folded; that means that the superfluous material of the folds underneath the top one was removed, the top panel only remaining, forming a long scarf or stole about twelve to fifteen inches in width by from twelve, fifteen or eighteen feet long.

Its division in two. It was at the beginning of the fifth century that the pallium branched off in two distinct directions—one, the secular or civil, which will be further dealt with under Byzantine costume; the other, the sacred or ecclesiastical pallium.

THE ECCLESIASTICAL PALLIUM

The fact that the pallium (himation) was worn by Our Lord and His Apostles invested it with a certain sanctity, and it became recognised as a garment of honour and dignity.

First worn by the clergy. As early as the second century A.D. it was a garment worn by officers or teachers in the Early Christian Church, by reason only of its being the distinctive dress of learned men. During the third, fourth and early fifth centuries, the pallium gradually became associated with ecclesiastical dignity, and, from the middle of the fifth to the end of the ninth, it was the distinguishing vestment of the Pope, archbishops and certain bishops of the Church of Rome, and has made sporadic reappearances down to our own time.

In course of time it had become considerably narrower, being about four inches in width, and was worn over the chasuble (paenula) as

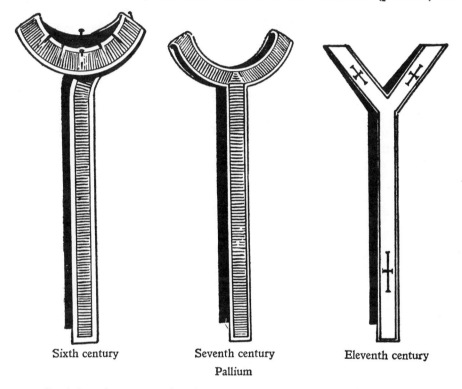

Sixth century	Seventh century	Eleventh century

Pallium

described in Fig. 42. In its lines across the shoulders it was supposed to symbolise the authority of the bishops, in imitation of the Good Shepherd carrying the lost sheep in this manner (*see* Shepherd, Fig. 48).

How it was fixed. In order to maintain the pallium in its right place, it was secured by three pins—at the back, in front, and where it crossed upon the left shoulder. Later, five pins were used in the same way, to typify the five wounds of Our Lord.

A change in shape. After the seventh century, the pallium—now but a single strip of cloth or silk—was made up in the form of a circle with the pendants before and behind, and in the eleventh century it took the shape of a double Y and was not more than three inches in width, usually decorated by six crosses, three in front and three behind. This is the episcopal pallium worn by archbishops of the Roman Catholic Church down to the present day. In the Greek Churches, both Catholic and Orthodox, the pallium is wider, similar to that shown in Fig. 47, and made of a mixture containing *wool*.

In its eleventh-century form it is seen on the armorial bearings of the See of Canterbury.

Its use as an honourable reward. This ornament of great honour indicated the highest dignity to the wearer and, dating from the eighth century, it was the custom for the Pope to confer it upon archbishops and a few bishops. Each pallium was first placed upon the shoulders of His Holiness before being sent, and was given as a token that the recipient participated in the plenitude of the Papal authority.

Some few bishops received it purely as an honour, but it carried no authority. If, however, an archbishop or bishop proved unworthy of possessing it, after it had been given, the offender was made to return it. Mention is made in mediæval writings of many such cases, which are not without humour.

(For the Secular Pallium, *see* p. 163.)

VARIOUS CLOAKS

The abolla came into more general use among the nobility under the Empire, but it was made of very fine linen and, towards the end of the Empire, of silk and other rich materials.

The paludamentum was appropriated by the Emperor and his

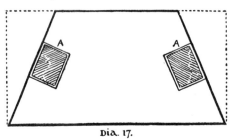

Dia. 17.

generals and worn over their armour during the first four centuries A.D. In the fifth century it became longer, reaching to the ankles. It then superseded the toga picta for full State dress. It retained its purple *colour*, although other rich shades were used, and in most cases it was fastened on the right shoulder. Instances have been known, however, of it being fastened on the left shoulder by a gold and jewelled ornament. Its *shape* underwent a change at this date. Originally a rectangular piece of stuff (see p. 44, Greece, and p. 71, Rome), the top corners were now cut off, converting its shape into that shown in Diagram 17 [1] and Fig. 60. (*To be continued* p. 148, Byzantium).

[1] Some books on Costume misapply the name of pallium to this cloak.

A cloak of the same shape, but of coarse material, was worn by common people, and called the *sagum*.

The laena remained a useful garment for the commonalty, the nobility using the *birrus* and the *lacerna*.

The lacerna, dating from the first century A.D., was frequently worn over the toga, as an extra covering, by senators when going to their official duties, but it was the rule for them to remove it when business began.

The same applied to *the paenula,* which, as before, was very popular with all classes, the nobility wearing it in a larger size than the ordinary working man. The usual *colour* for the paenula during the second and third centuries was of a dark tone of claret, inky purple, or brown, without decoration, except that occasionally the two bands of the angustus clavus were added.

It becomes a Church vestment, and eventually the chasuble. In the fourth century this paenula — now called the *amphibalus* on account of its size—was also worn by a new sect—the officials of the Church—as an ordinary outdoor garment for everyday use, and as a vestment when conducting Church ritual, even while celebrating the Eucharist. Because it covered the wearer entirely, as a "little house," it received a second name of "casula," which has been corrupted into the " chasuble," the sacerdotal vestment of celebrants.

During the fourteenth century its shape underwent a slight change. It was then cut on the plan of two diamonds, joined together on the upper arms, with the top points cut off sufficiently to allow the head to pass through.   Its original shape was sometimes used in the fifteenth century but more pointed back and front. The chasuble cut like the back and front of a fiddle is an invention of the sixteenth century.

The cope of the thirteenth century was nothing more than the paenula divided up the front, where it usually had very elaborate bands of embroidery. It was worn over the shoulders like a mantle and fastened by a clasp, "Morse," or a square of embroidery. The hood was made movable, special hoods being worn at different seasons.

In the sixteenth century, a flat piece of embroidery, semi-oval in shape, in imitation of the hood, took the place of the real thing.

THE CUCULLA

(French: *Cagoule*) was an overdress without sleeves, practically an oblong piece of cloth with a hole in the middle for the head. It was used by all classes as a protection from weather, and when travelling. It was prescribed by the sumptuary law of A.D. 382 to slaves, and in the sixth century (529) by S. Benedict to monks who followed the rules of his order—the Benedictines—and usually worn by them, and by monks of other orders, as a convenient garment when working in the fields. About the fourteenth century A.D. this ecclesiastical garment was given the name of the *scapular*.

A similar article of civil dress came into fashion in the thirteenth century, and was called the *cointise*, or *cyclas*.

The Subligaculum

The subligaculum was still worn as described under the Republic (*see* p. 72). During the period of the Empire this garment was the characteristic dress or livery of superior servants attending the nobility. As such it was made of rich material, and often highly embroidered. Slaves in the service of good families also wore it, and its richness was regulated by the grade of the wearer.

Gladiators, actors, joculators and dancers also wore this garment.

Hairdressing under the Empire—The Men

During the whole period of the Empire, men's hair was worn short, the maximum length of locks being from one and a half to two inches, and varying at different times from almost a close crop to wavy curls. The hair was combed and brushed from the crown of the head forward on to the temples. The method of curling and crisping the hair with tongs was very generally practised, especially by the fashionable, who bestowed much care upon their coiffure, using oils, perfumes and dye to enhance its beauty (*see* Figs. 32, 41, 42, 43, 44, 47).

In the early part of the first century A.D. a craze started for powdering the hair with gold-dust. Some of the most decadent emperors indulged in this fancy, notably Nero (A.D. 54–68) and Gallienus (A.D. 253–268). The period of time between the reigns of these two emperors (200 years) shows how long the craze lasted.

Beards and *moustaches* were essentially a Greek fashion, and would not be in favour with Romans of any patriotic feeling, not even those of humble birth. Elderly and old men of the unfashionable middle class might prove the exception to the rule by wearing a shaggy beard, and peasants might have a stubbly growth upon their chins that might pass as an unkempt beard.

In the second century A.D., the Emperor Hadrian (76–138) started a fashion by wearing a short curly beard, which remained popular with most of the succeeding emperors, and consequently with all men in the prime of life and of social position.

Whiskers. The patches of hair on the cheeks, worn by Greek men of fashion during the fifth century B.C., were copied by Roman patricians, and continued spasmodically as a popular facial adornment during the third century. These are well shown on the portrait bust of the Emperor Alexander Severus (222).

During the fourth century A.D., the hair was combed flat down on the crown of the head, without a parting, and the front hair or fringe was cut in an even line across the forehead. It was also a little thicker than before at the nape of the neck.

Shaving. Constantine revived the fashion of being clean-shaven, and for a long period beards and moustaches were abandoned by all men of importance and fashion.

Hair-dye and wigs. Men dyed their hair in various shades of dark and light hair-colourings, and they also wore wigs: Constantine the Great did so during the latter part of his life.

FOOTGEAR

This was practically the same as under the Republic, with the exception of those details in shoes mentioned under the various figures.

SHEPHERDS AND PEASANTS, 27 B.C–.A.D. 400

Fig. 48 is a young shepherd (third century A.D.). In appearance he is typical of peasants in general during the whole of this period. He is the type of figure used in early Biblical art to symbolise Our Lord in the character of the Good Shepherd (*see* Pallium, p. 109), and is frequently met with in the frescoes of the Catacombs at Rome. The method of carrying the sheep over the shoulders should be noticed, as it has been referred to under the ecclesiastical pallium.

This young man wears the now universal dalmatica, but, as was the custom with all men of the labouring class, the right arm is shifted out of the sleeve, which is allowed to hang at the side. The skirt part of the dalmatica is girded low down at the waist, obviously for convenience. Over this he wears the paenula, slung off his back to be drawn around him as night comes on, or for protection against the elements.

The *shoes*, made of thick untanned hide, open up the instep and fasten round the ankle. The legs are encased in strappings of hide cut in strips, and wound and crossed after the fashion of modern puttees. The bowl or pot he carries is an indispensable article of domestic use, for in it he keeps his worldly belongings, and in addition it serves him as a stew-pan.

Fig. 49 is another peasant, taken from a fourth-century fresco, and has the garb of a man of this class in use from about the beginning of the third century to the end of the fifth. He wears the tunica with long sleeves, and, rather unexpectedly, it is beautifully embroidered with a border and segmentæ, the latter showing a design of a Christian Cross. This proves that the peasants living in the Roman provinces

Fig. 48   Fig. 49

were not devoid of a sense of beauty, nor were they so poverty-stricken as one might believe. It is interesting to note at this very early period the beginnings of peasant art—an industry which developed later throughout the civilised world with such wonderful results.

Above the tunica is worn a cape of skin with the hair outside. It probably had a hood, to be used if required.

The *shoes* worn by this peasant are of thick felt with wooden soles, and his legs are covered with pieces of coarse linen, tied under the knees and round the ankles. This method of clothing the legs is still maintained among the peasant classes of Italy at the present day.

COSTUME OF THE WOMEN UNDER THE EMPIRE

27 B.C.–A.D. 400

Women's dress descends from classic simplicity to vulgar lavishness. Fashion-mongers of a luxurious age stick at nothing, however monstrous or lacking in good taste, to attain their ends. Consequently, in the manner of wearing garments, their form and decorations, fashion ran riot, and neither propriety, decency, nor good taste was observed.

Dating from the first century A.D., the guiding principles of simplicity and sobriety were gradually forgotten; and, although Roman ladies of fashion professed to admire the exquisite culture of their country's vassals (at the same time their masters in Art), and to imitate the elegance of their costume, over-decoration and a vulgar lavishness in dress were displayed by Roman society-women. What wonder when such a woman as Valeria Messalina was the first "lady" in the land!

FIRST AND SECOND CENTURIES A.D.

The stola. During the first and second centuries A.D., the Ionic version of the stola was the principal and practically the only garment worn by ladies of all ranks. The Doric form was worn at various times, as portraits of some of the empresses show.[1] Toward the end of the second century the neck-opening in the Ionic stola was gathered into a narrow band.

The palla. The variety in methods of draping the palla around the figure was endless (*see* Fig. 51). When of exaggerated length, it was wound many times round the body and over the shoulders; if the texture were of the filmiest, it would be wound many more times, with the two ends trailing on the ground or carried over the arms.

Fig. 51

[1] Portrait statue of the Empress Agrippina (Capitolian Museum).

Fig. 50. An empress of the second and third centuries wearing the stola and palla, in woven gold. The head-dress is founded on that of the Empress Sabina, wife of Hadrian (*see* p. 129, Jewellery). Her jewels are pearls and emeralds. The decorative pattern at the top is taken from the Mausoleum of Galla Placidia at Ravenna, and, although this example is of the fifth century, it is a very usual one in Greco-Roman Art (*see* Greek patterns, p. 35).

THIRD CENTURY A.D.

Stola superseded by the dalmatica. From the beginning of the third century, the stola was abandoned by degrees in favour of the garment which caused such a sensation among the people in general—the dalmatica (*see* Fig. 52). Worn by both sexes and all ranks, it was decorated by the angustus clavus in its original form, namely, a band of plain colour on both sides of the front and back. The dalmatica worn by women reached to above the ankles, or it was sometimes longer. The sleeves were wide at the openings, with one, and sometimes two bands of colour, and often edged with fringe. Under this at first was worn the

Fig. 52

Fig. 53

old-fashioned stola, which had no sleeves; but about the middle of the century long sleeves appeared, and these being added to the stola (now gathered into a band at the neck) converted it at once into the camisia (*see* Fig. 53).

The palla retires temporarily. With the advent of the dalmatica the paenula for utility took the place of the palla, which retired into partial obscurity. It was easy to arrange the palla gracefully and conveniently when the arms were bare and the figure clad in the close-hanging stola, but the wide sleeves and fuller skirt of the dalmatica made its drapery appear bulky. Consequently, a new article of attire—one better adapted to the conditions—was introduced, although it was but the revival of an ancient Greek fashion. *This was the VEIL.*

THE VEIL

The veil (Roman: "Ricinum"), a development of the κρήδεμνον or head-cloth worn by women of the Archaic Age in Greece, was a rectangular piece of lightly woven silk, wool, linen or cotton, of various dimensions, some long enough to hang gracefully on either side of a lady of quality (*see* Fig. 54), or, as worn by women of the people, only just long enough to cover the shoulders (*see* Figs. 52 and 53).

Of various colours, as worn by the wealthy they were sometimes richly ornamented with gold; and plain or with bands of colour by the poorer. Often the veil had a fringe to finish off the edges left in the weaving.

A veil of flame colour, or deep orange, was the special adornment of a bride of Pagan Rome. Christian brides wore veils of purple and white.

FOURTH CENTURY A.D.

The dalmatica improved. Improvements in the cut of the dalmatica were made, approximately, at the beginning of the fourth century, whereby it assumed the shape of a garment hanging in slightly radiating folds from the neck to the feet. This effect was obtained by cutting the sides, not on the straight as hitherto, but at an outward-sloping angle from the armhole to the hem. The sleeves lost their square effect by being cut also on the slant, in the manner shown in Diagram 18.

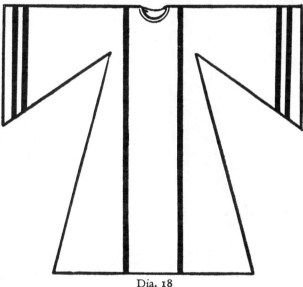

Dia. 18

The clavus elaborated. The bands —the clavi—were no longer restricted to any particular colour, and they became more elaborate, often having indented or fancy edges and the space between ornamented with rich embroidery (*see* Figs. 53 and 54).

The belt. Dating from this time a belt encircles the waist, giving the whole garment a more graceful appearance (*see* Fig. 54).

Special notice should be taken of the cut of this particular garment, as it served as the model on which women's and men's dresses of the future were all founded.

The camisia was worn under the dalmatica, but now for the most part it had long, fairly tight sleeves to the wrist, sometimes finished with a band of embroidery. This showed under the wide over-sleeve of the dalmatica.

The following is a description of the dresses worn by a group of five ladies, taken from a mosaic dated A.D. 352–366, in the Church of S. Maria Maggiore, Rome.

They are all wearing the dalmatica of the new cut (Diagram 18) and all, except the fourth, have it girded rather high, with a jewelled boss in the centre. One dalmatica is of emerald green, embroidered all over with white circles about six inches in diameter. Another is of orange, with the plain clavus in black. The third is of deep green, embroidered all over with three six-inch circles round a red centre in gold, blue and white. The clavus without any ornamentation is of gold. The fourth wears a white dalmatica, with the brown clavus, and the fifth is in deep blue, which has the appearance of a shot blue and green. The clavus on this is of plain gold. All show the toes of the shoes, which are scarlet.

Fig. 54. A lady of the fourth century, wearing the semi-folded palla over the new dalmatica.

In another mosaic two women are shown wearing the dalmatica, one red, the other blue, and both have the clavus in black.

These details prove that in the middle of the fourth century the dalmatica, with the clavus, was still the height of fashion, and they also give a good idea of the colourings and decorations then in vogue.

REVIVAL OF THE PALLA

Identical with the Pallium of the Men

The palla undergoes a slight change. With the alteration of the dalmatica, the wearing of the palla was revived by noble ladies of the Roman Empire. The same process of contabulation—folding—which the pallium underwent about the middle of the fourth century was applied to it (*see* p. 107 and Fig. 46).

How it was draped. This process only affected the first end of it —the part that hung in front. This was folded two or three times, according to the width of the material, into a width of about twelve inches, and the edge of the top fold turned to the left. Although this was unseen, it was passed through the girdle at the waist, for the practical purpose of keeping it in its place, more or less in the centre of the figure. From thence it passed over the left shoulder, either still folded and widening out further over the back, or slightly widening over the left breast and shoulder, according to the fancy of the wearer. It was then draped, after the method of the original palla, across the back, around the right leg, and over the left shoulder again (*see* Fig. 54).

Its *decoration* consisted chiefly of a border worked or woven in a contrasting colour, and it sometimes had a pattern dispersed over its whole area.

HAIRDRESSING—WOMEN OF THE EMPIRE

First Century A.D.

The hair was dressed in a variety of ways, but the style most favoured during the first century A.D. is shown in Fig. 37. The front was naturally or artificially waved or curled; in most cases the latter, forming rather

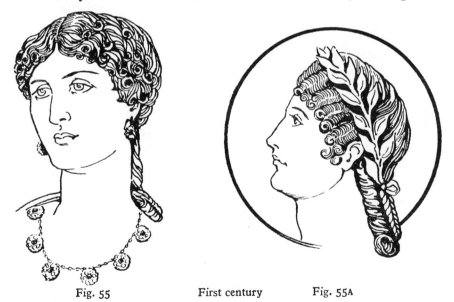

Fig. 55   First century   Fig. 55A

stiff waves or ringlets on the forehead, and leaving a division in the centre. The ends were twisted or braided into a knob at the back of the head, rather low down, as seen in Fig. 55. This method of dressing the hair was adopted by many of the Roman empresses of the first, second, third and fourth centuries A.D., a proof of its popularity, and it would be copied by all great ladies.

In Fig. 55A, the Empress Valeria Messalina, a long twisted tail takes the place of the knob, with the shorter ends of hair plaited and lying on top. A wreath of gold laurel, the Imperial insignia, is worn round the crown of the head.

The Empresses Livia and Octavia, according to their portrait busts, added a puff of hair on their foreheads, in the style seen in Fig. 51. Agrippina and Poppea encircled the back of the head with braids of hair, like a coronet.

A very extraordinary fashion was in vogue during the latter half of this century, and is seen in Fig. 55B. It was worn by the Empress

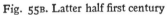

Fig. 55B. Latter half first century

Fig. 56. Second century

Domitia and Julia, the daughter of the Emperor Titus. The stiff curls were arranged on a pad or framework for support. At the back of the head the hair was arranged in waves, either across the head or from the front to the nape, the ends being gathered into a coil, or bound into a long tail hanging down the back.

Second Century A.D.

Fig. 56 is a style belonging to this century, and is taken from the portrait statue of the Empress Annia Galeria Faustina. The arrangement of the front waves is a little different from those of Fig. 37, but the chief feature is the plait of hair forming a high narrow coronet at the back of the head. In another portrait of her the palla is draped over it.

Fig. 56A wears the hair also plaited and arranged behind in a large thick circle, with a long ornamental pin passed through the centre.

Third Century A.D.

Another version of the last is seen in Fig. 57, but above it is worn a stephane of goldsmith's work and jewels.

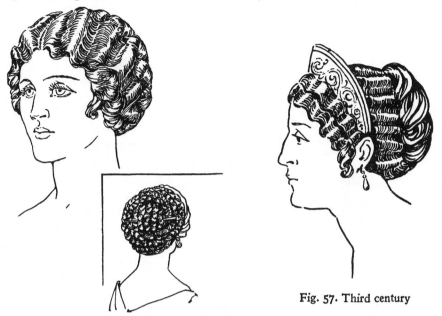

Fig. 56A. Second century

Fig. 57. Third century

Fig. 57A has the hair dressed in a twisted coil, low in the neck, and, like the preceding example, curls appear in front of the ears. This low

Fig. 57A. Third century

Fig. 58. Third and fourth centuries

twisted coil is quite a feature of the third-century hairdressing, and a modification of it is shown in Fig. 58—the Empress Helena, Saint and mother of Constantine the Great (247–328). Another style had a large square flat mass of braiding placed over the back of the head (the hair underneath dressed as in Fig. 58), and was worn by many empresses of the third and fourth centuries.

Fourth Century A.D.

Fig. 59. Fourth century

Fig. 59 is a very characteristic style of hairdressing for ladies of the fourth century, and is seen on many frescoes, mosaics and paintings of this period.

The hair was parted and waved, or else closely curled on the forehead and temples without a parting. The ears were often covered, but sometimes the lower part of them was exposed and adorned with jewelled earrings.

The back hair was either twisted into a coil and placed round the crown of the head in a large circle, or it was a plait of hair arranged in the same manner. Through this was sometimes stuck a large ornamental pin, and frequently a jewelled ornament was placed in front of it above the parting. When the veil was worn, it was placed over the whole coiffure and attached, if necessary, by the large pin (see also Fig. 54).

THE TOILET AND ITS ACCESSORIES

The improvement of the complexion is a vanity that has been indulged in ever since the world began; not only by women but by men. The Greeks were accustomed to anoint themselves with oil after the bath—the oil of the olive, for as yet sweet-smelling perfumes were entirely unknown. Fuller's earth was used instead of soap. For scraping down the body, a strigil of iron or wood was applied, and bathers took with them towels (if they were not supplied at the bath) to dry themselves.

The bath part of social routine. Among the Romans, attendance at the public bath was part of the social routine; and very magnificent buildings were erected for this purpose by important social and commercial magnates. Both hot and cold baths, and a sort of treatment like the modern Turkish bath, were taken after exercise and before meals. In the late Empire as many as eight baths per day would be taken by fashionable society.

The *art of making up* the face is also of great antiquity. The Egyptian ladies of the fifteenth century B.C. were expert at it. The face, eyes, eyebrows and hair all received their special treatment.

The ladies of Imperial Rome were as particular as the ancient Egyptians, or the ladies of to-day, in the details of the toilet. Paint, rouge, powder and cosmetics in general were all used. The use of patches upon the face and neck was not entirely unknown to the ladies of Rome, as well as to the decadent men.

Toilet-boxes. Many Roman toilet-boxes are to be found in various museums, differing but little from those used in modern times. The boxes were very beautiful specimens of craftsmanship, and contained bottles, generally made of alabaster, and scent-bottles, artistically shaped tubes from four to six inches long with tapering necks, for holding precious unguent or ointment. They were usually sealed, and the neck broken when its contents were required; *vide* "to break the box" (S. Matt. xxvi. 7).

Ointment-box

The teeth. The Romans prided themselves on their teeth, which they treated with a preparation called "Dentifricium," applied by a small brush; and after meals tooth-picks of gold, silver, or quill were employed.

Hair restoratives. Very costly oils and pomatums were brushed on to the hair. After the conquest of the Gauls, the Romans learnt the peculiar quality of a certain pomatum, used by the barbarians for giving a lustre and a more definite colour to red and yellow hair. This coloured hair became the rage in Rome on this account, and the pomatum received the name of "Sapo." It was found afterwards to have cleansing properties, and came into general use for washing—soap!

The comb. The use of combs dates back to a very remote period. They were mostly made of box-wood or ivory, and had the teeth set on one side, or both. If the latter, the set of teeth on one side would be larger than those on the other.

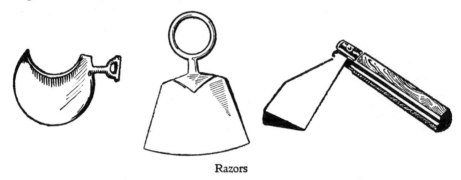

Razors

The earliest *razors* were made of bronze, and in shape very like a crescent with a handle fixed on one side. They were also of a spade-

Hand-mirror

Box-mirror

shape, with a handle fixed on the short edge. During the Roman period the blade took the shape of a knife, and very often had a folding-handle of wood.

Mirrors of polished metal were common, but mirrors set with looking-glass were rare. In some instances the glass had concave and convex reflectors, and there are some of this kind still in existence.

In shape the mirror was usually a circular disc of metal, with a handle attached. The back part was very highly decorated. Circular mirrors hinged to circular boxes were also common.

A method of *manicuring* the hands, almost identical with that we use to-day, was known to the Romans. Many instruments, such as nail-files, polishers, tweezers, etc., can be seen in collections at various museums.

The work-box. Needles, pins, bodkins, knitting-needles, scissors, the thimble—identical with ours—were all known to the Roman seamstress.

THE SUDARIUM. This was a small piece of fine linen, often embroidered with silk or gold, and equivalent to the handkerchief of modern times. It came into fashion about the first century B.C., but did not become very general as an item of the toilet until the period of the Empire. It was used for wiping the face and nose, and was carried either round the neck, in the hand, or in the sinus of the toga, which answered as a pocket.

An article of domestic utility analogous to the sudarium was THE MAPPA (see Consul, p. 161), or napkin, used at table for wiping the mouth and hands, after washing before and after a meal in a basin brought by a slave. In late Republican times the mappa was supplied by the host and laid on the table. In Imperial times each guest brought his own.

The sudarium and mappa were used in the Early Christian Church at the Sacrament of the Eucharist, when they were carried in the hand of the priest or sub-deacon, but later were folded, after the same manner as the pallium (see Pallium, p. 107), into merely a strip or band, used purely as a mark of honour by bishops, priests, deacons and sub-deacons, and held in the fingers of the left hand. By the twelfth century it was carried on the left wrist. As an ecclesiastical vestment it is known as the "maniple."

Another article similar to the former is THE ORARIUM, a larger napkin, carried by servants and slaves over the left shoulder, and used by them for cleaning vessels of all sorts. The plural for this is "oraria," and these napkins were often distributed to the audience at the play or the circus, to wave in token of applause. This *may* be the origin of " hurrah."

The orarium or orarion also became a vestment of the Church, and was worn by servants (deacons) of the Church over the left shoulder for the purpose of cleansing the vessels used at the Eucharist. In time it became folded like the pallium and the maniple into a strip of cloth, losing its utility but retaining its significance. After the eleventh century it was called *The Stole*, and was worn over both shoulders on top of the albe, and crossed on the breast, secured by the girdle, and under the dalmatica by bishops. By deacons it was worn over the albe, crossing the left shoulder and tied under the right arm. In modern times it is crossed in front when worn by priests over the albe.

In the Eastern Churches there are two distinct stoles—the orarion of the deacons as before described, and the epitrakhelion ($\epsilon\pi\iota\tau\rho\alpha\chi\acute{\eta}\lambda\iota o\nu$) of the priest. The latter is a straight piece of material about twelve inches wide, with a hole near one end through which the head is passed. It resembles a scapular without the back portion.

THE ART OF PAINTING IN ROME

Rome did not produce any native painters of repute. During the later Republican Period, Greek artists were sent for to instruct in this art, and most of the paintings, or "Old Masters," possessed by Romans were collected from other countries and from the conquered.

Portrait painting in coloured wax on small boards became very popular at the beginning of the Empire Period, and examples were often enclosed in the wrappings of mummies.

Mural paintings were carried to a high state of excellence during the Late Republican and Early Empire Period, in imitation of the Greek. The ruins of Pompeii and Herculaneum display many beautiful examples of this art.

Mosaic work also improved very considerably, both the marble tessellated variety and the glass. The production of beautifully coloured wall pictures in glass mosaic started, approximately, about the third century A.D., and reached its zenith in the Byzantine Era.

TEXTILES UNDER THE EMPIRE

"Almost every product known to modern textile art was produced in great perfection by the ancients." So states an authority on the subject.

Linen. Egypt still retained its supremacy as the most important centre of the linen-weaving industry, and supplied the demands of all the countries in the civilised world. Many examples of it exist, mostly obtained from Coptic graves in Egypt,[1] which date from the beginning of the second century A.D. to about the middle of the fifth. Garments made of this linen show decoration in colours, and the method employed in embroidering was of a simple nature. The part intended for the embroidery was either left blank in the weaving or the weft was cut away. The patterns were then worked in with the needle, or with the fingers only, upon the bare warp threads. Clavi, segmentæ, bands and borders were created in this manner.

The linen used at this period was always undyed, and frequently unbleached, and many of the garments worn by the wealthy were made of a superfine quality of this material, as a ground-work on which the

---

[1] The Copts were a sect of Egyptian Christians. S. Mark is said to have first preached Christianity in Alexandria in A.D. 69. Their doctrines were condemned as corrupt by the Council of Chalcedon, 451.

embroideries of borders and segmentæ showed up like jewels in a simple setting.

A particular kind of linen is spoken of as being woven in *three warps*, and another *with loops*, which gave a shaggy appearance like lamb's wool. This latter kind was used for making thick winter garments, cloaks, etc.

Linen was also manufactured at Malta, especially that of a fine soft make, and was much used for the tunica, stola, palla and, later, veils.

Cotton of the best quality and finest make was obtained from Egypt, and was in great demand for light garments such as the tunica, subucula, camisia and veil, chiefly in white, but sometimes dyed a colour, especially a brick-red. An inferior quality came from India. This was usually woven into muslin, and was called even in those days "Indian Muslin." It was of great price, as we are told by Pliny that Indian commodities were sold at Rome at one hundred times their original value.

Wool of various textures was used for many garments. It was skilfully woven into a very fine fabric, and used extensively for veils.

Felt was beaten into a heavy woollen material, and used for many purposes besides garments of extra warmth.

Silk was obtained more easily in the first century A.D., but at an exorbitant price, and by degrees silks of all textures, from the most substantial—satin—to that of the finest transparency, were much affected by patricians of both sexes. Sumptuary laws were passed by those emperors opposed to luxury, prohibiting men from wearing so *effeminate* a material. Tiberius (A.D. 14) attacked wastefulness in dress, and even forbade men to wear gold ornaments, but emperors whose tastes reached the other extreme encouraged a lavish use of silk. Heliogabalus (A.D. 218–222) was the first to dress himself entirely in silk. On his entry into Rome, his loose flowing robes—the dalmatica—of purple, made after the fashion of the Medes and Phœnicians, were of pure Chinese silk, heavily embroidered in gold. The succeeding emperor, Alexander Severus (A.D. 222), did all he could to check costliness in dress, but, as usual, without much avail (*see* History of Silk, Chap. V.).

Silk was very sparingly used by the middle classes even in the fourth century, and then it was mixed with wool for embroidering the borders, clavi, and segmentæ. With the advent of veils, fine silk threads were worked in decorative lines as borders upon them. Not until the sixth century, when the silk industry was established at Constantinople, was it used extensively for embroideries.

Pure gold was also woven into dress material and is mentioned in writings of the times. At a public ceremony in the year A.D. 52, the Empress Agrippina wore a stola and palla of this material. She was one of the few who were granted the privilege of riding in the Imperial

Gold Chariot,[1] drawn by four white Thessalian steeds richly caparisoned in gold and jewels, and she must have made an imposing spectacle when driving through the streets of Rome.

Heliogabalus also indulged his exotic tastes, not only by wearing this material at public functions, but even in the seclusion of his private chamber his robes were of pure gold.

Description of a toga picta. Virgil describes (*The Æneid*, 250) a mantle, probably the toga picta, of gold tissue, having a purple border with a double wavy edge on which gods and men, together with trees and beasts, were pictured in life-like fashion.

Woad. Apparently the discovery of the blue stain or dye, made by fermenting the pulped leaves of the herb called "woad," was not made until the last centuries before Christ. It was native to the lands of the Mediterranean and Persia, but evidently the Greeks did not know its use. It was left for the Romans to discover when they conquered the Celts of Britain.

JEWELLERY, ETC. UNDER THE EMPIRE

The Romans, like their "Masters in Art," the Greeks, excelled in fine goldsmith's work, and raised it to a very high standard during the first period of the Empire. In design they followed their masters to some extent. After this first period there was very little, if any, improvement or development in the art. It was an age of ostentation, and to overload the person with gems, jewels, and goldsmith's work of all periods and nationalities was the height of fashion.

During this period no restraint was practised by the aristocracy of Rome in their display of jewels, not only on their person, but on their accessories. After the lapse of twenty centuries we have acquired better taste (₹), and such ostentation is looked upon with contempt; but it must be borne in mind that, previous to the conquests in the Orient by the Roman forces, such things as sparkling stones were, with few exceptions, unheard and undreamed of. At this time these fascinating brilliant curiosities were only just coming into the possession of the very highest and wealthiest people in the civilised Western World, so they must be forgiven for their enthusiastic appreciation of such novelties.

The import of precious metals and stones increased enormously under the Empire, as a consequence of the extravagant tastes of the

---

[1] Possibly the chariot of Mithridates the Macedonian. (*See* Greece, p. 60; Rome, p. 83.)

Imperial Court. Twenty thousand pounds weight in *gold* was imported annually from Asturia, Galicia and Lusitania. *Silver* mines in Dalmatia yielded fifty pounds weight every day. *Diamonds* were brought from the far-off province of Bengal. *Pearls,* so highly prized by the Roman aristocracy, were obtained from the two great fisheries at Ormuz and Cape Comorin. *Amber* in great quantities was transported from the shores of the Baltic. The Romans set an immense value upon it, and special missions were sent to all the barbaric tribes living along the north coast of Europe, as far east as the mouth of the Vistula, to purchase it at a price beyond the expectations of the natives. Iron was one of the commodities exchanged for it.

A vogue. This yellow fossil resin was very freely worked into personal ornaments, furniture, and various other objects. It was a fashion for ladies to carry in the palms of their hands balls of amber for its delicate perfume, and pieces of rock crystal for its coolness.

Crowns. The Imperial crown of the first four Roman emperors was very simple—a wreath of laurel or bay leaves made in gold. This type of crown was used until Nero (A.D. 54–68) adopted the *corona radiata* (*see* Fig. 41), or sunrays, sometimes alternated with spiral horns. From this time onward it is frequently shown on the coins of successive emperors.

The Empress Sabina, the wife of Hadrian (A.D. 117), possessed a crown or diadem of wonderful workmanship (*see* Fig. 50) and valued at £240,000. Heliogabalus (218) was the first to wear a crown of pearls, which took the form of a circlet of two or three strands, fastened in front with a priceless gem. This type was subsequently much worn, with slight alterations, up to the reign of Constantine. When Heliogabalus entered Rome in triumph, he wore a tiara of successive crowns, the corona radiata, to the number of three, and his delicate arms were encircled with bracelets all flashing with jewels. Around his white neck were strings of perfectly-matched pearls.

The first Imperial diadem. Diocletian (284) was the most courageous and enterprising of all his predecessors, for he assumed that symbol of royalty so hateful to the Romans—the orthodox Imperial diadem, in imitation of the great autocratic sovereigns of the Orient. This crown, as worn by Diocletian, was a broad band of gold set with pearls, and it may be regarded as the foundation on which all Royal and Imperial crowns of subsequent monarchs have been built.

Head-dresses of noble ladies. Pliny, the historian of the first century A.D., mentions that the ladies of his time wore gold head-dresses. These were bands, coverings of network, the stephane, etc., and head ornaments copied from Greek models (*see* p. 61), made in gold and precious stones. They also wore elaborate ornaments in their hair, in the form of pins

surmounted by jewelled figures, and one still in existence is valued
at £10,000.[1]

This historian also tells us that the great ladies wore jewels of
inestimable worth, not only set in their bracelets, ear-rings, and finger-

rings, but in addition lavishly displayed upon their dress and
footgear. He describes having seen the Empress Lollia
Paulina, the wife of Caligula (A.D. 37), at a supper-party with
her neck, arms, hands, and girdle covered with emeralds and
pearls (*see* Fig. 50).

Ear-rings were ornamental drops, and frequently jewels
set in rings. It was not the general rule for men to wear ear-
rings, but it was evidently a custom of the third century, as
the Emperor Alexander Severus (A.D. 222) strongly opposed

Ear-ring   the wearing of them by men.

Necklaces were chiefly of pearls, usually wound several times
round the neck and fastened with a magnificent cameo.

Bracelets of three or four rows of pearls or other jewels, and bands
of gold set with gems, were worn by both sexes on
the upper and lower arms. Some of the emperors,
mostly the decadent ones—Caligula, Nero, Heliogabalus, Gallienus, etc., etc.—are represented wearing
them. Bracelets were used as a reward or "decoration" in the army. The paraphernalia of a general
making his triumph was not complete without them.
Bracelets of silver were awarded to soldiers for   Bracelet
good conduct.

Rings were universally worn as seals during the Empire. Precious
stones of all sorts, especially the ruby and the sapphire, were engraved
with a device and set in gold. The Emperor himself wore one
which was recognised as a seal of State. The Emperor Cocceius Nerva
possessed one, a diamond, which was handed down to Trajan and
Hadrian. Different families had their own particular signet rings,
and these descended from generation to generation. Rings worn by the
wealthy were very elaborate, and set with every kind of jewel, gem, or
precious stone. Cameos or intaglios, especially those engraved with a
portrait, were much used. Wedding rings at this time were made of gold.

It was a peculiar fashion at this period to wear rings on the upper

---

[1] It represents the Goddess of Plenty bearing in one hand the horn of Archelaus and
caressing a dolphin with the other.

Faustina's ring valued at	.	.	.	£40,000
Domitia's „ „	.	.	.	£60,000
Cæsonia's bracelet „	.	.	.	£80,000
Poppea's ear-rings „	.	.	.	£120,000
Calpurnia's „ „	.	.	.	£240,000

40,000 sesterces equals in value about £336,000.

joints of the fingers as well as the lower, evidently to enable the wealthy to make a greater display of their jewels.

The fibula or brooch of the Romans in its earliest form was on the same principle as described under Greece (p. 63). The pin attached to a spiral spring now gave place to a pin made movable by a hinge, but for a time it retained its bowed shape.

Early Fibula

During the first and second centuries it became much more like a brooch or ornament, with the pin fixed behind. In the following centuries

Brooch
Second century

the top part generally took the form of a disc, ornamented with enamels in bright colours, and all sorts of goldsmith's work, often set with jewels and gems. Grotesque animals and heads of animals were a very popular decoration.

Third century

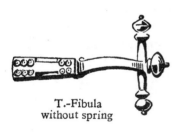

T.-Fibula
without spring

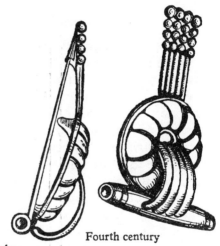

Fibulæ

Fourth century

A new brooch—*the buckle*—called by the Romans the "fibula," was a fastening now adopted for belts. It was of the same shape as we are accustomed to use at the present day, and either quite plain in gold, bronze or iron, or highly ornamented with goldsmith's work and jewels.

Jewels in general seem to have been dispersed over all parts of the person, according to descriptions given us by writers of the times, some of which have already been

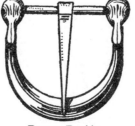

Bronze Buckle
First and second centuries

Bronze Hook and Eye

mentioned here. The sumptuous Gallienus (A.D. 260) was in the habit of taking his daily meal reclining on a gold couch set with precious wood, ivory, and jewels, and covered with roses especially brought from Egypt. He favoured the fashion of powdering his hair with gold dust, and his robes of silk, his girdle and his shoes glittered with an immense quantity of jewels.

In the year 270 the Emperor Aurelian, who was also a great general, conquered the Palmyreans and made their chieftainess Zenobia his prisoner, and brought her in triumph to Rome. The spoil comprised an indescribable treasure.[1]

Edicts issued from time to time held in check the extravagance of women of the middle class, and laws were passed forbidding unmarried women to wear precious stones, gems or pearls. So great was their passion for jewellery that marriages increased to a surprising degree. An unhappy marriage after all was more than compensated for by a string of pearls!

FURS UNDER THE EMPIRE

Before the Empire Period furs were very little used. The skins of native animals were used as additional *clothing* by the lower orders and peasants, and many of them were made into leather.

When the Romans came in contact with the fur-wearing barbarians of the north and north-east, however, a fashion was introduced of using the skins of the northern animals as rugs, both for the floors and for covering *furniture*. Hitherto, only the skins of lions, tigers and leopards, animals of the east and south, had been employed. These northern skins, chiefly taken from beavers, wolves, bears, marten, foxes and hyenas, and obtained from the forests of Scythia and the lands bordering on the Baltic, North Sea and Black Sea, were also converted into coats or tunicas for wear in winter and abroad. The custom of trimming a dress with fur was quite unknown.

[1] Along the flower-strewn streets filed the procession—an immense number of elephants, lions, tigers, leopards, and bears; cars laden with gold, silver, jewels, plate and wardrobe; the royal chariot of Palmyra, of gold studded with jewels—the spoil of the conquered, wending its way to the Capitol. In the column were captives from Ethiopia, Arabia, Persia, India, China, Gaul and Spain, "*all remarkable for their rich and singular costumes*" (Gibbon), but the most important of all was the "*lithe bronzed figure with brilliant black eyes and teeth like pearls*" of Zenobia (McCabe), "*esteemed the most lovely as well as the most heroic of her sex*" (Gibbon). She was led by a slave with a gold chain attached to a gold collar round her neck, bound hand and foot by heavy chains of gold, clothed for the last time in her massive gold ornaments and heavily jewelled robes as "Queen of the East." More from disappointed pride than fatigue (she had expected to be allowed to ride in the royal chariot), she complained bitterly that it was impossible for her to walk under so great a load of jewels.

Another captive who walked near her was Tetricus, the vanquished usurper of Gaul, wearing barbaric bracco, a saffron tunica and scarlet sagum.

Zenobia was treated leniently by Aurelian, who presented her with a beautiful villa in the Tivoli, where she lived and "*insensibly sank into a Roman matron, her daughters marrying into noble families*" (Gibbon).

THE GOTHS—A SHIFTING NATION

THE OPPRESSORS OF THE ROMAN EMPIRE

HISTORICAL DATA

The Goths were of the Teutonic family of Aryan [1] speaking peoples, and came originally from Scandinavia—Gothland. In the *first and second centuries* A.D. they were settled in the region north-east of the Vistula (Königsberg). This Gothic nation comprised several prominent tribes or races, the most important being:

1. The Eastern or *Ostrogoths*, who emigrated to the land situated between the rivers Don and Dnieper.
2. The Western or *Visigoths*, settled west of the Dnieper.
3. The *Gepidæ*, north of them both.
4. *The Langobards* (longbeards) were another race of Goths, located at this time between the rivers Elbe and Oder (Hanover and Magdeburg).

The government of the Goths was vested in a family or race of chiefs called the "Amala," who boasted descent from the gods of Norse mythology, Odin and Thor. All later Gothic chiefs and kings were descended from the Amala.

In the *third century*, under their chief, Cuiva, the Goths pushed southward across the Danube and raided the Balkans, defeating the Roman army and killing the Emperor Decius in A.D. 251. During these raids they also pillaged Thrace.

They were seriously defeated in 269, and again in the following year at Nish, by the Emperor Claudius II., who, on this account, received the title "Conqueror of the Goths." He died in the middle of the year and was succeeded by Aurelian, an able general. A gigantic attempt to invade the empire was made immediately by the Gothic nation as a whole; but Aurelian drove them back, although it was a costly victory to the Roman army. The conflict being indecisive, a treaty was concluded, whereby the Goths were to supply auxiliaries to Rome, in return for which service they were granted permission to settle in the province of Dacia, a part of which was occupied already by the Visigoths.

For some years there was peace, until the Goths renewed hostilities by plundering Bulgaria and Serbia, and were checked by Constantine the Great in 321.

Christianity had been preached to them during the third century, and a Gothic bishop is mentioned as having attended the Council of Nicæa in 325. A native bishop, Ulfilas, translated the Bible into the Gothic language. In religion they followed the Arian Faith.

The Arian Faith or Arianism, so named after Arius, a pastor of Alexandria and a theologian; born about A.D. 250; died about 330. He held the doctrine of the inferiority of the Son of God to the Father. Arian Christians left out the sentence "being of one substance with the Father" in the Nicene Creed, and substituted "being like unto the Father in such manner as the Scriptures declare." They also refused to repeat the words which assert the Godhead of the Holy Spirit.

The Athanasians took their name from the theologian Athanasius, born A.D. 298, died 373, who wrote chiefly against Arianism in relation to the doctrine of the Trinity. The Athanasian Creed, named after the theologian, was composed some time between

[1] A name applied to a group of languages, which must not be confused with the Arian religion.

the years 450 and 550. It was used by the Western Church, but was not sanctioned until after A.D. 800. It held the truth of the whole of the Nicene Creed drawn up by the Council of Nicæa, A.D. 325.

The Vandals, a race closely akin to the Goths, who, since the first century, had been located north of the Elbe (Mecklenburg), crossed the Danube (361) and settled in Pannonia. Simultaneously, the Ostrogoths went north, invading the Finnish and Slavonic tribes who dwelt in the upper reaches of the Volga, and, under their chief, Hermanric, they established a kingdom over a large extent of territory between the Black Sea and the Volga.

About this time (374) the Huns made their first inroad into Gothic lands, and, although the Visigoths acknowledged Hermanric's overlordship, they left him to fight the Huns unaided, with the result that the Ostrogoths were overthrown. The Huns then crossed the Danube and invaded the lands of the Visigoths, whom also they vanquished. Athanaric was the chief who led the Visigoths at this time.

At last (376) the Goths, in exasperation, asked permission of the Byzantine Government to cross the Danube and settle in Thrace. This was given on condition that they delivered up their arms. Many Goths received important positions at the Imperial Court, but this disarmament was obnoxious to their national spirit, and the unfair treatment they received from local government officials led them to revolt and lay waste the country. A battle fought in 377 between the Byzantine army and the Visigoths, under the leadership of Fritigern, was indecisive, and after it a general conflagration took place, in which the Visigoths were aided by many barbarian races, including Ostrogoths and Huns; and a victory over the army of the Emperor Valens was gained by their united forces, near Hadrianople, on August 9th, 378.

From the year 396, Alaric, the Visigoth chief, persistently annoyed the Government at Rome. He marched into Greece, but was met by Stilicho, the Roman commander, and turned back. During the following year the power of Alaric greatly increased, and under him the Visigoths and Ostrogoths were united. His ambition was to obtain control of Rome and its vast wealth. He crossed the Julian Alps (401), but the Gothic army was completely overthrown by Stilicho at Pollentia in a great battle in 402.

In 403, with great energy, Alaric prepared a desperate effort to advance on Rome. The city was saved by the diligence of Stilicho in 404, who met him at Verona and turned him back a second time.

Alaric, with the determination and destructive instincts of a Goth, achieved his ambition by besieging Rome and sacking it three times in 408, 409 and 410. In this last year he died, and was succeeded by his brother-in-law, Athaulf, who led a great part of the Visigoths into Gaul and Spain, making Toulouse their stronghold. Athaulf was a very handsome and intelligent man, and a barbarian only in name. He aspired to become Emperor of the West, and the husband of his prisoner, the Princess Ælia Galla Placidia (born 390). The latter he accomplished, and the marriage took place at Narbonne in 414; but he was assassinated in the following year when conducting an expedition into Spain to drive out the Vandals, Suevi and Alani, who had settled there five years previously.

Wallia succeeded him in 415, and was followed 419 by Theodoric I., son of Alaric, who had a prosperous reign of over thirty years. He was an ally of the Roman general Ætius against the Huns.

Theodoric I. met his death (451) in the battle of the Catalaunian Plains.[1]

The three brother Kings of the Ostrogoths, Walamir, Theudemir,[2] and Widemir Amala, together with Ardaric, King of the Gepidæ, were vassals of Attila, and fought on his side in his Western campaign. At this time the Vandals emigrated from the south of Spain into North Africa, took Carthage, and founded a kingdom there, with Genseric (or, more correctly, " Gaiseric ") as their king. A more complete conquest was effected in 439.

---

[1] The remains of some royal personage, together with various ornaments, jewels, and arms, were found near Povan on the Aube in 1842. Possibly they were Theodoric's.
[2] Father of Theodoric the Great.

Theodoric II. (455), son of Theodoric I. He murdered his elder brother Torismund, and thus obtained the Visigothic throne. He was a firm friend to Rome, which was taken, during his reign, by Genseric the Vandal; he quelled a rebellion in Spain, and was assassinated by a younger brother, Euric, in 466.

During the latter part of this period the Gepidæ took up their abode in the Hungarian Plains, until lately under the sway of Attila. The Ostrogoths migrated westward, and occupied the province of Pannonia, once a Roman possession.

(*Continued under* Byzantine, sixth century, on p. 154).

LIST OF AUTHORITIES CONSULTED FOR CHAPTER III

J. B. Bury
Cabrot and Le Clercq
F. Warre Cornish
Daremberg and Saglio
Rev. Percy Dearmer
Adrian Fortescue
Edward Gibbon
Thomas Hodgkin
Edward Hutton

A. F. Kendrick
Walter Lowrie
Joseph McCabe
A. H. Smith, British Museum
William Smith, Wayte and Marindin
Viollet-le-Duc
H. G. Wells
Mgr. Joseph Wilpert

CHAPTER IV

THE BYZANTINE EMPIRE [1]

NOTE

Although other chapters in this History of Costume are not carried (in this volume) past the Norman Conquest in England, it has been thought desirable to continue the historical data given in this Byzantine chapter to the middle of the fifteenth century, when the Empire fell.

Similarly, the details of Byzantine costume and arts are followed until the twelfth century—the period at which they ceased to have any marked influence on European fashions and culture. This has been done in preference to re-opening a Byzantine section in a subsequent volume.

It should be understood that the Byzantine Empire was known also as the East Roman Empire, the Eastern Empire, and the Greek Empire.

1. *The East Roman Empire*, because it was a transplantation to Constantinople of the original Roman traditions, government and culture, incorporating therewith Oriental influences. In the result it was merely a branch of the Roman Empire in the East.

2. *The Eastern Empire*, to distinguish it from the Western Empire—that of Rome.

3. *The Greek Empire*, because the national elements of Classic Greek culture, its art, literature, and intellect, became more and more the dominating expression of the people; and about the sixth century its traditions were the ruling force of the Empire. Its official language was Greek, and, when the Early Christian Church divided in 729, the Eastern portion at Constantinople called itself the Orthodox or Greek Church. Vast numbers of its inhabitants, who had maintained Roman character and traditions, were carried off by the Great Plague of 747, and were replaced by pure Greeks with no inheritance of Roman tradition behind them.

HISTORICAL DATA—TO THE FALL OF CONSTANTINOPLE IN 1453

A.D.

363. Valens is recognised as first Emperor of the Eastern Empire. Born in Pannonia (328). His elder brother Valentinian became Emperor of the West. Most of Valens' reign was occupied by war with the Goths, who, being pressed southward by the *Huns* (for Huns, *see* p. 175), were granted permission to settle in the empire, in lands south of the Danube. Incited to revolt, they took up arms against the Emperor, and defeated him in a battle near Hadrianople, August 9th, 378. It is said that he was trapped in a

A.D.

cottage and burnt with a few of his faithful soldiers. So ends the reign of the first Emperor.

During this reign a great controversy took place between the Catholics and the Arians. Valens was an Arian, and through him this faith spread widely through the East, and among the Teutonic races, especially the Goths.

379. Theodosius the Great (*see under* Rome).

395. The Emperor Arcadius. He married Eudoxia, the beautiful and high-spirited daughter of Bauto, the

[1] *See* footnote, page vi of *The Empresses of Constantinople*, by Joseph McCabe, 1913 (Methuen).

136

Frankish chief. John Chrysostom, Saint, and Patriarch of Constantinople (347–407), was one of the heroes of the Church, and antagonistic to the Empress Eudoxia. He assailed her to her face in Sancta Sophia, for which offence he was banished for a time. The minister Eutropius, a slave by birth, who rose to be High Chamberlain of the Palace, entirely dominated the Emperor.

408. Theodosius II., son of Arcadius. He was under the guardianship of his sister Pulcheria, who was given the title of Augusta in 415. Theodosius was a weakling, but learning was restored and the University of Constantinople founded in this reign, probably by the influence of the saintly Pulcheria. Public schools were first instituted at this time. Wars with Persia and the Huns.

447. Attila sent two ambassadors to the Emperor Theodosius, one the commander of his bodyguard named Edecon, a Scythian and father of Odoacer; the other his chief minister, a Roman and father of a future Emperor of the West, Romulus Augustulus (475–476).

A great earthquake took place in this year (447), and ruined the landward fortifications of Constantinople, overthrowing fifty-seven of its towers. The consequent danger to the Empire was appalling, owing to the menace of numerous barbarian inroads; but a threatened attack by the Huns under Attila was averted by the ratification of humiliating terms of peace by Theodosius II.

450. Death of Theodosius II. His sister Pulcheria proclaimed Empress in her own right. The first woman of the Western civilised world to attain the position of sole ruler. She married the senator Marcianus, or Marcian, who shared the throne and helped to reorganise the empire.

451. Fourth General Council of the Church at Chalcedon. Pulcheria and Marcian repudiate the Treaty of Peace with Attila, and Marcian marches an army to the assistance of Rome. He was in Moesia,[1] waiting to trap Attila on his return from the devastation of Northern Italy, when peace was arranged.

453. Death of Pulcheria. Leo I., the Thracian, raised to the purple by

Aspar, who became his chief minister. A constant feud existed between them until Leo murdered Aspar and his three sons, a deed which earned for him the title of Leo the Butcher.

474. Leo II. and Zeno the Isaurian, who married Ariadne, daughter of Aspar. This reign was troubled by the Ostrogoths under Theodoric the Great. Odoacer sends the Western Imperial insignia to Zeno, and informs him that the Western Empire ceases to exist.

527. Accession of Justinian I. on the death of his uncle Justin I. He was a man of great ambition and organising power. He married Theodora, a dancing-girl at the Hippodrome, who proved to be a woman of very great ability. A young officer, Belisarius, a Thracian, married the Empress's friend, Antonina, was appointed Governor of Dara, and became one of the greatest generals of the Byzantine Empire.

528. First Persian War.

532. The Nika sedition, a revolt of political factions who used the colours of the charioteers at the Hippodrome, the blues and greens, as badges. They took the word "Nika" (victory) as their war-cry. When the situation reached its climax, and the Emperor and his ministers became panic-stricken and contemplated flight, it was the Empress Theodora who rose to the occasion, and, in a powerful speech, exhorted them to stay by their posts and fight to the last. The Emperor and Council caught courage from this historic oration, and the revolt was suppressed.

533. Conquest of the Vandals by Belisarius.

536. Belisarius takes Rome, and Ravenna occupied (539).

540. This year marks the apex of Byzantine power in the reign of Justinian.

542. Terrible plague rages over Europe. The Second Persian War (540–546) and defeat of the Persians.

548. Death of the Empress Theodora.

553. The General Narses conquers Italy.

558. An army of barbarians—Slavs, Bulgarians and Huns—enters Thrace and marches to the gates of Constantinople. They are defeated by Belisarius.

565. Death of Belisarius and Justinian. The Avars [2] and Slavs begin to invade the empire.

[1] A province south of the Danube.
[2] From the north of the Danube and north of Serbia.

A.D.

626. First siege of Constantinople by the Avars.

628. Final defeat of the Persians.

636. Jerusalem taken by the Turks.

673. Second siege of Constantinople by the Arabs. They were repulsed in 677 by the aid of Greek fire.

717. Third siege of Constantinople by the Arabs, and their final repulse (718).

726. Worship of ikons prohibited.

741. Flourishing state of the Empire under Constantine V.

752. Ravenna taken by the Lombards.

753. Constantine V. persecutes the Iconodules or image-worshippers.

800. Charlemagne Emperor of "The Holy Roman or Western Empire." The Eastern or Byzantine Empire far gone in decay. "The Most Pious" Irene Empress.

810. The Pagan Bulgarians descend on Constantinople.

850. Rurik, leader of a band of Swedes, called in their native language "Ruotsl," raided the country south of the Gulf of Finland, and in 864 established himself as ruler at Novgorod and Kiev, and laid the foundation of modern Russia.

866. Re-founding of University of Constantinople.

867. The Emperor Basil I.

886. The Emperor Leo VI. the Wise.

907. The Russians attack Constantinople.

912. War with Bulgaria.

941. Second attack on Constantinople by the Russians, led by Prince Igor.

968. The monastery at Mount Athos founded.

969. War with Bulgaria.

976. The Emperor Basil II.

989. Vladimir, Prince of Russia, baptised.

1018. Complete conquest of the Balkans.

1025. Zenith of Byzantine power under Basil II.

1043. Last invasion by the Russians.

1054. In this year the Western or Catholic Church separated from the Eastern Greek or Orthodox Church, the bone of contention being the addition of three words to the Creed.

1067. The Empire on the decline. The Empress Eudocia Macrembolitissa.

1081. Robert Guiscard, Duke of Apulia, a Norman, invades the Empire.

1082. Treaty of Venice.

1084. Second Expedition of Robert Guiscard.

1096. The First Crusade.

1100. The Balkan Peninsula embraced in the Empire.

1118. Decline of trade owing to Italian competition.

A.D.

1147. The Second Crusade.

1180. Terrible state of the Empire.

1189. The Third Crusade.

1203. Complete decline of the Empire. The Emperor Isaac II. (1186–1195, restored 1203).

1204. The seventh siege of Constantinople by the Latins, who were undertaking the Fourth Crusade to the Holy Land under the leadership of Baldwin, Count of Flanders. The greater part of the crusading army was induced by the Venetians to conquer Constantinople for their benefit, under the pretence of quelling the Byzantine revolt. They stormed the city and captured it after slight resistance. Without cause or excuse, the Latins deliberately proceeded to sack it and massacre the inhabitants. Many monuments were destroyed, and the loss to art, crafts and literature was incalculable. Four bronze horses made by Lysippus stolen by the Doge, and erected in front of S. Mark's at Venice.

Baldwin formed a Latin empire at Constantinople and Nicæa. Thessalonica and Trebizond became a polyarchy.

1261. The Greeks take Constantinople from the Latins and re-establish their old régime.

1347. The position of the Empire becomes deplorable.

1370. John Palæologus, the Emperor, visits Venice, Paris and Rome, to solicit assistance from these Catholic powers against the heathen Turk.

The Turks were a constant source of anxiety for ten years. In 1400, Manuel II. also visited the West to procure aid.

1423. The Empire sinks to the level of a petty State, and is centred in Constantinople only.

1439. John VII. visits Lorenzo de Medici at Florence.[1]

1453. The ninth and last siege of Constantinople, the metropolis of the Byzantine Empire, was begun by the Turks under Mohammed II., on April 6th, 1453, and lasted 53 days. This glorious city was invested by 258,000 armed infidels and a park of 200 guns of exceptional calibre, with which the walls were battered, only to be repaired by the inhabitants—men, women and children toiling all night. On May 29th, the fatal blow to Christendom was hurled at a

[1] See portrait, Gozzoli's frescoes, Medici Palace.

breach in the inner wall, where it was met by the heroic Emperor Constantine XIII., supported by only three friends and a few loyal followers. His friends, fighting to the last, were cut down by the Janissaries, and Constantine met his death as "befitted an emperor and a faithful soldier of Christ." So ends the reign of the last Emperor.

The pillage of the city was granted by Mohammed to his soldiers, and disorder and rapine prevailed for eight hours. Few massacres took place, as the lives of the people were considered valuable for ransom. The build-

ings were preserved intact, and the Sultan made his State entry into the city through the West Central Gate of S. Romanus. At the principal doorway to Sancta Sophia he alighted from his horse and entered. He gave instructions for the immediate transformation of the Christian Church, wherein Constantine had received the Holy Sacrament the night before, into a Mohammedan mosque. The mosaics on the walls were "purified" with whitewash [1] and the Christian emblems removed.

"The Crescent had triumphed over the Cross."

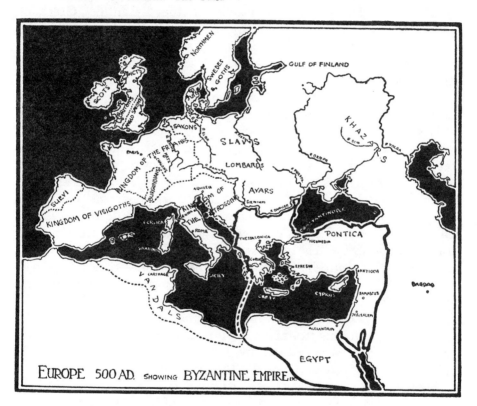

EUROPE 500 A.D. SHOWING BYZANTINE EMPIRE.etc

RISE OF THE BYZANTINE EMPIRE

IN the year 660 B.C. a small band of emigrants set out from the town of Megara, a port on the Isthmus of Corinth, whose inhabitants at a later period claimed to be the originators of Greek comedy. The destina-

[1] The Sultan Abdul Madjid ordered the complete restoration of the mosaics in 1837, and authorised copies were made by German artists. Later they were plastered over again.

tion of these emigrants was the promontory where Europe is divided
from Asia by the strip of water now known as the Bosphorus. There
they built their rude huts, and surrounded them with primitive fortifications, naming the place BYZANTIUM. This small colony of Greeks
existed through six centuries of continual warfare, but Byzantium was
eventually taken by Rome in A.D. 73 and finally reduced to ruins in
A.D. 196. This splendid position—a connecting link between the Western
and Eastern civilised worlds—recommended itself to Constantine
the Great, who founded a city in 328 upon the same site and called
it "New Rome," but later it received the name of its founder—
CONSTANTINOPLE, which was used alternatively with the original
name, Byzantium.

This new city became the capital of the Byzantine, Greek or
Eastern Empire, founded in 394 by Theodosius the Great, when he
divided the Roman Empire into the Eastern and Western. The Byzantine
Empire lasted for ten and a half centuries, and for a long period its capital
was the most important centre of civilisation in the world.

In the sixth century A.D. Constantinople presented a magnificent
spectacle, when viewed from the deep blue Sea of Marmora. Its outer
walls, seven feet thick and thirty feet high, connected a chain of towers,
and enclosed a second wall fifteen feet in thickness, and in places fifty
feet in height. This wall also connected high towers, ninety-seven in
number. Beyond these fortifications stood the city, upon a series of
gently sloping hills. The long oval-shaped Hippodrome contained,
amongst other ornaments, the four bronze horses made by Lysippus,
sculptor to Alexander the Great, which were transported thither from
Rome by Constantine. The immense Imperial Palace was at the north end,
and beyond that again the Basilica of Divine Wisdom—Sancta Sophia—
stood out conspicuously in its dazzling whiteness, surmounted by
cupolas of gold. The church of S. Irene, the baths of Zeuxippus,
the serpent column brought from Delphi, the obelisk erected by
Theodosius I., and his triumphal arch or Golden Gate—all these mar-
vellous buildings were backed by a vista of the Nicomedian Hills
and the snow-capped peaks of the Bithynian Alps.

Some details of the Palace of the Emperors have come down to us.
It was a city in itself, built upon the shores of the Bosphorus; and at
the water-stairs an Imperial galley was always kept in readiness, in case
of necessity for sudden flight! [1]

Inside, the golden roof of the audience-chamber was supported by
columns of pure gold and silver, and its walls were covered with hangings of silk and embroideries, and of pure gold glistening with precious

---

[1] The Bucoleon Palace. It took its name from a piece of sculpture representing a bull
and a lion which adorned the quay.

stones. The furniture of massive, quaint shape was of cedar-wood, overlaid with gold leaf [1] and upholstered with gorgeous materials.

Ornaments of goldsmith's work were intricately pierced and filled in with coloured enamels, and upon the marble floors were laid carpets of silk, of Persian make and strange design.

The centre of all was the Imperial throne, shaped like a tabernacle, all of gold, set with an enormous quantity of jewels. Over it was a cupola raised on four columns, surmounted by eagles with widespreading wings. Over the throne was a large bejewelled crown, with ropes of priceless pearls attached to it, suspended by golden chains from the ceiling. On either side of the marble steps that led up to the throne were two life-sized lions of massive gold,[2] which roared mechanically when it was considered expedient to overawe any suspicious or unwelcome suppliant. Behind these lions stood two huge Egyptian pylons, and directly behind the throne rose a golden plane tree, on the branches of which little birds of all kinds, wrought in goldsmith's work, jewels, and

Throne

enamel, sang for the amusement of the Court. In the midst of this exotic Oriental magnificence sat immovable an apparently diminutive figure, almost lost in costly robes of gold smothered in jewels and pearls: "My Eternity," "My Mildness," "My Magnificence"[3]:— *The Emperor!*

[1] An idea borrowed from the ancient Assyrians and Egyptians.
[2] Accredited by some to the Emperor Theophilus (829–842). In the ninth century, during a period of bankruptcy, these were melted down.
[3] Titles by which the Emperor signed himself.

A Spanish Jew, Benjamin of Tudela, visited Constantinople in the twelfth century, and gives a similar glowing account of the wealth and wonder of the place.

To this great city, which had become the emporium of the world, came the merchant galleys of all nations, East and West. Caravans from almost unheard-of districts of Northern and Eastern Asia journeyed over the arid plains and highlands, laden with vast wealth, which was poured into the storehouses of Byzantium; and, in return, Byzantine merchants distributed works of art, manufactures, and commodities of every description to far-off lands. This being so, it was not impossible for a piece of silk to travel from China to Britain *via* Byzantium.

Byzantine culture reaches the West, North and South. But a fact equally important was that the East, from whence civilisation and the arts proceeded, came into closer touch with Western lands. Foreign trade contributed largely to the spread of civilisation. In fact, the influence of Byzantine culture, and especially art (*see under* Art) was far-reaching and world-wide. In the West, Italy was the first to come under its power, its chief centres being Rome and Ravenna; later, Pisa, Venice, Padua, Parma and Messina. The Franks of the Merovingian Period, and later the Empire of Charlemagne (Germany), were affected by it. As early as the sixth century it penetrated as far as England, Ireland, Scotland, Scandinavia and Iceland. In the north it reached the Slavonic races of Russia and the Balkans, and in the south, North Africa.

Arts and Crafts

The fall of the Roman Empire in 476 marks also the fall of Classic (*i.e.* Greek and Greco-Roman) art. With new ideas and tastes, a new art—Christian art—was arising from the ruins of Paganism.

Early Christian art was founded upon Classic Greek principles; in short, a symbolic expression, for the most part represented by allegorical figures. During the early centuries of the Christian Era the Roman Government forbade the use of true representations, or likenesses, of sacred persons; but after the great persecutions, when Christianity became the recognised religion of the State, this ban was removed, and Christian art greatly developed, though mainly on Oriental lines. In this process much of the pure Greek sense of beauty of form, together with the less perfect Greco-Roman, was unconsciously lost and almost entirely disappeared, and the influence of the West was largely superseded by that of the East. In general character this was luxurious. Designs were very ornate, and backgrounds and surfaces were covered, in fact almost concealed, by scrolls and patterns, branches, leaves, flowers, and fruit, especially the vine, with its tendrils largely developed.

By the sixth century, under the rule of that patron of the arts, Justinian, the blending of the two — the Classic Greek and the Oriental — reached its zenith and flourished under the name of BYZANTINE ART.

Architecture, literature, painting (including frescoes), illuminated MSS. and mosaics, goldsmith's and enamel work and textiles, all underwent this transformation.

Greek artists in all branches of art were held in very high esteem throughout the world, and their work was eagerly sought on account of its superior technique, finish, and individuality.

The period following the death of the Emperor Justinian is one of considerable decline in the arts and literature.

The Iconoclastic persecutions of 726, 741 and 753 were not conducive to the development of art. This campaign against the worship of images and religious pictures came to an end in 842, after which the arts revived, and the ensuing period is conspicuous for great fertility in architecture, painting, and literature, and for luxurious costume.

Byzantium, as a centre of the arts, civilisation and fashion, ceased to have any influence over the West after the siege and sack of Constantinople by the Latins in 1204. Many priceless treasures of art and literature found their way into Western Europe, and these objects of Byzantine arts and craftsmanship were invaluable sources of inspiration to the artists and craftsmen of the West. This is proved by the fact that the art of all mediæval nations has some Byzantine element in its composition or fabric. Particularly is this the case with those nations under the legislature of the Orthodox or Greek Church.

The influence of these Byzantine or Greek artists was felt not only in the West, but extended to the East also. It had been borrowed from the East originally, and was now returned to them tenfold.

Architecture

Of all the Byzantine emperors, Justinian I. was the greatest as a patron of architecture on a magnificent and munificent scale. His most important work was the rebuilding of SANCTA SOPHIA, which was first founded by Constantine the Great in A.D. 360. The original church was destroyed by fire in 404, and rebuilt by Theodosius II. in 415, but was destroyed again during the Nika seditions of 532. With the help of the architect, Anthemius of Tralles, assisted by Isidorus of Miletus and ten thousand workmen, it was completed within six years (537). Procopius, the secretary to General Belisarius, gives a description of the richly coloured interior of Sancta Sophia. The vast dome, sectioned out into four smaller ones, was supported on four huge piers, and the deep recesses of the transepts to left and right were encircled with colonnades of pillars of green jasper; [1] porphyry,[2] variegated in purples, greys and white; alabaster; and marbles of green, crimson, rose and orange hue, set "like dancers in a chorus"; flanked with walls of mother-of-pearl, coloured marbles, and the golden brilliance of gorgeous mosaics, giving an effect of overpowering splendour.

Justinian himself, robed in white linen and staff in hand, frequently visited the building under course of construction, and encouraged the workmen with his appreciation and enthusiasm.

This perfect specimen of Byzantine art and architecture was taken as a model by the Turks, after their occupation of Constantinople in 1453, and on it they based all their Mahommedan mosques. The basilica of S. Vitale was built by Justinian at Ravenna, and is another excellent example of Byzantine architecture of this period, which now assumed a character more in accordance with ancient Greek traditions.

Justinian erected an enormous number of other buildings, both civil and military — churches, fortresses, hospitals, aqueducts, and military towers—all over the empire.

S. Apollinare Nuovo at Ravenna was built as an Arian Chapel Royal for Theodoric the Great, in the Byzantine style, by Byzantine architects and artisans. Originally it was dedicated to S. Martin,[3] Bishop of Tours (316–387). When Ravenna, the capital of the Gothic kingdom, fell into the hands of the Catholic Emperor Justinian in 552, he re-dedicated it and made several alterations. Another church of S. Apollinare in Classe was consecrated in 549, and is the finest basilica extant.

Greek architects were very much in demand in every country where the lure of art and culture had made itself felt.

Painting

Painting of various kinds had been practised previously by the Greeks of the Classic Age (see p. 52), and by the Romans, i.e. Greco-Roman. The Early Christians of the second and third centuries decorated the walls of their secret subterranean places of worship—the Catacombs —with frescoes, executed by artists of inferior technique, who used the symbolic method of expression for their subjects. None the less, the frescoes are of great value as authorities for costume of the late Imperial Epoch in Rome, and of early Byzantine times. They are also good examples of early Christian art, wherein the combined Greek and

---

[1] From the Temple of Diana at Ephesus.   [2] From the Temple of the Sun at Rome.
[3] It was dedicated afresh to S. Apollinaris, first Bishop of Ravenna, A.D. 75, when the relics of that saint were transferred thither in the ninth century from S. Apollinare in Classe, for safety during the Saracenic invasions.

Oriental elements can be seen and understood. These frescoes were carried out in tempera, or water-colour, upon the prepared plaster surface of walls or ceiling.

From this time onwards fresco painting became very general, and was used to a great extent for the ornamentation of churches.

From about the eighth century A.D., Greek artists were employed in the principal cities of Europe, chiefly in decorating churches with frescoes. Paintings of the same nature were often done on small panels of wood, first treated with a thin layer of plaster. These were mostly portraits. This kind of painting was much used for the decoration of ikons (sacred pictures, usually of the Virgin and Child, and of Saints), as was also the encaustic style (see p. 52).

The persecutions by the Iconoclasts, or image-breakers, of the year 741 were carried to excess. All pictures, images and decorations of a religious character that had escaped destruction hitherto were now effaced by scraping or whitewash.

Mosaics

Mosaic decoration had been practised in very early times, and followed the course of civilisation from Assyria through Egypt and Greece to Rome. In the first century of the Christian Era the art of glass-blowing very much improved, and the wealthy were beginning to have it set in their windows.

Mosaic work, in the first instance, was used as a floor decoration, carried out in small cubes of coloured marble, arranged in geometrical patterns of a floral nature, and introducing birds and beasts. About the end of the third century A.D. glass mosaic was introduced, and was used chiefly in wall decoration, marble still being utilised for floors.

Among the earliest mosaics of any great artistic merit are those depicting the histories of the patriarchs of the fourth century, in the church of S. Maria Maggiore at Rome. The mosaics of the life of Christ, with which the apsidal arch of the same church is decorated, are of the fifth century, and were erected by order of Pope Sixtus III. (432–440).

The mosaics in the mausoleum of the Empress Galla Placidia at Ravenna, of the fifth century, and those of S. George at Thessalonica, of the sixth, are well preserved, and are useful as authorities for the art and costume of the period. The processions of virgins (see Fig. 76) and martyrs, with which Theodoric the Great [1] decorated the long nave of his Arian basilica, S. Apollinare Nuovo at Ravenna, and many other churches in the same city, are elaborate examples of the mosaic work of Byzantine artists of this period. A pair of important mosaics, portraits

[1] Sir Thomas Graham Jackson believes these processions to be the work of Byzantine artists employed by Theodoric. Some authorities say they were put up by Agnellus, the Catholic bishop, in 560.

of Justinian, Theodora (*see* Figs. 66, 74) and Court officials, flank the apse of the church of S. Vitale at Ravenna.

In the eighth century, the Iconoclast war limited the style of design of mosaics somewhat, in obedience to edicts concerning the suppression of idolatry.

To enumerate all the best mosaics in the Byzantine style, composed during the course of the following six centuries, in Constantinople and other places, would occupy a book in itself. There are already numerous publications on the subject.

Goldsmith's Work, Sculpture and Bronze-casting

These arts were brought to a very high state of perfection during this epoch, and many examples can be seen in Europe to-day.

Illuminated Manuscripts

The numerous manuscripts illuminated by Greek miniaturists, in common with all examples of Byzantine art, had many Oriental characteristics. These originals, which later found their way abroad, were copied by the monks of Western Europe at a later date. Many of these illuminated manuscripts, of various nations and periods, are wonderful works of art, like their prototypes, the Byzantine, and are invaluable to us at the present day for their information as to costume, furniture, and hundreds of other details.

The Iconoclastic controversy is the cause of the present scarcity of illustrated manuscripts of the seventh and eighth centuries;[1] but those of a later period are more plentiful, and exhibit a certain continuity of tradition with those dating from the fourth to the sixth century.

A marked characteristic style of Byzantine work, especially in the drawing of the figures, is their apparent stiffness, due very considerably to the archaic treatment necessitated by working out the picture in mosaic, undoubtedly the models for many illuminations. This stiffness was also partly due to the artist's endeavour to impart to his figures a dignity and an intense feeling of veneration and spirituality.

The draughtsmanship is particularly masterful, and the drapery well arranged and defined, usually by indicating the folds with gold lines on brilliant colour. The backgrounds are often in gold, and, sometimes, especially in those of a later period, of a diaper pattern, all of which help to make the miniatures very ornate and decorative.

It was at the end of the ninth century that the leading principles of Byzantine illuminated manuscripts became firmly established, and the art reached its highest point of perfection during the tenth and eleventh centuries.

[1] Religion may foster art, but it also destroys it.

SECTION I

BYZANTIUM was the centre of fashion and civilisation from the fifth to the twelfth century.

Its influence can be traced in varying degree in the costumes and manners of the Courts of ruling princes, in the castles of the nobility and the homes of the people, in every civilised country throughout Europe, from the fifth century until late in the Middle Ages.

COSTUME OF BYZANTIUM

The Fifth Century A.D.

This period shows the beginnings of those extravagant tendencies which, increasing during the following centuries, were to culminate in the eleventh century in a wild orgy of sartorial magnificence.

Previous to the opening of the fifth century, the Eastern and Western Empires had become separate dominions (394). Constantinople was on the upward grade, but Rome, during the next eighty years (394–478), was flickering her last before final extinction.

One feeble effort was made during this time in the cause of costume. It had no immediate results, but it was the first stroke in breaking down the barrier of a long-standing tradition—a feat accomplished a century later (*see* p. 156).

A decadent people always strains after a new or eccentric idea. In the midst of the horrors of war, famine, pestilence and siege, a craze swept over the pleasure-loving, frivolous youth of Rome. It was during the terrible barbarian inroads into the Empire of the West, towards the end of the fourth and beginning of the fifth century A.D., that it became the fashion among Roman dandies to imitate the costume of their Teutonic invaders. Degenerate fantastics paraded the streets and public ways of Rome, and probably of Constantinople (although the Byzantines were of much saner mentality), dressed out in the loose *bracco*, fur tunicas, long hair, and barbaric ornaments peculiar to the Teutonic peoples. The Emperor Honorius (395–423) endeavoured to crush this ridiculous vogue by issuing three edicts, and he succeeded for a time; for these barbaric fashions were but freaks of a moment, and were not followed by eminent men or leaders of "Society."

The Paludamentum (*continued from p. 110*)

It has been noted already (*see* p. 93) that the paludamentum super-seded the toga picta for full State dress.

It was during the early part of this century that it became, without exception, the *Orthodox Imperial Mantle*. It was worn by the last emperors of the West, all future emperors of the East, and of empires to come.

In *colour* it was always purple, and its shape as shown in Diagram 17. Its length was greater than as used before, reaching to the ankles.

At first it was made of plain *material*—silk of the richest and heaviest quality obtainable. As each century dawned and faded, the material of which the paludamentum was composed became more and more rich and ornate. Often it was embroidered in heavy gold and encrusted with jewels, chiefly pearls—pearls by the million—until its surface was almost entirely covered. When the silk-weavers, installed at Constantinople by Justinian, became expert in the art of weaving brocade, this material was used, and was frequently superimposed with embroidery and gems. A distinctive feature of the paludamentum, or State mantle—for that is what it had now become—was the square or oblong decoration placed on the edge of the sloping side (*see* A in Diagram 17), back and front. This was called the TABLION. However rich the paludamentum might be, this particular piece of ornamentation surpassed it in splendour.

The paludamentum was worn not only by the emperor, but, in the sixth and following centuries, by the empress also. No other women were permitted the use of it.

It was worn by courtiers and high officials in the empire, in all colours *except* the Imperial purple, but not so richly decorated.

Henceforth, the various phases of the paludamentum will be noted under the description of the figures.

The Tunica

Details of the tunica were concluded under Imperial Rome (p. 105). No further change took place in its shape, but a few modifications occurred from time to time and are duly noted in this history.

The Dalmatica

The dalmatica, in the course of a short period, became merged in the tunica, the only difference being in the sleeves—close in the tunica and wide in the dalmatica.

The dalmatica was brought into use again during the latter part of the sixth century, as part of the Imperial robes of the emperor, as a

FIG. 60. AN EMPEROR OF THE EASTERN OR
WESTERN EMPIRE—FIFTH CENTURY, A.D.
(*see* p. 149)

FIG. 63. AN EMPRESS OF THE EASTERN OR
WESTERN EMPIRE—FIFTH CENTURY, A.D.
(see p. 152)

vestment of ecclesiastical significance. With men in general, it practically disappeared for about four centuries, when the wide sleeves peculiar to this garment reappeared among the Anglo-Saxons and the Carlovingians.

Women still continued to use the dalmatica concurrently with the stola until Saxon times, when it merged into the gown.

IMPERIAL COSTUME AND THE NOBILITY—MEN

Fifth Century

An emperor of this period is represented in Fig. 60, and it will be seen at once that the tunica is very similar to the Roman dress described in Fig. 44. He wears the tunica with close long sleeves, but it descends to the knee only, and is slit up the sides. In the original this is white, and is decorated on both shoulders with segmentæ in the form of squares, and a band of embroidery decorates the bottom edge, back and front, finishing at the ends with an upright motif outlining the slit, and enclosing another piece of oblong embroidery. The same embroidery outlines the wrists, and the tunica is belted low down on the waist. Over this is worn the paludamentum of deep purple, lined with the same colour, fastened on the right shoulder with a jewelled ornament, from which are suspended two strings of pearls. The tablion is of embroidery in red and gold, and set as a decoration on the front and back edge of the paludamentum. When it was necessary to free the left arm, the paludamentum was pulled up over the upper arm, thus falling in a point in front (see Fig. 66).

Fig. 61

The legs are bare, and on the feet are worn elaborate open-work boots that might be called sandals. They are of red leather and fastened by buckles at the ankle.

The usual Imperial diadem, a double string of pearls and a jewel, is worn.

Fig. 60. An emperor of the Eastern or Western Empire—fifth century—in tunica and paludamentum. The decoration is from a mosaic in the Church of S. John at Naples (fourth century).

Costume of a noble (*see* Fig. 61). This costume is taken from the celebrated ivory diptych at Monza, and is typical of that worn at Rome and Constantinople during the latter part of the fourth and early part of the fifth century. The portrait is generally believed to be Stilicho (350–408), with his wife Serena and their son. Some authorities, however, state it to be General Ætius (395–454). As far as the costume is concerned, the point is immaterial, as the two men were almost contemporaries. Both were great generals of the Roman or Western Empire.

General Stilicho wears the tunica to the knees, with close-fitting sleeves to the wrists. It is of a patterned material, worked with embroidery, most certainly not brocade. A border of a different design is

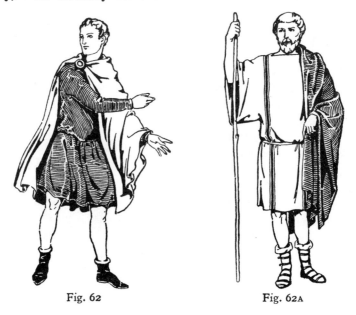

Fig. 62   Fig. 62A

shown at the hem and round the wrists. The paludamentum is of the same design and material, probably a very rich silk, and is fastened on the right shoulder with an elaborate fibula (*see under* Jewellery, p. 205). The presence of the sword and belt, together with the shield and spear, denote that he is in semi-military dress. His legs are bare, and his shoes (described hereafter) are of a special kind. Such a costume was worn by a general at Court functions.

The small youth shown in Fig. 64 is the son of General Stilicho. He wears a short tunica with long close sleeves to the wrist, and over it the colobium, now returned into fashion. Around him is draped the paludamentum. His legs are bare, and on his feet are shoes like those worn by his father.

Fig. 62 is a man of position. His tunica of woollen material is of a new shape, and is cut as shown in Diagram 19 with the sleeves all in one. It is of knee length, with long close-fitting sleeves. The upper part of the tunica fits the figure closely and falls in folds from the waist to the knees. This is the first example of a new style of tunica, which formed the basis of tunicas in general for many centuries, and it will be referred to many times in the future. Over the tunica is a short cloak, familiar as the abolla, made of cloth and fastened on the right shoulder with a fibula. His legs are bare, but he is wearing ankle boots (*see* p. 199).

Dia. 19.

Fig. 62A represents a man of inferior rank wearing the dalmatica, already fully described (*see* pp. 98, 99), but with this difference—it is here belted low down on the waist, almost on the hips. A loose piece of drapery, in the form of a rectangular cloak, is carried over his left shoulder. Many examples show cloaks of various colours, fastened at the neck in front with a circular fibula (*see under* Jewellery, p. 205).

COSTUME OF THE WOMEN OF THE FIFTH CENTURY

The Revival of the Greek Chiton

A strong national Greek tendency stirred the intellectual element of Byzantine society during the last decadent spasms of Imperial Rome, and was the cause of the revival of many traditional fashions of Classic Greece. Not the least important was the costume.

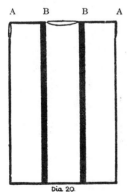

A B B A

Dia. 20.

It has been pointed out already that the Roman stola was identical with the Greek chiton (p. 81), but, with the advent of the dalmatica in the third century, the stola and palla sank into insignificance. It has been shown lately that the palla took a new lease of life in the fourth century.

The Greek chiton, *i.e.* the stola, returned at the end of the fourth or beginning of the fifth century, with slight modifications. It is shown in Figs. 63 and 64, but more clearly in Diagram 20. This new-fashioned stola still retained its original shape as a cylinder, but, instead of being entirely open at the neck and shoulders, the neck part was hollowed out and the arms were passed through the armholes *at the sides*, after the method of the kolobus (Diagram 10). It was also considerably wider, as the distance

Fig. 64

from the neck B to the edge of the armhole A was sufficient to allow the material to give the effect of a draped sleeve, the whole width being confined by a girdle worn rather high at the waist.

To this garment was sometimes added the very ornate latus clavus or the angustus clavus (*see* Figs. 63, 75, and 76).

Fig. 63 shows an empress of the fifth century. She is wearing at least four garments. First, an under-dress with tight sleeves to the wrist. Over this is a white stola of the new shape, the draped sleeves only showing. Over this again is a second stola, with the angustus clavus, and over all is draped the palla, with panel attached, and arranged as described under Fig. 54. The girdle is now worn over all the drapery.

The jewelled collar, with pear-drop pearls, is a new fashion which became a distinctive feature of Byzantine dress. Note the sudarium in the left hand.

Fig. 64 shows the costume of a noble lady at the end of the fourth century and first half of the fifth. The new shaped stola is worn, over an under-dress with close sleeves to the wrist, and is confined at the waist with a girdle. It is curious to find her with the palla draped in the old-fashioned Greek manner—a fact which proves how much this garment of antiquity was in favour, even at so late a date. Notice the prevailing fashion of carrying the sudarium in the left hand. The figure is that of Serena, niece of the Emperor Theodosius I. and wife of Stilicho, and is from the Monza diptych. It may be that the costume is not a representation of that actually worn by the lady, but a classic treatment of his subject adopted by the artist. This is doubtful in view of the very modern (fifth century) head-dress which she wears (*see under* Head-dresses, p. 169).

Fig. 65

Fig. 63. An empress of the Eastern or Western Empire—fifth century—wearing four garments: the decoration is from a mosaic at Milan (fourth century).

WOMEN OF THE PEOPLE

Fig. 65 shows a woman of this class. She is wearing the dalmatica, cut as shown in Diagram 18, with the angustus clavus. It could be worn girded at the waist or ungirded. The palla is worn over the head, a portion of the edge being fastened tight round the head. A fold of it is pushed to the front over this tight portion, and the bulk of the palla hangs on both sides of the figure. In this case the wearer has taken the right side hanging portion and draped it over the right arm and left wrist.

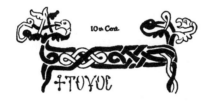

THEODORIC THE GREAT

"King of the Goths and Romans in Italy," vide *Italiani*.
"A lover of manufactures, and a great restorer of cities."—Thomas Hodgkin.

Theodoric the Great was the son of Theudemir, of the family of the Amala, King of the Ostrogoths occupying Pannonia.

The Ostrogoths were a ferocious people, whose spirit was unbroken by slavery. They were unthrifty, and consequently lived in a state of great poverty, but indulged in wasteful luxury, and when their resources gave out they ravaged and pillaged their neighbours.

Theodoric was born near Vienna in 455, and when quite young (463) was claimed as a hostage by the Byzantine Government to ensure the better behaviour of his countrymen. He was brought up at the Imperial Court, and educated in Byzantine culture. In the meantime, the Ostrogoths were subjected to raids by the neighbouring tribes—the Swabians, Sarmatians and Scythians—but eventually effected a final rupture with their previous overlords, the Huns.

473. It was arranged that Theudemir should attack Constantinople, and simultaneously Widemir was to advance on Rome. The expedition of the latter came to nothing, and he and his sons turned towards Gaul, and settled in the land of their kinsmen the Visigoths.

On the death of Theudemir in 476, Theodoric succeeded to the Ostrogothic throne. As ruler of these turbulent people, he became alternately a menace and a friendly neighbour to the Emperor Zeno. With the object of conciliating him, Theodoric was taken by Zeno into his service, and given the title " Magister Militum "; but, overruled by feelings of loyalty to his people, he alienated himself from the Emperor and intrigued openly and in secret against him.

At this period, a double of Theodoric comes upon the scene—the squinting Theodoric—a man of mean birth who had found favour with the Byzantine minister, Aspar. For some time this man set up in opposition to Theodoric, but they afterwards became reconciled, and joined forces (479) against the Empire; but Theodoric was won over by bribes. Again, in 483, he revolted and marched on Constantinople, but met with no success. The Emperor Zeno, wishing to be rid of so formidable a neighbour, willingly recognised the alliance Theodoric had made with the Rugians [1] against Odoacer. The Ostrogoths, led by their king, left the Balkans, crossed into Italy, and defeated Odoacer in battles on the

[1] A people living in the region of modern Bohemia.

Isonzo and at Verona. Gundobad, King of the Burgundians, descended into Italy as an ally of Odoacer (490), and the Visigoths under their King Alaric II., son of Euric, came to the assistance of the Ostrogoths. Odoacer left his stronghold, Ravenna, to meet them, and was hopelessly defeated on the Adda. He retired to Ravenna, where Theodoric besieged him for nearly three years, taking the city in 493. A treaty was drawn up by these two, whereby the government of Italy should be divided between them. At a grand banquet, given by Theodoric to inaugurate this treaty, Odoacer was stabbed to death as he sat at table, presumably by Theodoric himself. By this murder Theodoric became sole master of Italy, not without the reluctant consent of the Byzantine Emperor. For thirty-three years Theodoric ruled Italy, with Ravenna as his capital. He adopted a policy of wisdom and justice, and extended his dominions from Sicily to the Danube, and from Sirmun (Belgrade) to the Atlantic Ocean. He was an enthusiastic patron of the arts and architecture. In the cities of Italy he built and repaired many edifices, and adorned buildings and public places with works of art, thus gaining the appellation, *Theodoric the Great.*

He died at Ravenna in 526. His grandson Athalaric, aged ten, succeeded to the Ostrogothic inheritance in Italy, and Amalaric, another grandson, to that of the Visigoths in Spain.

Theodoric's tomb at Ravenna was erected by his daughter Amalasuntha, Athalaric's mother, who became regent, and governed with such prudence and wisdom as to gain the esteem of all the kingdoms of Europe. Athalaric was educated by her as befitted a Roman prince; but his subjects objected to their king being brought up by a woman, and preferred that he should be reared by them as a valiant Goth. After a life of debauchery under this tutelage, the king died at the age of sixteen, in 532.

Amalasuntha then attempted to occupy the throne. She married her cousin Theodatus, and they both intrigued for her recognition as reigning monarch of Italy. Unfortunately for them, their schemes were unsuccessful and they were eventually imprisoned. Later, Amalasuntha was strangled in her bath, and Theodatus was assassinated in 536.

Vitiges now became King of Italy, but the Romans resented an Arian as their ruler. Belisarius, the Byzantine general, entered the city of Rome unopposed, and the Gothic garrison evacuated it. Thus Rome was delivered from the barbarian yoke in 536.

In the following year, the whole nation of the Ostrogoths, under Vitiges, besieged Belisarius in Rome. Hadrian's tomb was then converted into a citadel, now known as the Castle of S. Angelo. The Goths, however, received a severe repulse from Belisarius, and Vitiges retreated to Ravenna. He was followed up by Belisarius, who took Ravenna (539), and finally subjugated the Goths in Italy. The king and most of the Gothic nobles were taken into the service of the Byzantine Empire.

Another revolt of the Goths took place under their king, Totila, who had recaptured Naples and the provinces of Lucania, Apulia, Calabria, and Rome, in 547, and Italy was brought under the sway of Totila.

S. Benedict, born at Nursia 480, died 544, was the chronicler of the Gothic kings, and founder of the Benedictine Order of monks. He did much to bring about a reconciliation between the Romans and the Goths, and considerably influenced Totila in his government.

Totila was defeated and slain by General Narses in 552, when the Goths were finally expelled from Italy. The Alemanni settled in France, and the Langobards, or Lombards, in that part of Italy now called Lombardy (565).

Recared, King of the Visigoths (586–601) in Spain, adopted the Athanasian belief, and became a convert to the Church of Rome.

711. The Visigoths of Spain were defeated by the Arabs, under their chief, Tarik, who landed at the fortress-rock Tarikrock—Gibraltar.

Note.—A description of the costume of these people is given under " Teutonic Tribes."

SECTION II

COSTUME OF THE SIXTH CENTURY

The sixth century is celebrated in the history of costume for three reasons: Firstly, the introduction of the *silk*-worm into Europe (*see* Silk, Chap. V.). Secondly, it is in this century that the practice of "faking" (a pernicious habit with modern dressmakers, to say nothing of theatrical costumiers) first came into use in the art of dressmaking. It started with the pallium (*see* p. 108) and the palla (*see* p. 118), so the blame rests equally upon both sexes. Thirdly, for the advent of *Trousers.* These abominable and disgusting garments, so long associated with depraved savages, were adopted by the highly cultured and respectable subjects of a great empire. Men of rank and position now wore close-fitting leg-bags called HOSA. These made their appearance even at Court, for they were worn by the Emperor and his officials. Possibly the fashion was set by that barbarian hero, Theodoric the Great, King of the Ostrogoths. Although the Roman Catholics obliterated Theodoric's portrait from among the mosaics [1] which decorated the walls of his Arian basilica of S. Apollinare Nuovo at Ravenna, they kept his trousers—for this time these garments had come to stay.

Asiatic trousers. Drawers, or trousers, besides being the distinctive garb of the barbarian races of the North and West, had been a part of the national dress of the Medes and Persians, the Parthians, Phrygians, Samatians and Dacians for many centuries before the Christian Era. The more refined Asiatics had them made of silk or cotton, and some were highly decorated with many patterns and stripes. The Magi, or Eastern Kings, are represented in mosaics and in art generally of the fifth, sixth and seventh centuries A.D. wearing these elaborately patterned trousers, to distinguish them as foreigners. By some nations of the East, especially the Persians, these trousers were worn close-fitting and had almost the appearance of long stockings.[2]

The Ostrogothic and Persian Wars of this epoch were factors which brought into favour the use of trousers; and it is at this period—the sixth century—in the history of costume that two names are found for the two kinds of leg coverings—commonly called by us to-day, drawers and trousers.

The old Celtic name of bracco became changed into " brôc," singular, and "brêc," plural, meaning loose or wide leg coverings. From this word is derived "breeks" or "breeches." In Frankish and old French it became "braies."

A new word now crept into the languages of Europe. In Latin and Teutonic this word was "hosa," meaning a tight or close leg covering. In Anglo-Saxon it became "hose." The name "hosa" is the one by which in future we shall know the tight-fitting leg covering worn during the next few centuries.

IMPERIAL COSTUME AND THE NOBILITY—MEN

The chief authorities for the costume of this century are the mosaics in the basilicas of S. Vitale and S. Apollinare Nuovo at Ravenna. The former are dealt with first, as they represent the nobility in Court dress.

The Emperor Justinian (A.D. 527–565) in State is seen in Fig. 66. The tunica is but slightly varied from that shown in Fig. 60 except in the arrangement of the segmentæ. The paludamentum is also very similar,

---

[1] *See* Sir Thomas Graham Jackson's *Byzantine and Romanesque Architecture.*
[2] Modern tights.

Fig. 66. The Emperor Justinian—sixth century—in tunica, paludamentum, and hosa. A development of the Imperial diadem is worn. The background suggests mosaics of the period.

but made of heavier and richer silk, specially woven for him on his own looms. It is fastened by a jewelled fibula with three strings of pearls attached, and is lined with silk of another colour. The tablion is of brocade or embroidery depicting birds in circles.

The most interesting point is that the Emperor is wearing on his legs the new hosa, made of silk. The shoes show the transition from the sandal of Fig. 60 to an indisputable shoe. The crown is of a new shape, much more elaborate, and is dealt with under Jewellery (p. 203).

Fig. 67 is that of the Emperor Justinian riding, and is taken from a silver disc found in a tomb at Kertsch in the Crimea in 1891, now in the Hermitage, Petrograd. He wears the short tunica, open up the sides, and embroidered with bands and segmentæ. The clavus of decorative needlework now terminates, above the waist-line, in leaf-shaped ends. (The clavus arranged in this manner continued in use well into the eleventh century.) The belt at the waist, and the sword belt over the shoulder, are decorated with goldsmith's work and set with precious stones. The coronet is composed of pearls, with a jewelled clasp in the centre; it is similar to that shown in Fig. 60, but now worn on semi-State occasions.

The hosa are plainly seen, and the feet are shod with embroidered leather shoes, fastened with a strap across the instep.

This dress would be worn at a semi-State function; and, for full State on horseback, the paludamentum would be added. This drawing gives the correct *horse furniture* of the time.

THE OFFICIAL DRESS OF THE CONSULS

The Toga Picta Contabulatum, the Secular Pallium and the Lorum

Consuls under the Roman Empire were the official representatives of the Senate. The title of consul was also an honorary one, conferred upon the governors of provinces outside Italy, who were elected by the Senate and sanctioned by the Emperor. The title continued in Rome and Constantinople until the sixth century A.D. About this time the office of the consulate was divested of its power. It reflected the glory of illustrious men who had gone before, and, as such, was much coveted as a title of honour. Foreign potentates, tributary and barbarian kings, princes and chiefs were propitiated by the title being conferred upon them.

The appointment of a consul was marked by much ceremony, and it was one of the customs for the consul, when assuming his office, to present his portrait, arrayed in his insignia, to the Emperor and to his

Fig. 67. The Emperor Justinian. The details in the corners are taken from segmentæ.

Fig. 67. THE EMPEROR JUSTINIAN

friends. These portraits were carved in ivory, with the donor's name and other representations in bas-relief, and were formed of two (sometimes more) tablets or panels, hinged together, and called "diptycha"—diptych.

Writing utensils.—Diptycha. The word in Greek, δίπτυχα from πτύσσω, meaning "to fold," applied originally to two wooden lids, hinged together, in which black wax was run for the purpose of writing on with a "stilus," which left a white line upon the black wax. The stilus was like a pencil, made in bronze, iron, wood, or ivory, with a point at one end, and a knob, to be used for obliterating what had been written, at the other. This was called by the Romans "Tabulæ." Another Roman name for two panels hinged together was "Diplomæ"; and these were letters-patent, conferring government grants, passports, certificates, etc., and were generally of bronze with the name and wording cut in.

Diptych and Stilus

The *insignia of a consul* consisted of the tunica talaris, with long, fairly close sleeves, generally embroidered at the wrists. Over this was worn the tunica palmata, which descended to half-way below the knee. The sleeves were wide, and came to just above the elbow or wrists. On the feet were boots—calcei— following the pattern given on p. 75.

In his left hand he carried the "Scipio Eburneus," a sceptre of ivory surmounted by an eagle, and used by a consul or magistrate only at the games.

Fig. 68

Fig. 69

In his right hand he held the "mappa" (*see* p. 125) (usually shown in diptycha folded like a pad) of white, which he used only at the circus, to give the signal for the games to begin (*see* Figs. 68 and 69).

The most important part of the paraphernalia was the toga picta.

First method used till 450 (see Fig. 42). Up to the middle of the fifth century, the toga picta was worn after the manner of the toga umbo (*see* Fig. 42), but instead of allowing the end at point F to hang behind or trail on the ground, it was brought round the front of the figure, draped over the right thigh, and the end carried over the bent left forearm (*see also* Fig. 41).

Second method used about 487. Later—that is, towards the end of the fifth century—the toga picta was put on first in the usual way, and, according to the diptych of Boethius, consul in 487 (*see* Fig. 68), the pallium is separate, and placed on top. It started at point A in the centre-front, passed over the right shoulder E, but where it next went is a matter of conjecture; probably it took the same course as shown in Fig. 70. The toga picta also started at point A underneath, and, having passed over the left shoulder B, it crossed the back, passed under the right arm C, over the front, and the remainder draped over the left shoulder and forearm D. The sleeve of the tunica palmata is seen at F.

Consuls in office after this date (*see* Fig. 69) used the same insignia as previously described, but the toga picta, now necessarily very much reduced in width — *not length* — was worn in a slightly different manner (*see* Fig. 69A).

Fig. 69A

Third method used after 517. No separate pallium was used, but the toga was folded along its straight edge, and the bottom point A was started at the feet, as before, and brought up the centre-front (Fig. 69A). It then passed, still folded, over the right shoulder B, was looped in the centre of the back at C, and passed over the left shoulder D to the front and across the breast, under the right arm E and passed through the loop in the centre of the back at C. From this point the toga was opened to its full width, returned under the right arm F, and draped over the right thigh, the end being carried over the left arm G.

The ornamentation of the toga picta was the same as described on p. 93, with the addition of a band of embroidery *on the inside* to match the rest of the design worked on the straight edge. Being folded back, this gave the panel effect which was so like the pallium. There is no doubt that at this stage of development the band of embroidery was fixed on, as we fix on a cuff or fix up the bottom of trousers to-day.

Later, in all probability for the sake of convenience, the arrangement of the last method was faked. The toga picta may have been cut in two unequal parts across the segment (*see* Diagrams of toga, Diagram 11), and the front or larger portion supplemented by a band, until it reached that point where it passes through the loop at C. Here the remaining or smaller part of the toga picta was pleated on to the end of the band.

Unfortunately, the same design of ornament was used for the decoration of both the toga picta and the pallium. This, together with the fact that the backs of the figures of the consuls never can be seen, makes the arrangement very difficult to understand, even by careful study of the diptycha.

After the abolition of the office and title of consul in the sixth century, the panel, or pallium as it was in reality, became entirely detached from the toga picta, and evolved into a mere scarf or band, most gorgeously decorated with gold, jewels, and great quantities of pearls. It measured from nine to twelve inches in width, and about eighteen feet long. This secular pallium, or as it was sometimes called, the LORUM (*see* Fig. 70), from the Latin "Limbus" (Gr. παρυφή), meaning a border, band or scarf, became an item of Imperial insignia, and was much used from the eighth to the twelfth century as an ornament worn with Byzantine Court costume.

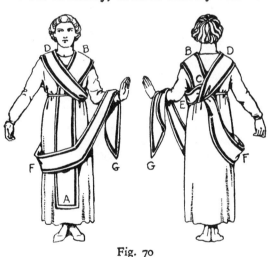

Fig. 70

How it was put on. As usual it started at A, then it passed over the left shoulder B, making a loop at the back C, and returning over the right shoulder D; thence across the chest, under the left arm at waist level to the back, it passed through the loop at C. The remainder was brought round the right thigh F, across the front, and carried on the left forearm G. This arrangement could be reversed, the lorum passing first over the right shoulder, round the back to the left shoulder, under the right arm, through the loop, and returning under the *right* arm, across the front, and carried as before on the left wrist (*see* Fig. 85).

The costume of a courtier is shown in Fig. 71. He wears the short tunica (embroidered with segmentæ—a design for a square one is shown in the top corner), already described under Fig. 60 and Fig. 66, and above it the paludamentum descending to the ankles. Both the tunica and paludamentum are frequently shown in white in mosaics; in one

Fig. 71

Fig. 71A

case a sulphur-coloured one is depicted, with the tablion in plain purple. The tablion shown in this figure is more ornate. On his legs are the hosa, and he wears shoes of a new shape.

Fig. 71A is also a nobleman of this period, wearing ordinary dress. The tunica is longer than usual, and the manner of girding it with a small scarf to form a pouch—"kolpos"—at the sides should be noticed. This nobleman is wearing the toeless boots described under Footgear, p. 200.

Fig. 72 shows the costume of a man of some position, wearing the tunica, girded at the waist, from whence hangs a POUCH, pocket or wallet. The cloak is a rectangle, fastened as usual on the right shoulder. On his legs are high cloth boots.

Fig. 72A is that of a young man of the middle class. The dress does not vary much from that worn by the peasant shown in Fig. 49, but it would

Fig. 72   Fig. 72A   Fig. 72B

be made of much better material. The clavus, it should be noticed, is of the new design, and extends only to just above the waist-line.

Fig. 72B is an older man, and one of decided religious convictions. On the end of his waist-belt or scarf is worked a cross. His legs and feet are bare, quite a usual occurrence even at this time.

HAIRDRESSING OF THE MEN, A.D. 400–1200

350. The first example of the style of hairdressing in vogue throughout this long period is described under Imperial Rome, fourth century, p. 113, and shown in Fig. 44. This fashion of wearing the hair continued during eight centuries, the length, fulness, and crispness varying slightly at different times, as shown in figures illustrating the costume of this epoch.

400 to 800. In Fig. 73 is seen a head of hair dressed in the customary way. It is cut to form a fringe over the forehead, and sufficiently long at the back to allow it to puff at the nape of the neck.

Fig. 73

With the brush and comb it is arranged to radiate from the crown of the head. (The segmentæ and neck-band of the sixth century are worthy of notice.)

741. Constantine IV. (668–685) arrived at Constantinople after his accession, a youth with a sprouting beard, and in consequence the nickname "Pogonatus" has clung to him through history. His portrait at Ravenna shows him clean shaven.

800. Until the ninth century, it was quite the exception to wear beards and moustaches. The emperors (Figs. 80 and 85) and the noble (Fig. 81) show that by this time (900–1000) the wearing of beards and moustaches was the correct thing.

1200. Patches of hair on the cheeks were now obsolete.

IMPERIAL COSTUME AND THE NOBILITY—WOMEN

SIXTH CENTURY

Fig. 74 shows the State costume of the Empress Theodora, the details of which are taken from the same source as those of the Emperor (*see* Fig. 66), *i.e.* S. Vitale, Ravenna.
The stola of white is ornamented with gold and emeralds, following the lines of the decoration seen upon the tunica worn by the Emperor. Over this she wears, by special concession, the paludamentum of purple, lined with blue, and embroidered inside and out with a rich border in gold. On the outside, above the lower border, are embroidered figures of Asiatic character—the Magi—in gold. Surmounting the paludamentum is a heavily jewelled collar, and upon the fashionable head-dress is posed the Imperial diadem in gold, pearls and emeralds. Ropes of pearls, ending in fine specimens of pear shape, hang from the diadem (*see* Jewellery, p. 203).

Fig. 75

Fig. 75. The Lady Antonina (from the same mosaic) is wearing

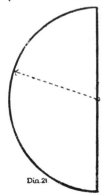

Dia. 21

either a dalmatica or the stola. The sleeves are not indicated very clearly in the mosaic, but the presence of the highly decorated angustus clavus points to the garment being the dalmatica. In the original, it is of a red purple, with the gold clavus embroidered with red, white, and green flowers. Over this is worn a garment differing slightly from any hitherto described (unless the paenula is taken into account)—a semicircular cloak (*see* Diagram 21), for such it must be, as it resembles very closely the paludamentum, the regal garment prohibited to any woman except the empress. It is of

Fig. 74. The Empress Theodora—sixth century—showing her in full State dress. The architecture in the background is founded on details from S. Vitale, Ravenna.

patterned white silk material, and, since brocades were not woven in Byzantium at such an early date (*see* Silk, Chap. V.), it is possibly of Chinese or Persian origin. Segmentæ in red and gold are embroidered in the two corners.

Description of costume of noble ladies. The mosaic at Ravenna also shows six other ladies in attendance on the empress, three of whom are in the background. They are dressed in a similar fashion, but the colourings of their garments differ.

The second lady is wearing the stola of white, figured in blue, with segmentæ in gold, white, and green. The cloak is of gold, embroidered with red roses of Byzantine design, slipped green.

The third wears a cream stola, worked in green—possibly a Chinese brocade. It has a deep border, and the segmentæ are in black and white. The cloak is of white, with gold segmentæ in the corners.

Rose

The fourth wears a green stola, figured with red, and a cloak of red flowered with green and gold.

The third and fourth ladies show the white ends of the scarves that are tied round their waists, and all seven of them wear the fashionable head-dress.

Mosaics at S. Apollinare Nuovo, Ravenna, represent twenty virgin martyrs, who are depicted in the costume of noble ladies of the sixth century. One of them (S. Agnes) is shown in Fig. 76. All the twenty wear practically the same dress, with slight variations. It consists of an under-stola, showing only the close sleeves to the wrists. Over this is worn the new chiton in white (Diagram 20), cut wide enough to form draped sleeves well on to the wrists. It has the angustus clavus in black and gold. Over all is the gold palla, with a border of sapphires and pearls, the panel of blue edged with red being attached to it. It is arranged as shown in Fig. 54, but with a *difference which is new.* Having crossed the left shoulder for the first time, as usual, the palla is drawn across the back, and pulled over the right shoulder, and a bit of its top edge is caught down to the belt in front. The bulk of the palla falling behind the right arm is pulled across the front, having passed *under* the right arm, and flung over the left shoulder. It will be found that by this arrangement a cape-like sleeve is formed on the right shoulder. At this stage it is belted over all by a rich girdle, with a large ornament of jewels in the centre, but leaving the long end free to hang down the back. The figure is holding this end in the right hand. It should be noticed that a small portion of the white chiton is visible at

Fig. 76. S. Agnes. From the mosaic at S. Apollinare Nuovo, Ravenna, showing the costume of a noble lady of the sixth century.

FIG. 76. A NOBLE LADY OF THE SIXTH CENTURY, A.D.
(*see* p. 168)

the chest. At the neck the border of jewels forms an apparent necklace.

The hair of these twenty women is dressed after the fashion shown in Fig. 59, but a band of gold and jewels is worn round the top, and the hair is puffed out above it. From this band hangs a white gauze veil with fringed ends.

MIDDLE-CLASS WOMEN

Fig. 77 shows a woman of the middle class, wearing the shaped dalmatica, ungirded. The sleeves of the stola are seen at the wrists. On the head is worn a cap, following the shape of the head-dresses worn by the nobility, but this one is made of plain white linen, with a roll brim and soft crown.

WOMEN'S HEAD-DRESSES

Towards the end of the fourth century, a head-dress of a curious nature came into fashion. Decidedly of Eastern origin, it resembled the Oriental turban, and it remained an official and fashionable coiffure for several centuries.

It was a circular roll or pad, with a close-fitting cap inside it, and is described more explicitly by comparing it to a skull-cap surrounded by a miniature motor tyre.

Fig. 77

A.D. 350. In its first stage of development, the cap part of this head-dress was of larger dimensions, and is seen in Fig. 64. In this example the roll, which fits close to the head, is ornamented with narrow bands set at equal distances from one another all round. Similar bands are also set over the rather large cap or crown. This large cap did not remain long in fashion, and it soon gave place to a close-fitting skull-cap with the roll surrounding it. Head-dresses of this shape are worn by the group of ladies seen in the mosaic at S. Maria Maggiore at Rome, dated 352–366. The figures are all wearing the dalmatica, and are described under Imperial Rome, p. 118. A description of this head-dress has been reserved for this chapter, as it is particularly characteristic of Byzantine dress, although it was worn also at Rome.

A.D. 400. The empress in Fig. 63 is wearing this kind of coiffure, but with the difference that the Imperial coronet is placed on top, thereby masking the cap from view.

Fig. 78 shows this head-dress. The bands are now reduced to five in number, and are about one and a half or two inches in width, edged with pearls; and above the roll, masking the cap, is placed a jewelled coronet. The profile drawing shows the cap without the coronet. No hair is visible, but sometimes two small curls were worn on the temples,

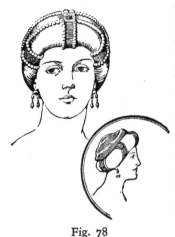

as if to establish the fact that the wearer had hair, and of a certain colour. The roll is shaped to fit the head, forming a drooping curve over the forehead, and fitted close in front of the ears, entirely covering the top of them but leaving the lobes exposed.

During the sixth century this coiffure became a recognised part of the insignia of empresses and Imperial ladies; and it continued in use as such, with slight modifications, during the whole period of the Byzantine Empire. There were, however, restrictions with regard to its colour. For Imperial use, the roll was of black, purple,

Fig. 78

or red. The cap and roll were usually different colours. Many drawings of this period show the roll black and the cap red. Lighter colours only were worn by women of less exalted position. Over the back part of this head-dress was often draped a veil.

The Empress Theodora (*see* Fig. 74) shows the roll in black, with bands of gold enriched with jewels and pearls decorating it in five places, one in the centre of the forehead and two on either side. There are probably others at the back which are unseen. This is surmounted by the elaborate Imperial diadem, with many ropes of pearls attached to it (*see* Crowns).

Fig. 75 wears the same type of head-dress as seen in Fig. 78. The Empress Irene (*see* Fig. 82) wears above the roll a further development of the Imperial crown. The roll is also worn by the empress in Fig. 91.

In course of time the shape of this head-dress was adopted by women of the middle class. Theirs was but a simple version of the original, and made chiefly of white linen. A woman of the sixth century is shown in Fig. 77. The woman in Fig. 94A shows how the cap had developed and the roll diminished in the course of a few centuries. By the tenth century nothing more than a rolled brim remained (*see* Fig. 92).

Fig. 7. A Celtic chieftain in civil dress
(*see* p. 12)

Fig. 17. The Doric chiton

(*see* p. 33)

FIG. 26. THE CRINKLED CHITON AND THE CHLAMYS *(LEFT)*
FIG. 25. THE CHITON *(RIGHT)*
(see p. 42)

FIG. 41. AN EMPEROR OF THE THIRD CENTURY, A.D.

(see p. 93)

FIG. 50. AN EMPRESS OF THE SECOND AND THIRD CENTURY, A.D.
(*see* p. 115)

FIG. 66. THE EMPEROR JUSTINIAN—SIXTH CENTURY, A.D.
(*see* p. 157)

Fig. 74. The Empress Theodora—sixth century, a.d.
(*see* p. 167)

FIG. 80. A BYZANTINE EMPEROR OF THE EIGHTH AND NINTH CENTURIES, A.D.
(*see* p. 181)

FIG. 82. THE EMPRESS IRENE (A.D. 797-802)
(*see* p. 183)

FIG. 85. A BYZANTINE EMPEROR OF THE TENTH,
ELEVENTH AND TWELFTH CENTURIES, A.D.
(*see* p. 186)

FIG. 91. AN EMPRESS OF THE TENTH, ELEVENTH AND TWELFTH CENTURIES, A.D.
(*see* p. 195)

Fig. 98. Represents King Arthur wearing the characteristic costume
of a British chieftain of the sixth century, a.d.
(*see* p. 223)

FIG. 109. HENGIST, CHIEF OF THE ANGLES (A.D. 449)
(*see* p. 241)

FIG. 115. THE EMPEROR CHARLEMAGNE IN FULL STATE DRESS (A.D. 800)
(*see* p. 258)

FIG. 118. A FRENCH KING OF THE CARLOVINGIAN OR CAPETIAN DYNASTIES
(*see* p. 262)

FIG. 128. AN ANGLO-SAXON QUEEN
(*see* p. 274)

THE RISE OF MONACHISM

As early as the third century A.D., or even before that, a few Christians of exceptional godliness withdrew themselves entirely from the world, for the better devotion of their lives to spiritual contemplation. They had no fixed abode, but wandered in wild and uninhabited places, and were called *Anchorites*, *Hermits* and *Monks*. They did not become very numerous in Europe, owing to the rigorous climate, and eventually disappeared altogether. In the warmer climates of the East, and in Africa, this cult developed, especially among the Copts of Egypt, a country renowned for the great number of Anchorites living in the wild and desolate parts. A desire to lead a lonely ("Monus") life, devoted to prayer, the glory of God, and the teaching of His Word, inspired many men and women to retire to some cave, or hollow in the ground, or thicket. They wore little clothing except the coarsest of linen or cloth, and the skins of animals. They deprived themselves of every conceivable comfort, and starved and mortified themselves into states of spiritual exaltation. Later these ascetics made for themselves small cubicles or cells, and living together were called *Cenobites*.

In 271, a young man, a Copt born at Koma in Egypt in 251, disposed of all his worldly belongings, in obedience to a divine injunction, and retired to the wilderness. He became celebrated for his sanctity —S. Anthony.

First monastery. In answer to the prayer of many Cenobites who wished to live under his guidance, he inaugurated (A.D. 305) at Fayoum, near Memphis, a system of living together in separate cells in one enclosure, called a "laura," meeting only for common service. He died in 356 at the age of 105 and was canonised in the Roman Catholic Church.

This system—Monachism—developed in the East and spread westward. It was the origin of those religious orders which became such a great power spiritually and educationally in many lands:

The Benedictines, founded by S. Benedict (480–543) at Mount Cassino in 529:

The Cistercians, by Robert, abbot of Molesme, Burgundy, at Citeaux (Cistercium) in 1050. They were re-formed by S. Bernard of Clairvaux (1091–1153) about 1145:

The Carthusians, by S. Bruno (1050–1101), and named from La Chartreuse, near Grenoble, Vienne, in 1086:

The Franciscans, by S. Francis d'Assisi (1182–1226) in 1210; and many others.

Dress. At the time of the foundation of Monachism, no definite uniform was worn by these religious people—the monks and nuns—but just the ordinary clothes of poor people. The shape of their garments has been retained until to-day; and as time went on, and the fashions of the people in general changed, these garments became quite distinctive.

By the sixth century the men wore only the tunica of coarse cloth, reaching to the ankles, with fairly wide sleeves—a modified dalmatica

Monks.

Franciscan. Cistercian.

—and often a shirt of hair-cloth under it. Their feet were bare, being shod only with sandals.

The paenula, with the hood—the cucullus—was used if necessary; otherwise their heads were bare. The practice of shaving the head was in use among the Egyptian priests of the Early Dynasties, and was copied by the Coptic Christians in the form of the TONSURE—a round shaved patch on the top of the head—adopted later (in the sixth century) by the clergy in general as a mark of distinction from the laity. There were two forms of tonsure: that of S. Peter, in which a circle of hair was left by shaving the top of the head and the nape of the neck, was in vogue in Italy, Spain, Gaul, and the Early

English Church. The other form, that of S. James, used in the Early Scottish Church, was made by shaving all the head in front of a line drawn from ear to ear.

This uniform was international. The clergy who brought Christianity to England in the seventh century wore the garments described on p. 102 (Rome), and the monks the garments described above.

By the tenth century a few more details were added and the uniform may be said to be thoroughly established.

The garments worn by monks at this time were:

THE FROCK ("Froc," Norman-French, meaning a coarse stuff), a garment cut all in one, with long loose sleeves. It was a development of the tunica. The width of the sleeves varied with different orders; also their length, some being long enough to reach the knees. The superfluous material was used to cover the hands.

THE COWL. A name originally used for a bag, and later adapted for an article of dress of the same shape, i.e. the cucullus (see p. 74) or hood. The name of hood denoted a head-covering for the laity; that of the cowl, a distinctive head-dress of monks.

There were three varieties of the monk's cowl:

No. 1 was a separate garment having a short cape-like collar, called the capuce.

No. 2 was attached to the paenula or cloak.

No. 3 was attached to the cuculla or scapular.

In all three examples it was spoken of as the cowl.

The colours of the garments worn by the various orders were:

The Benedictines. Black serge frock, with cowl attached to the scapular. This latter garment was worn by the Benedictines under the frock, the hood emerging at the neck. No girdle; shoes instead of sandals.

The Cistercians. Grey frock for everyday use, pure white in church; black scapular with cowl (No. 3) attached. Sandals.

The Carthusians. White frock, white scapular with bands at the sides to connect the front and back portions; cowl (No. 3) attached. Sandals. Novices wore a paenula with cowl No. 2, or a short scapular, unjoined at the side, over a white frock.

The Franciscans or *Friars Minor.* The original colour [1] of the frock was a light brown or a natural hue. When a band of these friars came to England in 1224, their dress was of a greyish colour and the name of Grey Friars was given to them. Cowl No. 1 was worn. This Order introduced the cord girdle.

---

[1] The original colour has been the subject of great controversy, but no decision has been reached. Discussion became so embittered that the Pope issued orders that it should cease.

The Dominicans—Friars Preachers. The nucleus of the institution was founded by S. Dominic (*b.* Calaroga, Old Castile, 1170; *d.* 1221) in 1214. White frock; white scapular (lay brothers wore a black scapular); black mantle or paenula, with cowl No. 2 attached, or sometimes a black capuce. They came to England in 1221 and were called Black Friars.

Nuns of the different Orders wore the same frock and in the colours of the Orders. Instead of the cowl they wore a veil over their heads, shorn of all their hair. The paenula was used out of doors. Novices wore a white veil; professed nuns a black one.

THE HUNS

Brief Historical Sketch of the Huns and Attila

The original race of Huns, or Hi-ung-nu, was of an Ural-Altaic people, occupying the north-western border of China, the plains of Tartary, and Mongolia,[1] as far back as the year 2000 B.C.

Only two contemporary records of the Huns exist. One is a description given by Priscus, the rhetorician, who was sent on a mission to Attila by Theodosius II. The other graphic account is by Jornandes, who lived in the following century. We may gather from these accounts that the Huns, in appearance, and to a certain extent in their dress also, were not unlike the Finns, Kalmuks, and Buriats of the eighteenth century.

Appearance. In physique these nomadic people were of great size, but had very short legs, large round heads, small black deep-set eyes, prominent cheeks, unadorned by beards, flat noses, brownish-yellow complexions, long straight black glossy hair, and broad chests (*see* Fig. 79).

It was their custom to tie down the noses and compress the skulls of their children with binding bands, and to slash the cheeks of their baby boys to prevent the growth of hair.

Agriculture was understood to some extent by the Huns, but cattle-breeding was their chief pursuit, and wealth was gauged by the size of their herds of cattle. They were expert horsemen and hunters, and lived in the saddle from early morn till night. They were renowned for their bravery, were intensely warlike, and very cruel.

During the third century B.C. the Huns threatened the Chinese Empire, which caused the Great Wall of China, 1500 miles long, to be built, 298–211 B.C.

Mete was the name of one of their chiefs, and under him the Huns made their first migration (in 177 B.C.) in a western direction, and a further development of their dominions took place. Mete died in 170 B.C.

In 165 B.C. they came still further west, and settled in Siberia. The Hun nation now being divided, the eastern portion broke through the Great Wall, and became absorbed in the population of the Chinese Empire during this century.

The western portion marched further west about 50 B.C. beyond the Ural Mountains, and by the middle of the first century A.D. were settled in Europe around the Caspian Sea.

The eastern Hunnish Empire had almost disappeared by A.D. 84, only a few tribes remaining in Mongolia.

During the first century A.D. the power of the western Huns steadily increased; and by the second century A.D. the Huns disappeared altogether from the regions bordering on China; those tribes who had drifted in the wake of the western Huns gave up all idea of reconquering their old territories in Mongolia, and joined their kinsmen on the borders of Europe.

In the fourth century A.D. they were established in the country watered by the Volga, subjugating the native Alani of the river Don and the Sea of Azov.

During the year 363 they broke into the Balkan peninsula and ravaged the whole country north of Hadrianople, and in 376, under their chief Balamir, they

---

[1] The oldest settlements of the Mongols were west of Lake Baikal.

invaded Hungary, driving out the Goths, under their king Hermanric, from the Danube into Roman territory. Partly helped by the Goths, they menaced the Empire, and at Hadrianople defeated the Byzantine Imperial army, led by the Emperor Valens.

In 396 the Huns crossed the Caucasus and raided Armenia, and in the year 409 they were led by their chief Uldis across the Danube, and advanced into Bulgaria, but they were overthrown.

Roua was King of the Huns in 432, and he was succeeded by his son, "The Scourge of God," Attila (in Magyar Myth called Etele; in Teutonic lore, Etzel). This great barbarian leader had his capital in some locality situated between the rivers Danube and Theiss. This consisted of a vast camp of huts and tents, surrounded by stockades.

The *houses* of the Huns, when they were sufficiently settled in one place to build them, were huts of wood. The houses of the important people were quite elaborately constructed of the same material, and ornamented with carvings, and the whole structure beautifully built and polished.

The *Palace of Attila* was a vast circular enclosure, containing the houses of his wives and families. These were surrounded by a stockade, and in the centre arose the house of the king himself, surmounted by several high towers, all of wood and elaborately carved and polished.

His personality. Attila has been described as a very grave man, possessing a certain amount of Byzantine refinement. At any rate he was sufficiently cultured to indulge in a bath now and again, and for this purpose he had one built after the Roman fashion. Incongruous as it may seem, though important perhaps, it was the only stone building in his domain. No contemporary portrait of this mighty savage exists; only a pen-portrait by a writer of a century later.[1] He is described as a savage without parallel; short, with a large head and huge chest, with the typical Hunnish flat nose, deep-set eyes, sallow complexion, black hair, and a long narrow beard about his mouth. He dressed simply, and—cleanly! As a general he commanded rather than led, and preferred diplomacy to battle. His greatest weapon was prevarication.

Evidently he was not without a fascinating personality, and there must have been about him a romantic atmosphere which interested society in Rome and Constantinople, as we know that an Imperial princess, Honoria, daughter of the Empress Galla Placidia and mother of the Emperor Valentinian III., so far forgot her dignity as to lose her head in admiration, and sent him a letter and ring claiming him as her husband and deliverer.[2]

Under the sovereignty of this hero, the savage Huns attained their greatest power, and were the terror of the civilised world. Attila's empire extended from the Baltic to the Danube and the Rhine, and from the North Sea to the Caucasus.

The year 437 saw them vanquishing the thriving kingdom of the Burgundians, centred about the Rhine, and in 441 they burst into the Illyrian provinces, and later into Thrace.

446. Attila's expeditions into the Eastern and Western Empires.

451 is the year of his great advance into the West. He was accompanied by the three Ostrogothic kings, and the King of the Gepidæ, who formed his staff. On his way he burnt Metz, sacked Rheims, and murdered the officiating bishop S. Nicasius before his altar; marching on through the territory now known as Belgium[3] unchecked until he reached Orleans, which he besieged. The town was on the point

---

[1] Jornandes, a Goth.

[2] She was only following the example of her mother, who married first Athaulf, King of the Goths, and secondly Constantine, the Roman commander and father of Honoria. Galla Placidia received the title of "Augusta" in 421.

[3] History repeats.

of capitulation when the general Ætius, accompanied by the Gothic king Theodoric I., son of Alaric, arrived from the south and saved it. After this Attila retreated, followed by the Imperial army, until he reached the Catalaunian Plains, where a terrific battle took place, resulting in the complete victory of Rome at Châlons-sur-Marne.

Having reinforced his army during the year, Attila set out, in the spring of 452, to destroy Rome. Crossing the Danube into Pannonia, and over the Julian Alps, he laid siege to Aquileia, the capital of Venetia. After three months the city fell, and its inhabitants, leaving it to the destruction of Attila, fled to the marshes and lagoons which fringed the Adriatic coast, where they settled and founded the city of Venice upon three islands and many islets. Altinum, Concordia, Padua and Modena were ravaged and burnt. Vicenza, Verona, Brescia, Bergamo, Milan and Pavia received him, but these cities were sacked, and the inhabitants also fled to the lagoons. Rome was saved by the mediation of the Pope, and the policy of Pulcheria and Marcian of Byzantium. Attila then retired to his palace by the Danube, and died suddenly in the year 454.

After the death of Attila, his empire declined. His people, barbaric and nomadic in nature, were not disposed to be ruled by his successor and son Ellak, a man educated in Roman culture and Roman military tactics. They revolted, and Ellak was murdered.

The Huns still retained some of their power in the region of Asia Minor and the Caspian Sea, and, when the empire broke up after the death of Attila, many Hunnish tribes found a refuge in the old habitations of the Huns and Alani.

The successor of Ellak made an alliance with the Goths in 462, and little is heard of them for nearly a century, until an army of mixed barbarians, chiefly Huns, made a raid into Thrace, and came very near Constantinople; but Belisarius met and defeated them at Melantias in 558. Peace and quiet followed, and from this time onward the original race of Huns disappeared.

The Avars. A race of savages, the Avars, a Tartar horde who were akin to the Huns and possessed some traces of the Hunnish characteristics and physique, had reached the Danube in A.D. 565. In 572 they ravaged Moesia, and defeated the future Emperor of Byzantium, Tiberius II. In 583 they gained a solid success over the empire by the capture of Sirmium, and, about the same time, these Avars or Slavs penetrated into the Balkan provinces and settled there, taking the town of Singidunum (Belgrade). During the next reign—that of Maurice the Cappadocian (582–602)—they were bought off by the empire. Later (611) they allied themselves with the Persians against the Emperor Heraclius I. (610–641).

Extinction. This race eventually settled in various wasted districts and, with the erratic instincts of barbaric nomads, overran Central Europe. They vanished about the ninth century A.D.

A remnant of these Avars, Slavs or Huns were subject to the Empire of the Khazars, which fell in 969, when the Khazars became completely subjugated by the Russians.

COSTUME OF THE HUNS

The clothing of the Huns consisted chiefly of a tunic. In shape it was like the original tunica, of which so many examples have already been given (*see* Diags. 10 and 13). The materials used were of various kinds. The wealthy had theirs made of cloth woven from the hair of the Bactrian camel, the dromedary, or the yak. These animals were peculiar to the part of Asia to which the Huns originally belonged. The wool of goats and sheep, and linen woven from flax, were also in general use. There is no doubt that some of the most important people, like chiefs and their numerous wives, sometimes were able to obtain silk from China. Although their tastes were very primitive, and they did not appreciate the refinements of the Roman world during the earlier periods of their existence, it must be remembered that their territories were not very far removed from those of their distant and more cultured cousins, the inhabitants of China. The lower classes of the people and slaves wore garments made from the fibrous bark of trees and plants, woven into a sort of coarse hemp. This barbarous nation had particularly dirty and nasty habits, for we are told, amongst other things, that they never put on a clean shirt or tunic, but continued to wear this one and only vesture until it decayed and fell off altogether.

Evidently the vermin of those days were of abnormal size, for we are told by the Roman historian, Marcellinus, that the Huns often made clothes by using "the skins of field mice sewn together, and this both at home and abroad." Tunics composed of this fur would have the rich effect of moleskin.

Tunics of the better classes, and presumably the robes or gowns of the women folk, were decorated with borders of needlework, wrought in crude colourings in curious semi-Oriental, semi-Archaic patterns. This embroidery was done for the chief or master of the house by the large collection of women who were his concubines and household. Embroidery was not limited to the ornamentation of clothes, but used for decorating the furniture and also the walls of their apartments, if the skin of a large beast was not available.

Furs were used extensively both as garments and trimmings. The hair of the yak, in particular, was considered most chic, as an adornment to the helmets of warriors, or on any part of the person where it showed to best advantage.

Metals—bronze, iron, copper and silver, were worked into all sorts of articles and shapes as armour, arms, ornaments, utensils, etc. The Huns were expert smelters and workers in metal, like their kindred, the Finns.

These articles of metal-work were quaintly decorated with coloured stones, such as are natural to the northern part of Asia and the Ural Mountains. The turquoise, found in Persia, was a favourite ornament, used in its rough or uncut state.

A simple garment like a cloak would be known of course to these people; often, like those used by races of an earlier epoch, the skin of some large beast, fastened round the shoulders. On the head, surmounting the long, straight, glossy, black hair, they wore caps, in shape often round and sometimes square. These caps were of bright colours, with a roll or upstanding brim of fur.

Their nasty hairy arms and legs were bare, except for a few articles of barbaric jewellery with which they were sometimes decorated, and on their feet they wore clumsy shoes of hide, with or without the hair, cut in one piece, but slit at the back of the heel and on the instep, the toe-point thereby acquiring a decided point upwards. The shoes were laced with thongs of leather. For riding, the legs would be covered with pieces of hide, with thongs binding them round the legs.

The *arms* carried were knives, short and long, of curious curved shapes, carried in scabbards of leather hung by thongs, or chains of metal, from the waist or hip-belt, or over the shoulders. The spear and bow and arrows were very important. They carried shields of a round shape, covered with skin

Fig. 79

and metal adornments. The hair of the yak, and the yak's tail, were graceful and conspicuous ornaments.

A man of the middle class is represented in Fig. 79.

SECTION III

SEVENTH, EIGHTH AND NINTH CENTURIES

The prosperity of the empire fluctuated very considerably during the whole of this period, thus somewhat retarding the development of fashion. Consequently, this part of the history of Byzantine costume cannot be dealt with so fully as the preceding sections, and embraces three centuries. The scarcity of records of facts relating to the years between 641 and 717 makes this period the most obscure in the history of the Byzantine Empire.

The seventh century began with a series of misfortunes. Constantinople experienced the unpleasant ordeal of being besieged by hordes of barbarians on three separate occasions. In the eighth century, the Iconoclastic persecutions, inaugurated by the Emperor Leo III. (717–740), commenced the era of discord and strife which lasted for a hundred and twenty years. These troubles were relieved from time to time by spasmodic intervals of moderate good fortune, especially during the reign of Constantine V.[1] This tendency towards improvement continued more or less until the close of the ninth century.

THE DÉBUT OF THE JESTER

As early as the first century B.C. it had been the custom for well-to-do people to maintain in their house a comic actor, to cheer the family circle, and to enliven the hours spent in domestic employment or at meals. The name of "balatro," and later "buffare" (to puff out the cheeks), was given to this artiste.

In the ninth century A.D., mention is made of buffoons or jesters being attached to the Court of the Byzantine emperors, their business being to make the time pass as pleasantly as possible with their antics, quips and gibes and cranks—an onerous and difficult post in those depressing days.

No distinctive costume was worn by the jesters of this period. It was not until the Middle Ages that the office became so important and the costume assumed those familiar peculiarities known to everyone.

---

[1] Sometimes called Constantine VI., owing to faulty chronology of this time.

IMPERIAL COSTUME AND THE NOBILITY—MEN

SEVENTH TO NINTH CENTURIES

In spite of national calamities and periodical bankruptcy, the emperors not only dressed well, but displayed prodigious extravagance, particularly on Court dress and Court ceremonial.

Gold, purple silk, and rubies, emeralds, diamonds, all of enormous size, set in a welter of priceless pearls, are the outstanding features of Imperial Court costume of this and the later period.

Constantine IV. (668–685) is shown in a mosaic at S. Vitale, Ravenna, wearing a costume almost identical with that worn by Justinian (*see* Fig. 66), and his courtiers are wearing clothes similar to those depicted in Fig. 71, which proves that little change occurred during the course of a hundred years.

When we come to the ninth century, we find an emperor, Theophilus the Unfortunate (829–842), notorious for his love of lavish display, who wasted his undeniable talents by adding to the Court luxury copied from Persian despots. His exotic tastes have been compared to those of the decadent emperors of Rome—Nero and Heliogabalus—and he can be quoted as the pioneer of superlative extravagance in dress.

Fig. 81

Fig. 81A

Fig. 80 is an example of the State dress of an emperor of the ninth century. He wears a dalmatica, with wide sleeves displaying the close ones of the tunica underneath. In this instance it is made of very rich

Fig. 80. A Byzantine emperor of the eighth and ninth centuries. The design in the background is from a panel, temp. Basil II. (976).

gold brocade, with an embroidered border round the neck and the upper part of the sleeves and at the bottom edge, and girded at the waist by a jewelled belt. The paludamentum is very ornate, being composed of purple silk, woven with eagles in blue enclosed in circles of gold, and the tablion is one mass of gold embroidery and jewels. The paludamentum is lined with silk of a contrasting colour and fastened on the right shoulder with a jewelled brooch.

The noble shown in Fig. 81 appears very simple after the elaborate outfit of the emperor. The tunica is made of a very rich material, plain silk or brocade, with an ornamental border, and over it is the paludamentum or semicircular cloak which was coming into very general use at this period. The collar is a separate article, and is of rich embroidery to match that on the bottom of the tunica. The head-dress is an innovation, and is dealt with under Head-dresses.

MIDDLE CLASSES

Fig. 81A shows a man of the middle class, wearing a tunica with all its decoration concentrated on the neck-band. The design comes a little way down the front, edging the opening, and the tunica is fastened by a small button or two on the chest. It would depend upon the social position of this person whether or not he would wear hosa and shoes tied round the ankle. A man of the peasant class would wear the same kind of tunica, but without embroidery. His legs usually would be bare, but he might wear hosa of a coarse make. In either case he would have rough shoes upon his feet.

IMPERIAL COSTUME AND THE NOBILITY—WOMEN

SEVENTH TO NINTH CENTURIES

The women were equally extravagant in their clothing, and especially in the matter of Court costume.

Fig. 82, taken from an ivory in the Musée du Bargello, Florence, represents the Most Pious Irene, an Athenian of noble birth, and "destined to a terrible celebrity in history, and to a very undeserved sanctity in the Church." [1] She became the wife of Leo VI. (775–780) and mother of Constantine VI. (780–797). She usurped the throne on the death of her son, and reigned with a great show of splendour for five years. With the idea of reuniting the Eastern and Western Empires, Charlemagne sent legates to ask for her Imperial hand in marriage, but without success. In the year 802 she was deposed and sent a prisoner to the Isle of Lesbos, where she died nine months later.

She is here shown wearing a dalmatica of cloth of gold, ornamented according to the latest dictates of fashion with a series of square plaques in gold filigree, set with emeralds, rubies and pearls. In place of segmentæ, plaques of gold, enamel and jewels are used. Details of the paludamentum are taken from the ivory of the Empress Eudocia, 1067, and, although of a later date, the decoration is that used at this period. The groundwork is of the usual purple silk, embroidered in circles of gold, set with pearls and emeralds, with a border and tablion of the same. It is lined with a contrasting colour, and fastened on the right shoulder under the heavily jewelled collar. Its unusual length adds to the dignity of the wearer. She carries the ivory sceptre, now an attribute of royalty, and the cross-surmounted orb in gold and jewels. The elaborately developed head-dress and diadem are dealt with under their respective headings.

Fig. 83

Fig. 83 is a noble lady of the eighth century. The dalmatica is

[1] See *The Byzantine Empire*, by Edward A. Foord.

Fig. 82. The Empress Irene (797–802). The costume is derived chiefly from an ivory of the Empress and partly from other sources.

clearly defined, but the arrangement of its decoration is quite different from that hitherto seen. It encircles the neck, descends the front, and borders the hem of the skirt. Bands of similar decoration are placed half-way up the wide sleeves, which are edged with a small border. The semicircular cloak is draped over the left arm, and envelops the hand, which holds some precious object: this was the usual method of covering the hand holding a votive offering. The drapery on the right side of the figure normally would be caught up over the right shoulder. It is here allowed to hang to display the dalmatica to better advantage.

Middle-Class Women

Fig. 84 is a woman of the middle class (eighth century). The tunica, girded at the waist, and having close sleeves to the wrists, has a border of a different colour; and the semicircular cloak, lined with a contrast-

Fig. 84   Fig. 84A

ing colour, is fastened in front with a disc-brooch. Over her head is draped a veil, secured to the head by a band or fillet.

Fig. 84A shows another woman of rather humbler status. She wears the girded tunica. Over the head is draped the palla, caught round the head by the method described under Fig. 65.

SECTION IV

THE TENTH, ELEVENTH AND TWELFTH CENTURIES

At the beginning of this period, the improvement in the political, commercial and artistic outlook of the empire, foreshadowed in the ninth century, continued particularly under the rule of Basil I. (867–886) and Leo VI. the Wise (886–912). It reached its culmination in the reign of Basil II. (976–1025). The empire's prosperity at this time could be favourably compared with that of Justinian's reign. From the first quarter of the eleventh century onward, the glory, power, and fame of Byzantium were on the downward grade. This gradual decay continued until the worst was realised in the year 1204, when the Latins took Constantinople—a terrible calamity for the Byzantine Empire, but a godsend to the peoples of a later date and our own time. The sack of this city—this repository—this museum—had the effect of releasing vast stores of priceless treasures of art and literature, which were distributed practically throughout the whole world.

IMPERIAL COSTUME AND THE NOBILITY—MEN

Judging by the many representations of emperors which are still extant, no definite rule existed as to the costume to be worn on State occasions. Each emperor seems to have adopted the style most pleasing to himself. Nicephorus III. Botoneiates (1078–1081), one of the most extravagant and luxurious emperors who sat upon the throne, always dressed very magnificently, despite the fact that ruin and depression threatened him on all sides. For the want of something better to do, he changed his dress ten times a day.

No doubt these magnificent royalties were very careful of their clothes, and, like a certain lady of the sixteenth century, stored them in spacious wardrobes, where they accumulated, to be brought out and worn by their successors; for we learn that in the twelfth century Isaac II. (1185–1195), a despicable and weak man, intensely vain, possessed numerous wardrobes of costly garments. This wretched, highly perfumed dandy was deposed in 1195, had his eyes gouged out, and was shut up.

After the taking of Constantinople by the Latins in 1204, the

Crusader generals sent envoys [1] to the Imperial Palace. When they entered the throne-room of the Blachernæ Palace [2] they found that the Byzantine populace had resurrected Isaac from his dungeon. He had been dressed up in his splendid garments of State. "So richly clad that you would seek in vain throughout the world for a man more richly apparelled than he," and propped, eyeless, upon the golden throne to receive his "deliverers."

Geoffry de Villehardouin further relates that "by his side (sat) the Empress, his wife, a most fair lady, the daughter of the King of Hungary; and of great men and great ladies there were so many that you could not stir foot for the press, and the ladies were so richly adorned that richer adornment might not be."

Emperors continued to wear the paludamentum over the dalmatica, as seen in Fig. 80. At the same time, representations are found in MSS., ivories, etc., of certain variations adopted by emperors, one of which is indicated in Fig. 85. It is interesting to note the liberties which were taken with what had been hitherto the regulation Court dress. The elaborate decorations of the dalmatica worn by the emperor in this figure are practically the same in character as those seen upon the tunicas in Figs. 60 and 66, and remained as a distinctive feature upon the dalmaticas of European kings until the end of the twelfth century.

The emperor in Fig. 85 is wearing the lorum (described on p. 163), made of cloth of gold, encrusted with rubies, emeralds and pearls, with a fringe of large pear-drop pearls on both sides. He does not wear the paludamentum, although examples of its use with the lorum are found. This emperor is holding the orb in one hand, and in the other the HOLY LANCE.

THE HISTORY OF THE HOLY LANCE

There were two Holy Lances.

The one which pierced the side of Our Lord upon the Cross was kept, together with the Crown of Thorns, in the basilica on Mount Sion. When Jerusalem was captured by the Persians in 614, these holy relics were carried off, but they were recovered and brought back to Jerusalem in 629. The point of the lance became broken from the spear-head, and half of it was set in an ikon and both pieces deposited in S. Sophia.

---

[1] The envoys were two Venetians and two French knights, Matthew de Montmorency and Geoffry de Villehardouin, marshal of Champagne. It is from the Chronicles of the last-named knight that the descriptions quoted above are taken.

[2] In the N.W. corner of the city just inside the walls.

Fig. 85. A Byzantine emperor of the tenth, eleventh and twelfth centuries, wearing the lorum over the tunica. He is holding *The* Holy Lance in his hand. The design in the background is from an ivory cross of the period.

This ikon was given by the Emperor Baldwin II. to Louis IX. of France, who enshrined it at S. Chapelle.

The remaining half fell into the hands of the Turks when they took Constantinople in 1453. The Sultan presented it to Pope Innocent VIII. in 1492, since when it has never left Rome, and is now kept in the dome of S. Peter's.

The other portion of the spear-head and shaft was removed from Jerusalem some time before the tenth century to Constantinople, and used by the emperors as part of the Imperial insignia (*see* Fig. 85). It is shown in an illustrated MS. portrait of Basil II., in the library of S. Mark, Venice. The present location of this part is unknown.

The second holy lance is that of S. Maurice, the leader of the Theban Legion, who was martyred for his Christian faith in 287. It enshrines a nail from the True Cross—encased in the enamelled head-piece—and was used by the first emperors of the Holy Roman Empire as an emblem of investiture. After 1273 it was used at their coronations (*see* Fig. 119). It is now in the Imperial Treasury at Vienna.

THE VARANGIAN GUARD

At the end of the tenth century the Varangian Guard, an Imperial bodyguard, were a conspicuous, picturesque, and useful adjunct to the Byzantine Court. They were recruited from the most perfect specimens of manhood found in Scandinavia. Previous to this date (980), they were serving the chief of their kinsmen, the Ruotsl (Slav: Rüs = Russians: *see* p. 138), but this chief or prince of the Russians, Vladimir the Great (980–1015), finding them somewhat self-assertive, suggested to his neighbour Basil II. that they should be taken into his employ —a proposal which he adopted. The Varangian Guard were bound by oath ("vár" = Scandinavian for "oath") to the emperor's service, and were in constant personal attendance on all occasions, ceremonial or domestic. They remained loyal to the reigning emperor, and upheld the Byzantine throne to the bitter end.

COSTUME OF THE VARANGIAN GUARD
(*and for Viking Chiefs from the Fifth Century onwards*)

The costume of one of these guards is shown in Fig. 86. His outfit consists of a tunic called the "kyrtil," of the same shape as the colobium. Over this is probably a shorter one of skin called a "hjup," and on top the coat of mail, "brynja," made of leather and covered with metal plates or iron rings sewn close together. Over this again several metal ornaments are placed, and the sword-belt is slung over the right shoulder. A large skin hangs from the shoulders. The legs are covered with bracco (Scandinavian: "braekr") cross-gartered all the way up the leg, and shoes of leather of primitive make (*see* p. 12) are worn on the feet.

The helmet, "hjalm" (*see also* Fig. 110), is of iron, with very large bull's horns — a decoration much affected by Teutonic peoples — attached to it, and flanges on each side of the face. The most important men had helmets of gold. Long fair hair fell from under this helmet, and long beards and moustaches were worn. The shield was sometimes round, and sometimes as shown in the illustration, made of wood covered with leather, braced with a rim, and furnished with a boss of iron or bronze. It was decorated in a fantastic manner.

Weapons carried were: (i.) The *spear*, the iron head often being richly ornamented, and inlaid with gold and silver. The shaft, made of ash, was eleven feet long and rarely exceeded one inch in diameter. (ii.) The *axe*, a very formidable weapon with a heavy double-bladed head, was slung from the belt or carried in the hand. (iii.) A *sword* of iron, with an elaborate hilt of iron, bronze or gold, inlaid with stones or ivory, and richly engraved, was carried in a scabbard of wood covered with skin, and bound with leather and metal studs.

Fig. 87

COSTUME OF THE NOBILITY (*continued*)

Young nobles of the tenth and eleventh centuries wore the tunica shorter than previously, *i.e.* to just above the knee. Here it was finished with a wide piece of jewelled embroidery, which was repeated at the neck, but not on the wide over-sleeves if these were worn. Close sleeves were often the only kind worn, but in either case a piece of narrower embroidery finished off the wrists of the close sleeves, and bands of embroidery, often set with precious stones and pearls, surrounded the upper arms. The tunica was girded at the waist.

The figure in Fig. 87 is wearing a richly decorated semicircular cloak, fastened at the neck in front with a jewelled fibula. The cloak has an ornate border which goes round its edges, including the neck, and the weight of the border helps to ensure the cloak being worn in the right way; that is, falling open from

Fig. 86. A SCANDINAVIAN OF THE VARANGIAN GUARD

the clasp at the neck and draped on the arms. (At the same period, the familiar paludamentum, with tablion, was worn.)

The legs show a reversion to the early bracco, and are cross-gartered to the knee. Bracco were often worn without cross-gartering, in which case the fulness below the knee formed transverse folds or rucks round the calf and ankle.

Another vogue in leg-covering at this time was the use of ordinary hosa, with a sort of long sock drawn over it, and turned down a few inches below the knee. The origin of this leg-covering is found in the national dress of the Franks, a nation who had risen to great importance since the coronation of their king Charles in 800 as Emperor of the Holy Roman Empire in the West. These outer leg-coverings—called PEDULES—were now in constant use; they were a kind of short hosa, made of cloth or leather, seamed up the side and cut to fit the foot and ankle as closely as possible, yet sufficiently large to allow them to be drawn over the foot and heel (*see* Fig. 90). This is another example of the manner in which a barbarian notability or nation has influenced the fashions of a thoroughly established and cultured State.

Older men of the nobility wore the tunica decorated in the same way as described under Fig. 87, but reaching to just above the ankles, with the paludamentum or the semicircular cloak over it.

The rectangular pallium, of smaller dimensions, was in moderate

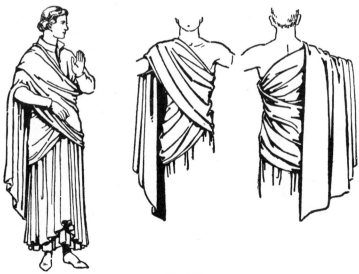

Fig. 88

favour, but not worn in the old-fashioned manner. One corner of the long side having been attached at the waist, probably to the belt on the right side, it was wrapped round the lower part of the figure, across the front, round the back and over the left shoulder, the end hanging down in front. The left arm was usually enveloped in it.

Another method of wearing this garment was to start with one corner behind the right shoulder, pass it across the back, under the left arm, across the abdomen, right hip, back to left hip, drape it across the front, over the right shoulder and then allow the remainder to hang down the back (*see* Fig. 88 and Diagram showing method of draping).

Fig. 89 represents a noble attired in quite a new style, which came into fashion about the end of the eleventh century, and was the mode on which Byzantine Court dress was based for the remaining four centuries of the empire's existence. The tunica and dalmatica have been blended. The over-tunic, of a large-patterned brocade, has moderately wide sleeves, showing the close ones of the under-tunic. Note the decorated plastron worn on the chest.

Fig. 89

The paludamentum has given place to the semicircular cloak, fastened in front; and the tablion has become less important — a stage in the process of elongation which resulted eventually in its retention merely as an ornamented border.

The head-dress is noticeable, and after this date it formed a characteristic feature of Byzantine Court head-gear, remaining in fashion until the end of the fifteenth century. It is a high-crowned turban-shaped hat, with an upstanding brim. There were variations of this (*see* Fig. 81). Sometimes the crown was not so high, and in other instances it was shaped like a pointed bag, having a tassel at the apex which hung on one side of the face. It was made of silk. The brim was sometimes of the same material, or of gold set with jewels; or, again, it was often of fur. These caps remained in use for Court dress among the Russian nobility to the beginning of the eighteenth century. They were adopted as the head-dress for many uniforms down to the nineteenth, and variations of them were in use among Russian peasants up to 1917.

Fig. 90 is a young nobleman in every-day attire, or a gentleman in his best. His tunica would be made of silk or cloth, and the richness of

Fig. 90   Fig. 90A   Fig. 90B

the embroidery on the borders would depend upon his means. Often jewels were set in these borders.

The semicircular cloak is fastened either on the right shoulder or in front with a fibula. On the legs hosa are worn, and over them soft boots or pedules. The four lines on the pedules seen in the drawing suggest folds, and are reproduced from frequent indications in illustrated MSS. The hat, usually of a brilliant colour, is now a universal head-covering—another fashion of barbarian origin.

MIDDLE CLASS

Fig. 90A is a citizen, wearing a simple tunica of linen or cloth, buttoned at the neck and belted at the waist. He carries his cloak on his shoulder ready for use. His legs are covered with hosa, and over them white woollen pedules, cross-gartered with bands of leather or cloth. Shoes, to which the bands of the cross-gartering can be attached if desired, are worn.

Fig. 90B is a man of the well-to-do peasant class. He wears an ordinary tunica, decorated only by a band at the neck, but he has caught up the bottom side edges and attached them to the belt, a common practice at this time, evidently adopted for the sake of freer action. On his legs he wears wide hosa, really identical with the barbaric bracco, of exactly the same shape as those seen in Diagram 3. On the feet are rough boots of leather or untanned hide, reaching to the calf. The cap, a new feature, is cut funnel-shape, with the edge turned up to form a brim.

IMPERIAL COSTUME AND THE NOBILITY—WOMEN

Some interesting Byzantine empresses belong to this period—women of ambition and greed for Imperial power. To be the wife and share the throne of one emperor was not sufficiently exhilarating. Most of them married two and some three. But it must be remembered that emperors cropped up and disappeared with remarkable rapidity. Theophano is one of these notorious pluralists. The daughter of a tavern-keeper, she married first the Emperor Romanus II. (959–963) and was the mother of a future empress of Germany; secondly, Nicephorus Phocas (963–969). She is credited with being a triple murderess.

Later, two sisters, the daughters of Constantine IX., occupied the throne. First Zoe (1028–1050), who married three times after she had attained the age of forty-nine. Each of her husbands enjoyed the privilege of being co-emperor with her. She was renowned for her simple yet exquisite taste in dress. The younger sister, Theodora, retired to a convent, but, by the desire of the people, was recalled to share the throne with her sister: a unique occurrence. Theodora became sole empress on the death of her brother-in-law Constantine X. in 1054, and reigned nineteen months. These ladies were the last of the Macedonian Dynasty.

The family of Comnenoi then ascended the Imperial throne. Eudocia, the daughter of Macrembolites, a Byzantine noble, was a double empress, having married two husbands—the Emperor Constantine XI. Ducas (1059–1067) and the Emperor Romanus IV. Diogenes (1067–1071). Part of her costume is described in the last section.

From an artistic point of view the most important woman about this time was only an Imperial princess—Anna Comnena (1083–1148), the daughter of Alexius I. (1081–1118) and wife of Nicephorus Byrennius, the historian. She herself was an authoress of no little repute. Her chief work was the *Alexiad*, a history of the life and times of her father.

An empress of this period is represented in Fig. 91. The costume differs in several particulars from the State garments of empresses of an earlier date.

The dress consists of a foundation of heavy silk, cut on the lines of

Fig. 91. An empress of the tenth, eleventh and twelfth centuries wearing the lorum. The border of the background is adapted from details on the cover of a psalter of Byzantine work (Egerton MSS. (1139), British Museum) which belonged to Melisenda, Queen of Jerusalem, 1131–1144.

the dalmatica, but narrower in the skirt. On this is superimposed a shot blue and gold gauze, a diaphanous silk fabric of Byzantine manufacture (referred to on p. 216), slightly fulled to the foundation, and retained in place by bands of embroidery round the neck and edges of the sleeves, and at the bottom by a much wider, heavier, and richer border. Over this is worn the lorum, and round the neck is a jewelled collar.

An event took place in the year 972 which had important results on costume—particularly women's—in Germany; namely, the marriage of the Princess Theophano, daughter of Romanus II., to Otto II. Her

Fig. 92

Fig. 93

trousseau was sumptuous, and her garments of gold, encrusted with jewels and embroidered with pearls, created a great sensation among the people of Aix-la-Chapelle, already accustomed to lavish display on the part of their emperor.

The bridal dress of another Imperial princess is described as being of cloth of gold, bordered with heavy embroidery of pearls and diamonds upon a purple ground.

On the death of her husband, an empress put on her *mourning robes* of deep violet, unrelieved by any ornamentation whatsoever. An ample veil of the same colour was surmounted, on special occasions, by the Imperial diadem.

It was not until much later that royal widows renounced the world and retired into a convent, but we hear of many Byzantine empresses who were compelled, through disgrace, to exchange their Imperial garments for the black gown, black veil, and shorn locks of a nun.

Fig. 92 is the costume of a noble lady of the eleventh century, wearing quite a new garment, which follows the lines of the dalmatica; in cut it is almost the same. It is made of brocade, red on a gold ground, with crimson borders set with jewels. The waist-belt is the same as the borders, and through it the skirt part is drawn up in front. The deep red under-dress has wide sleeves, and the white close sleeves of another under-dress are seen at the wrists. There is nothing new about the head-dress, although it is worn rather differently from those shown in the sixth century (*see* Figs. 75 and 78).

A new fashion. Fig. 93 shows an entirely new style of costume. It is taken from a tenth-century textile, and represents allegorically the Empire of Byzantium. It is typical of the costume of a royal lady of that period and of the two following centuries.

The under-dress closely resembles the stola, with long tight sleeves, and is ornamented with bands set with jewels. Over this is a short garment, cut with large armholes. It is fastened at the neck with a fibula, and a border of jewels finishes the bottom edge. The waist-belt has two ornamental ends hanging from it, and fastens in front with a large clasp. A small scarf or palla, bordered in the same manner as the under-dress, floats from the shoulders. The most striking features are the freedom of the hair (*see under* Hairdressing) and the coronet (*see under* Jewellery).

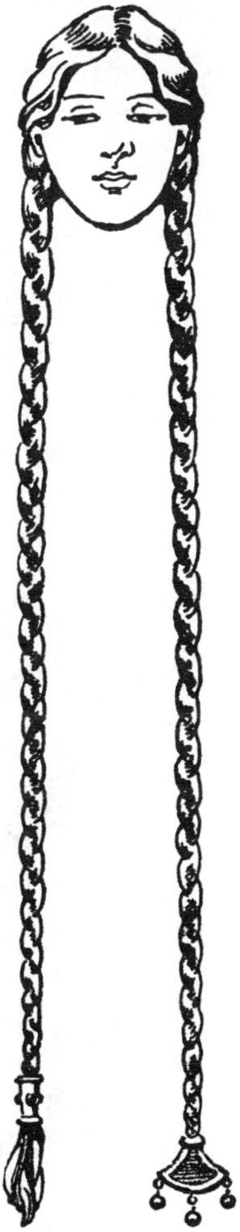

Noble Ladies' Hairdressing

Eleventh and Twelfth Centuries

The women of the Byzantine Epoch were like the women of the present day. They hid their greatest charm—the hair—under a head-dress pulled down tight over the head (*see* Fig. 78). In one respect they were unlike—they chopped off their long tresses *only* when, as a penance for their misdeeds, they retired into a convent, either voluntarily or perforce! It was not until the tenth century that the Byzantine woman of fashion realised the mistake her ancestresses had made, for at this time hair waved upon the temples became the vogue (*see* Fig. 92).

Fig. 93A

By the end of the tenth century it was the fashion among the upper classes to wear two long plaits. The hair was parted, from forehead to nape of neck, into two portions. Each portion was divided into three, and plaited into a long tail hanging on each side of the face and down the front (*see* Fig. 93). Of course, if a Byzantine beauty had only a

moderately ample head of hair, she did not hesitate to enlist the aid of artifice, so that she might compete with others. These tails were finished off with metal and jewelled cylinders surrounding the ends, or terminated in heavy jewelled ornaments to make them hang straight [1] (*see* Fig. 93A).

WOMEN OF THE MIDDLE CLASS

Fig. 94 shows a gentlewoman wearing a dalmatica long enough to fall in folds over the feet, with sleeves very wide at the wrists and ornamented with bands on the upper arm; a similar band encircles the neck. A shorter dalmatica, reaching only to

Fig. 94

the ankles, could be worn if preferred. Either variety could be worn girded or ungirded. A veil over the head completes this costume.

Fig. 94A. This woman of the well-to-do middle class wears a modified

Fig. 94A

Fig. 94B

dalmatica. It is cut on the lines shown in Diagram 18. A band of another colour edges the neck, sleeves and skirt, and a belt encircles the waist.

[1] This fashion has continued in use among the Russians until the present day.

The close sleeves of the under-garment would show on the forearm. If desired, a small palla might be added, put on shawl-wise across the shoulders, and draped over the arms. The head-dress is a development of that shown in Fig. 77.

Fig. 94B is taken from a representation of the Blessed Virgin, who is dressed as an ordinary woman of the people. The ample stola, with close sleeves, is bound round the waist with a cord, from which the sudarium is seen hanging on the right side. Over the stola is draped the palla. Its folds over the head should be noted, as they are characteristic of this period. The palla is put on by placing its centre edge on the head, with equal parts hanging on either side. The left-hand part, except for a loop draped in front of the armpit, is taken back over the shoulder and hangs behind. The right-hand part is draped in the same manner, but its front corner is thrown across the chest and over the left shoulder.

10th Cent.

FOOTGEAR

First Section—Fifth Century

The first section of this period deals with the footgear worn both at Rome and Constantinople, and shows the transition between the sandal of the ancients and the shoe of more modern peoples.

The elaborately perforated shoes or sandals shown in Fig. 60 are excellent examples of this transition. They are of leather, coloured a brilliant scarlet, and are fastened on the outside of the ankles with buckles.

Those seen in Fig. 61 are decided shoes, cut rather open on the instep and secured by a strap and buckle. Leather of various colours, chiefly red and often gold, was used for this kind of shoe, which was ornamented with gold and sometimes set with jewels.

Fig. 62 is wearing Udo (referred to under "Republican Rome," Fig. 34), but, being worn by a man of position, the uppers are made of soft leather, with a leather sole, and lined with another material, probably silk, of some contrasting colour (*see also* Fig. 72A).

Fig. 62A is a man of the people, who wears a foot-covering in general use among this class. It is a short boot or sandal of leather, worn over loose coverings of linen, and fastened by a series of straps and buckles.

Shoes worn by the women at this time are hidden to some extent by the folds of the dress, but their shape is the same as the men's. Ladies of high rank are always depicted with *red* shoes peeping out. Those worn by the middle classes were of cloth or leather in various dull colours, and the poor had them made of untanned hide.

Second Section—Sixth Century

This century marks the general use of the shoe in preference to the sandal. A beautifully shaped shoe is illustrated here, made of a soft

leather or material, ornamented on the toe and fastened by jewelled clasps at the ankles. It is worn by the Emperor Justinian (*see* Fig. 66). Another kind is also shown, made of cloth, leather or silk, and decorated with gold. It is cut very low at the sides of the foot, but is high enough at the back to encase the heel entirely. It is fastened by two straps round the ankle. Other kinds are shown in Figs. 67 and 71.

This one of black leather is worn over white pedules by ordinary people.

A peculiar foot-covering was in vogue at this time. It was an ankle boot without a toe-cap, leaving the toes resting upon the sole exposed to view (*see* Fig. 71A). Sometimes the upper part was laced up the front, and at others it was fastened at the side. Good strong serviceable boots of leather are shown in Fig. 72; they reached very nearly up to the knee.

Third Section—Seventh, Eighth and Ninth Centuries

No particular new shape is met with during this period. A more lavish display in dress resulted in footgear being more elaborately decorated. Those worn by the emperor in Fig. 80 and the empress in Fig. 82 show jewels set in circles of pearls, mounted on gold. Similar richly decorated shoes were worn by the nobles of the Imperial Court, and by the aristocracy of lesser importance.

A shoe for ordinary use is shown here. It is of leather with three straps attached to one side of the sole, and fastened with a buckle at the opposite side of the ankle.

Fourth Section—Tenth, Eleventh and Twelfth Centuries

Fig. 85 is an example of very richly embroidered shoes in which pearls play an important part. In the portrait of Basil II. (976–1025), he is shown wearing top boots, cut at the top like those of a Life Guardsman of the present day. They are made of red leather sewn over with pearls.

Although Fig. 87 shows a noble wearing shoes of an old shape, his legs are cross-gartered in the fashion adopted by the Franks. This style is seen also in Fig. 90A.

At the end of this period shoes and boots developed a decided point in the toe, and were without decoration (see Fig. 89).

Women's footgear has passed without much comment owing to its being seen so seldom, but attention is called to the shoe worn by the woman in Fig. 94A. It is cut low at the sides, with a strap up the instep, and fastened by another round the ankle attached to the heel part.

10th Cent.

BYZANTINE JEWELLERY

Up to the end of the fourth century, the craft of Byzantine gold-smiths exhibited the same qualities both of design and workmanship as that of the Greco-Romans, but after this date the technique and elaborate designs of the Oriental goldsmiths were adopted. Consequently, the jewellery of the period following is characterised by lavish ornament, superficial display and slighter construction.

Gold was the chief metal used, being more suitable for the very intricate and delicate piercings, and for the setting of precious stones. To some extent the methods of the goldsmiths of Classic Greece were followed in the decoration of gold-plate. Fine wire, twisted together into coils, formed minute motifs on plain gold ground-work. Stones were at first set in plain raised settings, but about the sixth century mounts were perforated, setting the stones clear, and fixing them with claws. Often large stones were threaded on gold wire, to be suspended (*see* the Earring).

Raised Settings

Claw

The favourite jewels were the *emerald* and *sapphire*; next, the *ruby* and *diamond* — all polished, *not* faceted. *Pearls* ranked as supreme favourites, and were used in alternation with coloured stones, as a contrast. Pearls were usually mounted on the plate or foundation by being perforated and fixed by a threaded gold wire. Rows of pearls, such as are seen on costumes in the various illustrations, were threaded on gold wire and fixed to the material by loops at intervals.

Mosaic work. Articles of jewellery were frequently set with mosaic work in stones—chiefly garnets—glass, and vitrified paste, in addition to jewels. This style of decoration was also introduced from the East. It became very popular with Byzantine jewellers (*see* Frankish circular agrafe), and was much used for ikons. Another kind of decoration for jewellery was an engraved design on the gold, the incisions being filled in with black alloy. The whole surface was then burnished. This art, called *niello* work, is of great antiquity, and reached its highest point of perfection in the fifteenth century. During the sixteenth century it disappeared, but has been revived since that time.

The introduction of enamel into jewellery for personal wear was not very general, although it was used to some extent for the decoration of diadems for emperors and kings.

The art of the Byzantine jewellers reached its climax in the sixth century. Between this date and the tenth century there was a great demand for this work all over the civilised world.

Sixth-century Diadem

Crowns. The Emperor Justinian struck out in a new line with regard to his Imperial diadem. Until this time, emperors of the Eastern and Western Empires (save for Diocletian, *see* p. 129) wore the circlet, composed of two rows of pearls with a jewelled clasp in front (*see* Fig. 60). The crown now took the form of a band, from three to four inches deep, and fitted the head, sloping outward to its upper edge. It was decorated with jewels and rows of pearls on the top and bottom edges. A feature most typical of his and later Byzantine crowns was the ropes of pearls which hung from each side, falling over the ears. Any number of ropes were used, and they usually finished with a pear-shaped pearl or jewel. This type of crown remained in use until about the eighth century. It was then made up of a series of plaques of gold, connected together by links. Each plaque was richly ornamented with quantities of precious stones, and often with enamelled panels depicting saints, surrounded by borders of jewels. A cross usually surmounted the front plaque. About the ninth century an arch was added, springing from

Eighth-century Imperial Crown

the front to the back. Irene the Pious (ninth century) was empress in her own right—or by usurpation—and she probably introduced the arch. She not only wears one, but a second spans the sides of her crown. The Emperor Henry II. of Germany (1002: *see* Fig. 119) is wearing only one arch, and from this time it became a usual decorative detail.

Another kind of crown came into use during the tenth century, and its shape is best understood by referring to Fig. 93. In shape it was a truncated cone, comprising two bands (sometimes three or four) of gold, richly decorated with jewels and enamels.

Tenth-century Crown

Extending beyond the upper (wider) band came a border of radiating points, terminating in some examples in balls or other ornamental features. It was worn by many empresses, and princesses of the Imperial family from the tenth century onward, and is seen in many illuminated manuscripts, and frescoes of this period. The Virgin is often represented wearing a crown of this design.

With empresses the most important item of the regalia after the crown was the thickly jewelled *collar*. It had its origin in the deep neckbands worn by Egyptian ladies of the pre-Christian centuries. The illustrations—Figs. 63, 74, 82, and 91—show this collar better than it can be described.

Ear-rings

Ear-rings of large size were worn by noble ladies. The first one shown here is four inches in length, and depicts the method of threading a jewel on gold wire as a pendant. Other kinds of ear-rings were circular, square, triangular, and crescent-shaped plaques of gold, pierced with various designs; and some were solid, being engraved, or decorated with jewels and niello work. The third one has the cross treated in this manner.

Waist-belts were either of leather covered with gold and jewels, or entirely made of gold plates, hinged together. These were chiefly worn by emperors and empresses in full State.

Waist-belt Ends

Bracelets took the form of ornamental bands, many set with jewels or large plain gold rings, strings of pearls or other gems.

Bracelets

They were usually worn outside the tight sleeve of the stola and above the ornamental band at the wrist. Bracelets were frequently made to open with a hinge. The one shown here is not quite a circle; the front part which opens is straight. It has a cameo or a piece of enamel in the centre.

Fibulæ of Byzantine workmanship did not differ from those of the 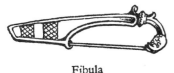 Roman Period. They were made of gold and gilt bronze, of the various forms already alluded to, from the ordinary safety-pin type to the T-shape, but with more ornament and detail added to them. Circular-topped

Fibula

fibulæ or brooches were used for fastening the paludamentum and cloaks of the nobility. These had strings of pearls attached to them—at first two (*see* Fig. 60) and later three (*see* Fig. 66). Fibulæ of all shapes were decorated with mosaic work and set with gems and jewels.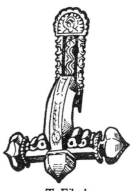

Rings. Plain rings in bronze, silver or gold were engraved with inscriptions, monograms, and the favourite sign of the cross. The commonest form of monogram used between the eighth and tenth centuries had a cross with the letters of the name distributed on or be-

T–Fibula

tween its members. They were used for betrothal, marriage and gift  rings. Some were worn as amulets for protection against disease or misfortune. Intaglios and cameos, either portraits or otherwise, were much used as bezels of rings.

A new item of jewellery came into fashion during the first part of this period, and remained in constant use among all classes of religious persons for many centuries. This was the *reliquary,* a receptacle for holding some sacred relic. These reliquaries took various forms, chiefly that of the cross, and were made to be carried upon the person as a charm or amulet. They were wonderful little specimens of art, and the most costly materials were employed in their fabrication. The one shown here is of enamel on gold, set with jewels, and has a square receptacle, covered by a jewel, to hold some portion—a tooth or a hair—of a martyr, or a thorn, or a piece of the True Cross.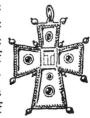

Reliquary

Crosses hung by chains around the neck were very rich and ornate, being carried out in enamels, jewels, or niello. The most usual decoration was Our Lord upon the Cross, surrounded by four saints, all executed in cloisonné ware.

Pectoral Crosses

ENAMELLING

The art of enamelling was known to the Chinese and Japanese before the Christian Era. The Romans had some knowledge of its use, and mention is made of enamel-work produced by them in the third century A.D. The craftsmen of Byzantium improved upon this third-century product, adopting a method copied from the Persians. For the particular style called cloisonné enamel, the pattern or design is delineated by strips of fine gold-plate, soldered edgewise to a gold foundation, and the enamel of different colours is run in to the various compartments. It is then fired, and the enamel is complete. Often the whole surface of the object to be decorated is covered in this manner.

Enamel was not much used for articles of personal jewellery, but, dating from the eighth century, it was frequently used to decorate circular or square plaques for ornamenting dresses (*see* Fig. 82). The backgrounds of these plaques were often of plain gold, with the design only in enamel; or alternately its whole surface was entirely covered.

A good deal of this enamelling was carried on at Constantinople, and it reached a considerable degree of excellence by the sixth century.

Cloisonné enamel was also made at Limoges, France, under the direction of S. Eloi.

BYZANTINE INFLUENCE ON RUSSIA

One sunny afternoon in July 860, when the rank and fashion of Constantinople were taking their languid saunter along the promenades skirting the Bosphorus, the attention of the crowd was suddenly focussed on an approaching flotilla of queer canoes, numbering two hundred, presently found to be manned by a rabble of quainter folk. They were savages who had braved the rapids of the Dvina and the Dnieper, crossed the wide expanse of the Black Sea, and arrived to terrify the inhabitants of Imperial Byzantium.

These barbarians were soon repulsed, but not before they had caused considerable panic in Constantinople. This was the first visit of the Russians.

In 864 Rurik founded Novgorod, and a number of his Swedish warriors came further south and settled at a place on the Dnieper—Kiev.

Eventually this stronghold was taken in 882 by Oleg, Rurik's successor, who thereby became master of the territory between the Black Sea and the Baltic.

A second visit to Constantinople was paid by the Russians in 907 —this time a much more formidable host, led by Oleg. Finding the harbour in the Bosphorus closed, he fitted his ships with wheels, and, setting sail in a north-west wind, he "flew" to Constantinople on the landward side! The city was saved by a barrage and the desperate policy of the Emperor Leo VI. The Russians were bought off at £6 per ship in addition to many handsome presents.

Novgorod retained its Scandinavian character, but Kiev was dominated by Slavonic influence; the latter became the principal stronghold of the early Russian chieftains. In 944 Prince Igor made a commercial treaty with Byzantium, and a trade route was opened down the Dnieper to the Black Sea. By degrees, Byzantine civilisation permeated Russian life, and very materially influenced the manners, customs, costume and traditions of the Russian people. The widow of Igor—Olga—was the first of this race to become a Christian.

In 977 Prince Vladimir assumed sole government. He married Anna, sister of the Byzantine Emperor, whose ally he became. Under Byzantine influence he adopted the Greek Faith and established the Orthodox Church in Russia, and after his death in 1015 was canonised. During his reign Kiev became the chief town of Russia.

Under Jaroslav (1019–1054) war was declared against the empire in 1024, but the Russians were hopelessly defeated. Jaroslav adopted the policy of Vladimir, and encouraged art and civilisation in every possible way. Kiev reached its zenith under his rule. Magnificent churches were erected by Byzantine architects and builders, and artists, scholars and teachers flocked thither, and soon this city on the Dnieper rivalled in its splendour the city on the Bosphorus. Byzantine fashions and Court dress were followed with such punctilious thoroughness that their character dominated the costume of the Russian nobility throughout the Middle Ages.

Moscow was founded in 1147. In 1414 the Grand Duke of Moscow's daughter, Anna, married John Palæologus, Emperor of Byzantium. After

Fig. 95 Fig. 96

the marriage, in 1472, of Ivan III. with Sophia Palæologus, niece of Constantine XIII.[1] (which followed the fall of Constantinople), a great rejuvenescence of Byzantine culture, refinement, and costume occurred in the Muscovite Empire. Much of the best that escaped the massacre of that fearful night of May 29, '53, had taken root in Russia; and numbers of Byzantine artists, architects, and artisans found employment—principally at Moscow—in building, decorating (exteriors and interiors), furniture, arts and crafts, and costume.

[1] Historians are at variance as to the sequence of emperors named Constantine. According to Gibbon, the son of Constantine XI. (Ducas) was Constantine XII., and the one here mentioned would appear, therefore, to be Constantine XIII.

In right of his wife, Ivan considered himself heir to the Byzantine throne, and therefore adopted its double-headed eagle as his arms.

Up to the time when Peter the Great (1689) introduced Western civilisation, and the Empress Elizabeth (1741) and her Court adopted French culture and fashions in every detail, Russian Court and national costume were purely and simply replicas of Byzantine modes.

The peasantry of Russia retained the Byzantine elements in their peasant dress right down to the year 1917, and they may do so still!

Figs. 95 and 96, representing a noble and a noble lady of Russia of the sixteenth and seventeenth centuries, are given to show the great similarity to the fashions of Byzantium.

LIST OF AUTHORITIES CONSULTED FOR BYZANTINE SECTION
CHAPTER IV

Hugh Arnold
Fred. W. Burgess
Prof. J. B. Bury
Cassiodorus—Secretary to Theodoric the Great
Paul B. du Chaillu
Smith-Cornish
Daremberg and Saglio
Charles Diehl
Edward Foord
Edward Gibbon
J. A. Herbert—Ill. MSS.
Dr. G. F. Herzburg
Thomas Hodgkin
Edward Hutton
Sir Thomas Graham Jackson
M. G. Julian
H. M. Kondakov

J. Lemprière
Walter Lowrie
Joseph McCabe
Ammianus Marcellinus
M. André Michel
M. Van Milligen
M. Emile Molinier
M. Antoine Munöz
Priscus
Procopius—Secretary to Belisarius
Rothay Reynolds
Rudolph von Scala
Gustave Schlumberger
Alexander Speltz
A. H. Thompson
H. G. Wells
Joseph Wilpert

CHAPTER V

HISTORY OF SILK FROM THE EARLIEST TIMES TO A.D. 1600

SILK is the strongest, most lustrous, and consequently the most valuable of all textile fabrics.

CHINESE SILK

The silkworm was a native of China, and its fibroin was first discovered and utilised by the Chinese about 3000 B.C.

China boasts the most ancient literature, and the first mention of silk in its records occurs about 2500 B.C. The emperor at that time, W-Hang, was a great patron of agriculture. His empress was the first to cultivate the silkworm, and to her is attributed the invention of the silk-weaving loom. So jealously did the Chinese guard their secret that for three thousand years they preserved a monopoly of the silkworm and the art of weaving silk material. Quite a quantity of silken goods found their way into other lands. At first these luxuries were enjoyed only by the countries in close proximity to China, and chroniclers prior to the Christian Era make mention of this precious stuff. The Western world was mystified as to its origin—whether vegetable, animal or mineral they could not tell. Herodotus (448 B.C.) concludes it must have been the fibre of some tree or plant. Aristotle (304 B.C.), tutor to Alexander the Great, and various other writers during many following centuries, asserted that it was derived from the fleece of animals, or from vegetation on trees and flowers, confusing what they had heard of the rearing of silkworms from mulberry trees, with the growth of cotton and flax on shrubs. Some went so far as to suppose that silk was obtained from beetles or spiders.

Embassies were sent to China to discover this State secret, and to persuade the authorities to open more direct commercial intercourse with the West; but without avail; so they had recourse to the purchase of plain silken material, and unravelled it for the sake of the silk thread. This was first practised by the inhabitants of the Island of Kos, off the coast of Asia Minor. The threads were re-woven into lengths of silk, and much of the silk materials used in Greece, Rome, Byzantium, and in the East generally outside China, was obtained in this manner, being exchanged for more than its weight in gold.

For many centuries the Persian traders were the channel of communication between the West and China. Their caravans traversed the whole of Asia from China to Syria, and they monopolised the trade in raw and woven silk.

Silk was very little known in Europe before the first century B.C., only very small quantities reaching Rome by long and circuitous routes. This very much enhanced its value, and it was obtainable only at a price prohibitive to all but the most wealthy. In the first century A.D. silken draperies of various textures, from the most substantial to those of the finest transparency, were much indulged in by the luxurious ladies of the highest Roman society.

Satin (Chinese: "Sou Twan") or *samit* was a thick, rich, closely-woven silk, invented by the Chinese and much coveted by the ancient Greeks and Romans, and for it they paid fabulous prices. It is mentioned in Classic literature.

Sericum, the Latin name for silk, derived from "Seres," the designation given by the Romans to the inhabitants of Sereinda, a remote region of Eastern Asia, *viz*. China.

Sub-Sericum was a cheaper substitute for pure silk, and therefore in more general use by men and women of Ancient Greece and Rome. The very costly silk was unravelled from the imported material, and interwoven with some cheap filament—either cotton or wool.

A sumptuary law was passed by the Roman Senate about the beginning of the Christian Era, prohibiting men from debasing themselves by wearing silk. It was thought to be only fit for women.

The emperors Vespasian and his son Titus (A.D. 69–81) were robed partly in silk at the time of their triumph, and Heliogabalus (220) was the first emperor of Rome to clothe himself entirely in pure Chinese silk. The price of this material being so high—it was worth its weight in gold—this act is recorded as wanton prodigality.

JAPANESE SILK

The Japanese were the first to discover the secret of the silkworm and the art of silk-weaving. An embassy was sent to China to bribe or capture four Chinese silk-weavers and bring them to Japan to teach the industry to the Japanese. From this time—the third century A.D.—to the present, the culture of the silkworm and manufacture of woven silk material in Japan became a very important and individual industry.

INDIAN SILK

There is a legend that the discovery of the Chinese secret to the people of India was brought about in the year A.D. 300, by the marriage of a Chinese princess with an Indian prince; and in one of the head-dresses of her trousseau were concealed the eggs of the silkworm. The larger proportion of silk produced in India comes from the tussor moth, the caterpillar of which feeds on the oak leaf, and this is commonly known as tussore silk.

During the fourth century A.D., the manufacture of silk from raw material imported from China was an important industry, carried on at Antioch, Alexandria and Antinoë. Persia became another important centre. King Shapur II., having conquered Syria in A.D. 355, brought back some Greco-Syrian silk-weavers and established them in his kingdom, where they developed the industry to a high standard. Persian fabrics of the Sassanian Period (226–651) were in great demand, and their patterned silks, first introduced about the close of the fifth century, are characterised by a frequent use of designs depicting animals, horse-men and hunters, enclosed as a rule in circles.

A certain amount of silk-weaving was carried on at Constantinople during the fourth century, but progress was seriously handicapped by the limited supplies of raw silk. The Persians still controlled the west-ward trade routes from China, and these were closed to the Byzantines during the Persian Wars of the fourth and fifth centuries.

In the year 399 the Chinese reached Ceylon, and here their junks deposited their wares—lacquer, jade, etc., and chiefly raw silk—to be collected by merchant galleys for transportation to Persia, Arabia, and Syria, *via* the Arabian Sea and Persian Gulf.

Patterned silks. Silk woven with a pattern was first made, out-side China, Japan and India, during the fifth century A.D. in Syria, Egypt, and particularly Persia. The first patterns employed were copied from old Greek designs of the fifth and fourth centuries B.C. (*see* pp. 55, 58, Greece).

Brocade—a name often misapplied—was a weft and woof of silk, sometimes intermixed with gold or silver, on which a pattern was superimposed by an independent weaving with the shuttle. Made in China and, after the introduction of the silkworm, in Japan and India; from the fifth century onward at Antioch, Alexandria, Antinoë, and in Persia.

Damask, a patterned silk, supposed from its name to have been originally made in Damascus. Known during the Merovingian Epoch (420–752). It was woven in elaborate patterns of foliage, flowers, scrolls, trees with parrots on each side of the trunks, peacocks and lions. The pattern was the same colour as the ground-work, but woven in such a manner that it took a lighter or darker shade.

BYZANTINE SILK

In the sixth century two Persian monks, who were working as missionaries in China, made it their business to understand the whole art of silkworm culture and the weaving of silk. They came to Constantinople and laid their scheme before the Emperor Justinian; and, inspired by the promise of great reward, they returned to China, eluding the vigilant jealousy of the Chinese, and succeeded in obtaining a quantity of silkworms' eggs. These they concealed in a bamboo tube, and returned to Constantinople in the year A.D. 551. From the silkworms thus pur-

loined all subsequent generations which stocked the Western world were produced; and for six centuries the Byzantine Empire monopolised silk manufacture in Europe.

The most beautiful silks, some woven with gold or silver thread, and some figured with patterns of animals, flowers and scrolls in gold and silver, were made in the factories of Constantinople.

Byzantine brocades are characterised generally by the use of a diversity of patterns—lions, dragons, birds, human figures, and hunters on horseback spearing wild animals—enclosed in decorated border circles, usually linked together by smaller circles. Inscriptions in Greek, Arabic or Persian were often woven in these circles.

Many authorities are of the opinion that Byzantine silks of the sixth century, still extant, are of Persian manufacture. Be that as it may, the designs are almost entirely Persian, or very much influenced by Persian characteristics.

12 th. CENT.

The greater part of these materials were prohibited as exports to the West, and reserved for the use of the Byzantine emperors and for diplomatic presents to any foreign potentate they thought fit to propitiate. This was the custom borrowed from the emperors and high dignitaries of the Chinese Empire.

Justinian himself controlled the manufacture of silken goods in the precincts of the Imperial Palace. He augmented his revenues very considerably by selling the products at prices prodigiously beyond those which he had formerly prohibited as excessive! An ounce weight of the fabric thus manufactured could not be obtained under the price of six pieces of gold.[1] The article was thus rendered eight-fold more expensive than it had been before the silkworm was introduced. This was the price demanded for common colours, but when dyed a royal blue or purple the fabric immediately assumed a quadruple value.

We hear of a king of the Burgundians in the sixth century entering the city of Lyons clad in a white silk tunica. This may have been made from material re-woven at Kos, or from a length of silk of Byzantine or Persian manufacture: more likely than not it was the former.

Soon after this time the Venetians opened commercial relations with Byzantium, and for many years continued to be the channel for supplying Western Europe with silken material.

In Charlemagne's time the Jews joined the Venetians, and, with their usual enterprise and discernment, opened branch establishments for the distribution of these Byzantine and Oriental fabrics in France, and even England, but at a price too great to allow anyone but those of the highest rank or fortune to purchase. The trade was very extensive, and carried on by representatives travelling all over Europe.

Branch factories for the production of silk materials were established within the Byzantine Empire at Corinth, Thebes, and Athens; but, prior to the twelfth century, Byzantium alone among the countries of Europe had possession of the silkworm.

At the beginning of the tenth century a material was introduced which became very general during the succeeding centuries. It was woven in camel or goat hair mixed with silk, and was a very fine and supple fabric. Often threads of gold or silver were woven in the woof,

[1] The gold coin in use in Byzantium during this and later periods was the "Besant"; and this was placed upon their shields as a charge for heraldic distinction by certain Crusaders when in the East.

forming stripes and sometimes intricate geometrical designs. These fabrics originated at Boukhara, and were called "Boquerant" or "Bougram." For the cheaper market a material using cotton in place of silk was made, and, in the first instance, woven in India. Afterwards this cotton and hair mixture was manufactured in Europe.

The Crusades undertaken in the twelfth century contributed considerably to the distribution of silk stuffs throughout Europe, during this and the following century.

Baudekyn—a material composed of silk interwoven with threads of gold. The web was of gold, and the woof of silk; and it had the effect of a coloured silk shot with gold or silver. Made originally at Baldeck or Baldacus, other names for Bagdad, whence it derives its name. Baudekyn was also made with patterns. These were either worked or woven on the surface in coloured silks or gold threads. In either case it resembled a brocade. Known in the East about the ninth or tenth century, but not introduced into England until the thirteenth century. This very expensive material was used to cover furniture, as well as in the making of regal costumes.

Cendal—a name for a silk of thinner texture and not so expensive as samit, used for men and women's robes in the twelfth century. It was of all plain colours, the most popular being a scarlet. It was also striped in two or three shades. Often used for lining, and very much used for flags, banners and pennons of spears called "gonfalons" and "oriflammes."

SICILIAN SILK

There is mention of silk-weaving carried on in Sicily during the ninth and tenth centuries, but it could not have been very extensive. After the expedition of King Roger of Sicily into Byzantium in 1131, he took measures to establish this industry in his kingdom, and with the aid of his admiral, George of Cappadocia, sent Greek (*i.e.* Byzantine) weavers from Athens, Thebes and Corinth to Sicily, and installed them at Palermo with orders to teach his subjects the art of silk-weaving. Twenty years after, the silks of Sicily are described as having attained a decided excellence, being of divers patterns and colours, some fancifully interwoven with gold and silver; and they were held in higher esteem than silks of Byzantium.

One of the two tunics preserved at Nuremberg and *said* to have belonged to Charlemagne, is of Sicilian manufacture, and the date 1181 is woven into one of the borders.

The introduction of Greek, Arabic and Persian inscriptions into brocades, copied from the earlier method, was much practised by the weavers of Sicily and Italy during the twelfth and thirteenth centuries, in order to deceive buyers into the belief that they were of Persian origin. It was generally believed that the Persians excelled in the manufacture of silk; therefore their fabrics were considered superior to any other, and commanded a higher price.

Gauze is mentioned in 1300, but it is evident, from sculpture and illuminated MSS., that it was used in the tenth, eleventh and twelfth centuries.

ITALIAN SILK

From Sicily the art found its way into Italy—no great distance—in the twelfth century; and the Italians, like the Chinese before them, managed to keep the secret and monopoly of silk production and weaving for four centuries.

Modena, Genoa, Florence, Bologna, and Venice were the chief cities of manufacture.

A flourishing manufacture of brocade was carried on at Lucca in the thirteenth century. These artisans were driven to Venice in 1310, where they resumed the manufacture.

Camocas brocade, with raised design in gold on a background of black, white, blue, green, purple, grey, mauve, crimson and shaded colour. The design usually represented birds. Manufactured at Cyprus.

Pailes.—Latin: "Pallium," "Purpura," signifying in general any rich cloth; Old Norman: "Pell"; Old English: "Paell," "Pell"; French: "Paille." Hence the modern English: "Pall," a rich cloth. The name given to very rich silken stuff from various countries, *e.g.*, pailes of Byzantium, pailes of Syria, pailes of Persia, pailes of India, and pailes of Damascus.

The warehouses or exchange depôts for these fabrics were at Alexandria, whence they were exported to the West.

Pailes of Damascus. This name had no relation to damask as we know it. It refers to silk fabrics of various colours, figured with gold and silver. The price in 1316 was fifty-five crowns per piece.

Shot silk, sometimes mentioned as *pailes roe*—a silk in two colours, the woof of one colour and the weft of another contrasting colour. It was of Eastern manufacture, and in use in the twelfth century.

This material was at first considered very wonderful, and all sorts of strange ideas were current as to its origin. The most common story was that it was made in some far-off island inhabited only by women weavers who were directed in their process by fairies. Others related that this material was actually woven by the dwarfs and gnomes of fairyland. Shot silk was much used for women's clothes during the twelfth, fourteenth and fifteenth centuries. It was manufactured at Venice and several other Italian towns, and later in Spain and France.

Frise—cloth of gold—was considered very precious. Mention is made of it in romances from the twelfth century onwards. It is a corruption of the name " phrygia." No manufacture of cloth of gold existed in Friesland, a province of the Low Countries, at this date!

Crêped silk, a very fine silk manufactured in the East, very similar to crêpe-de-chine of to-day. It was one of the materials brought from the East into Western Europe during the Crusades of the twelfth century, and was much used for the " bliaut " worn by noble ladies between the years 1130–1200.

Sarsnet, thin silk of Oriental origin, in all plain colours. Much used in the thirteenth century.

Pourpre, a rich quality silk manufactured at Tyre and Venice in 1248. The colours used were Indian purple, vermilion, indigo, crimson, black and white.

L'Ecarlate, similar stuff to pourpre, but a little inferior in quality.

Siglaton, a material very like samit, but much esteemed during the thirteenth century in the belief that it was of Eastern or Spanish (Moorish) manufacture.

Velvet, a silken fabric, woven with a looped surface which is cut, forming a thick close-set pile. First mentioned in 1277, and made in Lucca and Genoa. Existing specimens of earlier date than the fourteenth century are extremely rare.

Velvet upon velvet, made in the same way, but with two piles, one (the pattern) higher than the other.

(*Pell*, a similar material *made of cotton* and treated in the same manner. It had the appearance of modern cotton plush. In use among the Scandinavians as early as the ninth century.)

ENGLISH SILK

The earliest record of silk-weaving in England is in the fourteenth century. An Act of Parliament was passed to protect "certain old-established silk women against the Lombards and other Italians." The little that was made was manufactured from raw silk brought into this country. The trade developed somewhat in the reign of James I., but silk manufacture in England was not brought to perfection until 1688, when the Edict of Nantes drove many French refugees to this country. They settled in Spitalfields, and their descendants are living there to-day. A silk-throwing mill was set up at Derby in 1714 by Sir Thomas Lombe, a merchant of London.

———————

Velvets, brocaded, either with a gold pattern on the velvet ground, or a velvet pattern on a gold ground, and

Shot velvets were in use in 1353.

Samit en graine, richer quality samit. In 1353 it cost twenty crowns per piece—double the price of cendal.

Caffard, caffa, malicques, were names given to satin in the fifteenth and sixteenth centuries.

Zatoni, a kind of satin or samit, mentioned in the fourteenth century.

Tiercelin—Cendal, but of better quality than ordinary cendal; used for armorial surcoats, on account of its strength. Fifteenth century.

Tabby or *taffeta,* a thick silken stuff with a soft nap, mentioned in 1487. It was in use at a much earlier date, for part of the robes found in the tomb of William Rufus (1087) were of taffeta.

Cafoy was a coarse taffeta, used mostly for hangings.

Tinsen, a kind of glossy satin, temp. Henry VII.

Tiffany, a kind of thin transparent silk, like sarcenet.

SPANISH SILK

It is thought that silk-weaving was carried on in Spain at an early date, though not before A.D. 709, when the Arabs settled there. Mention is made, however, of silk being woven in Spain in the ninth and tenth centuries. When Ferdinand V. conquered Granada in 1492, he found there many Moorish establishments for the production of silk fabrics, which were rivalled by others carried on in Murcia and Cordova. At this time considerable progress in the production and manufacture of silk material was made in Spain, but as a result of Moorish influence it retained its Oriental character for a long period.

FRENCH SILK

Although some authorities declare that silk-weaving was practised in France at the end of the twelfth century, it has been stated by others that the first introduction of silk-weaving into that country was due to Louis XI., who obtained workmen from Genoa, Venice and Florence and established them at Tours in 1480. Little progress was made in the art until the reign of Francis I. (1515–1547), when many artisans were brought from Milan, a duchy then belonging to the French monarch, and installed at Lyons, where they made rapid progress, and Lyons rapidly became the most important centre of silk-weaving in France. It was during this reign that the silkworm was first introduced into France; and Henry IV. (1589–1610) propagated mulberry trees and silkworms throughout the kingdom. From this date to the present time, France has held first place in the silk-weaving industry, a position held earlier by Italy for over four hundred years.

From the fifteenth century onwards, the craft of silk-weaving and the art and design associated with the production of silken materials have become so important and involved that a considerable literature dealing with these matters has been called into existence.

For further information, therefore, a reference to various works on specific periods or details is recommended.

In the reproduction of ancient costumes for the modern Drama or Pageant, the following substitutes for materials used are suggested:—

Materials	*Modern substitutes*
Linen	Cotton crêpe, linen, lawn, cambric.
Linen Woven in Olive Oil	Said to be "like the skin of a dried onion." Silk proper should not be used, but there is no objection to sateen, or to a mercerised cotton, both of which crush very considerably.
Wool	Cashmere, merino, fine cloth, domette, or the modern government silk.
Coarse Cloth for Peasants	Serge, soft hessian, sacking, wide-mesh canvas, frieze.
Silk	Soft satin (wool back), merv, Jap silk, crêpe-de-chine.
Muslins	Muslins, ninon, crystalline.

LIST OF AUTHORITIES CONSULTED FOR HISTORY OF SILK, CHAPTER V

Dr. Bock	Luther Hooper	J. R. Planche
F. W. Fairholt	A. F. Kendrick	Howell Smith
Otto von Falke	W. R. Lethaby	E. Viollet-le-Duc

CHAPTER VI

THE BRITONS OF THE DARK AGES, A.D. 428–700 [1]

Britain was evacuated by the Romans in the year A.D. 428. It had been a part of the Roman Empire for over three centuries, and, during that period, those Britons who had submitted themselves to Roman rule had prospered. The civilisation, tastes and refinements introduced by the conquerors remained behind after their departure.

During the latter part of the Roman occupation, the country in the north had been harassed by the Picts and Scots. These people were of the original Celtic race in Britain, who, at the time of Cæsar's invasion, fled to the north and west, beyond the limits of Roman power. These unconquered Celtic Britons were called "Caledonians" by the Romans and by the more civilised Britons, and were divided into two nationalities—the Picts in the north of Britain, and the Scots in the north-west of Ireland.

As late as A.D. 207 the Caledonians are described by Dion Cassius as being a naked, half-wild race, with large limbs and red hair.

HISTORICAL DATA

S. Ninian, Apostle of the Picts, b. 350, of royal parentage; d. 432. A disciple of S. Martin of Tours (d. 397).

S. Patrick, Apostle of Ireland. A native of Britain, b. 387. Educated in Gaul. Founder of the Irish Church; d. 458.

A.D. 429. Hitherto the Caledonians had been kept in check by the Roman garrisons; but when in due course these were withdrawn (in 428), they descended in full force upon their more cultured kinsmen.

During the fifth century, the Scots, an Irish race, migrated to North Britain and founded a kingdom called Scotland.

A.D. 446. After the departure of the Romans, the administration of the country devolved upon the Britons, who, being unable to cope with the truculent barbarians from the north, appealed for help, through their British chief, to Ætius, the Roman general. Rome, however, had her hands full with her own internal troubles and refused assistance.

A.D. 449. In this year a band of Jutish sea-rovers, under the leadership of Hengist and Horsa, landed at Ebbsfleet. As a last resort, the British chief, Vortigern, pressed these two leaders into his service. With their help he defeated the Picts and Scots; but when this was accomplished, these mercenaries, either from pride or discontent, devoted themselves to their own interests, and after a while established themselves in Kent with Hengist as their king (454). It is said that for love of Romwen, Hengist's daughter, Vortigern betrayed his country, and gave them the kingdom of Kent. Vortimer and Catigern, his valiant sons, fought four battles against the Jutes, in one of which, at Epsford, Catigern and Horsa fell in a hand-to-hand fight.

[1] Until the publication a few weeks ago of Mr. Gordon Home's scholarly work, *Roman York* (1924), the date of the Roman evacuation of Britain was believed to be A.D. 410. Mr. Home's researches now fix the date of the last official evidence of Roman activity in Britain at 428.

At Vortimer's death the Britons fled, leaving Hengist master of Kent.

Ambrosius Aurelianus (successor to Vortigern), a Romanised Briton and an upholder of the old Roman discipline, drove back the Jutes, but was eventually defeated by them.

A.D. 465. The success of Hengist encouraged the Saxons to invade the country, under their chiefs, Ella and Cerdic. The former became king of the South Saxons, and Cerdic, king of the West Saxons, or Wessex.

A.D. 490. S. David, apostle of the Welsh Church, b. about 490.

A.D. 495. Last of all the marauding visitors came the Angles, and these three races, Jutes, Saxons and Angles, waged terrific warfare in the land. The Jutes came from Jutland, the Saxons from Holstein, and the Angles from Schleswig, and all were of Teutonic origin. They were known among themselves as "Angles"—the remaining Celtic population of Britain called them "Saxons"—hence the term "Anglo-Saxons."

The Britons had imbibed during the Roman occupation considerable elements of culture. To them, these Teutonic marauders appeared no better than barbarians, and all Roman civilisation was lost in the relentless struggle for supremacy. The arts were forgotten, and it is believed that by the time the Saxons had established their power, the Celtic-British race was almost completely exterminated, excepting those who had fled to Wales, Cornwall, the north-west coast of Britain, and that part of France still called Brittany.

The conquest of Britain by these composite tribes took nearly two centuries to complete, namely from about A.D. 450 to A.D. 613. At last there came a gradual settlement, and the various chiefs took possession of the parts of the island which they respectively had conquered. Each chieftain formed his own government, and there arose a number of small kingdoms. These became known as the *Heptarchy*, a word derived from the Greek "Hepta," = seven, and "arche" = sovereignty. The seven kingdoms consisted of:

	OCCUPIED BY	LOCALITY	FOUNDED BY	YEAR
Kent	Jutes	Modern Kent	Hengist	457
Sussex	South Saxons	Sussex and Surrey	Ella	490
Wessex	West Saxons	Counties west of Sussex and south of Thames, except Cornwall	Cerdic	519
Essex	East Saxons	Essex, Middlesex and part of Herts	Ercenium	527
Northumbria	Angles	North of Humber to the Forth	Ida	547
East Anglia	Angles	Norfolk, Suffolk and Cambridgeshire	Uffa	575
Mercia	Angles	Central Counties	Cridda	582

These seven kingdoms were in a continual state of flux, from time to time one gaining supremacy over the other.

The first Anglo-Saxon kingdom to acquire definite superiority was that of Kent. Northumbria rose later, and supplanted it.

King Ethelbert, A.D. 560–616, was the first prominent king, being not only king of Kent, but overlord of England to the Humber. He married Bertha, daughter of Childebert, king of the Franks.

A.D. 563. S. Columba, Apostle of the Scottish Highlands, b. 521, of royal parentage. Left Ireland with a body of monks, and established a monastery on the Isle of Iona.

A.D. 596. S. Augustine, founder of the English Church, arrived in Kent; d. 604; buried at Canterbury.

Power transferred to the north. Edwin of Deira became king of Northumbria (617). Married (625) Ethelburga, daughter of Ethelbert and Bertha. This led to the conversion of Northumbria.

A.D. 626. Paulinus was a priest in her retinue, who brought about the conversion.

A.D. 633. Edwin vanquished by king of the Welsh, and Penda, the heathen king of Mercia. Edwin's wife became a nun. Country relapsed into heathenism until Edwin's nephew, Oswald, King and Saint, brought S. Aidan, a Scottish bishop, and founded the See of Lindisfarne on Holy Island (642). Oswald lived at Bamborough. Penda slew Oswald at Maserfield (643).

A.D. 634. Wessex converted by Birinus.

A.D. 635. S. Cuthbert lived at Lindisfarne and converted the whole of Northumbria; d. 687.

A.D. 664. East Anglia converted by S. Wilfred, abbot of Ripon, son of a Northumbrian noble, b. 634; d. 709.

In less than a hundred years the whole of England had been converted to Christianity.

A.D. 668. Organisation of the Church effected by Theodore of Tarsus, sent over to become Archbishop of Canterbury.

Benedict Biscop. An important person of the seventh century was Benedict Biscop. Born of noble parents in the year 628, he was, as a young man, a courtier of Oswy (642–670), king of South Northumbria. Later, he accompanied S. Wilfred to Rome, and studied there for ten years, returning to Britain in 668 with Theodore of Tarsus. He eventually became abbot of the monastery of S. Augustine at Canterbury. He founded the monasteries of (Monk) Wearmouth and Jarrow, and built other churches, bringing masons who understood the use of stone for that purpose from Gaul, and glass-blowers who made glass for the windows. He paid five visits to Rome, and on these occasions collected numerous examples of Byzantine arts and crafts, which he brought back to his native land—books (*i.e.* illustrated MSS.), relics, and ornaments of goldsmiths' work, rich vestments, and clothes of all descriptions, ivory carvings, and pictures. Those depicting religious subjects he hung upon the walls of his churches, thereby teaching the illiterate parishioners the Life of Christ; much to the delight of the simple folk. Very few of such works of art from the East had been seen in Britain since the days of the Roman occupation, and even the Roman art then known was inferior to the Byzantine work brought by Benedict Biscop. The monks devoted themselves eagerly to the reproduction of illustrated MSS., goldsmiths' work, and other objects of art from these models, for the decoration of their churches. This fact explains the very noticeable Byzantine influence in the technique and workmanship of the Anglo-Saxon and Early English Period. Benedict Biscop also introduced singing into his services, having brought back an Arch-Chanter from Rome to teach the choir. The last ten years of his life were spent in company with young Bede at Jarrow. This great patron of the arts died in the year 690.

S. Hilda, abbess of Whitby, great-niece of Edwin of Northumbria; d. 680.

Caedmon, the first English poet, a cow-herd on the Abbey lands at Whitby, was contemporary with S. Hilda.

Costume in General

DURING these troublous times there was no opportunity for the development of costume. It is generally admitted that the sixth and seventh centuries are the period of history concerning which we have least definite knowledge. Everything was subordinated to warfare, and no arts or literature flourished. Costume achieved no progress (at least very little record remains to enlighten us on the subject), and we must conclude that the Briton of the late fifth and early sixth century wore the Roman-British costume described in Chapter III, Section ii, p. 85.

449. From the few chronicles handed down to us we learn that the *troops of Vortigern* wore the "lorica" (Saxon: "lluryg"). This is the tunica referred to under Roman Britain and shown in Fig. 97. This man is dressed as befits a soldier of the Roman army of the past and present, except that, being a Briton of no importance, his hair is worn after the

British fashion; and he is wearing shoes which have taken the place of sandals in general use.

500. Coins, sculpture, and foreign chronicles conclusively prove that the Britons of this period had very nearly the same appearance as their neighbours, the Franks of the Merovingian Period.

560. Aneurin, the Welsh bard, a contemporary of the traditional King Arthur, and probably present at many battles for liberty fought by his country-men, tells us that the "warriors fighting against the invading Saxons *wore gilded armour, harnessed in scaly mail, and four-pointed helmets.*"

Fig. 98 represents King Arthur, wearing a costume founded on the best available authorities. The mixture of "barbarian" or British charac-teristics with Roman features is interesting, and the illustration shows an excellent example of the amalgamation of the two. He wears the lorica of leather and scales of gilded bronze, held over the shoulders by leather straps fastened by bronze ornaments to a breast-band. This is worn over the tunica, embroidered round the edge and round the rather wide sleeves with a Celtic design. Over all is a rectangular cloak, fastened by a fibula. The lower

Fig. 97

part of the legs is covered with cross-gartered studded straps over the bracco. A sword of native workmanship is slung over the shoulder, and

Arthur's Helmet

Square Helmet

he holds a gilded bronze spear. The helmet, of the square variety, is of gilded bronze, surmounted by a dragon of Celtic design.

Fig. 98 represents King Arthur wearing the characteristic costume of a British chieftain of the sixth century.

Square helmets of this type appear to have been common to all tribes warring in Britain, and their use must have continued for two hundred years, possibly longer, as they are seen on the heads of warriors depicted in Charles the Bald's Bible (840).

Amplifying these few details, we must consider two other and external influences which played their part in the costume of Britain towards the end of this period. These were the Franks of the Merovingian Epoch and the Saxons—both were of Teutonic origin.

The Franks dwelt on the other side of the Channel in France, and their close proximity must have resulted in frequent intercourse between the two countries.

As regards the native dress of the invading Saxons, we have the researches of German authorities to help us. By the end of the seventh century there is to be found in Britain an amalgamation of the characteristics of Frankish and Saxon dress. This fact is proved by illuminated MSS. of the eighth century, which still exist, and are the *earliest known illuminated MSS. giving records of British costume.*

THE FRANKS OF THE MEROVINGIAN EPOCH, A.D. 240–752

RISE OF THE KINGDOM AND HISTORICAL DATA

The Teutonic race as a whole inhabited that part of Europe which is bounded on the north by the Baltic Sea, on the west by the Rhine, the south by the Danube, and on the east by the eastern limits of modern Prussia.

The tribes comprised in the Teutonic race were:

The Franks of the Lower Rhine and Weser	The Jutes of Jutland
The Chauci of Brunswick	The Angles of Schleswig
The Cherusci of Hanover	The Saxons of Holstein
The Chatti of Hesse	The Suevi of Swabia

The Goths originally from Gothland but now settled in Prussia.

These rude tribes of Germania [1] were practically devoid of civilisation, and had no knowledge of the arts, and when they first came to the notice of the Roman Empire, about the beginning of the Christian Era, they were considered barbarians of the lowest type—with the exception of the Franks, who were considerably ahead of their kinsfolk.

The Franks were governed by chiefs, and by the year 240 they had become a powerful confederacy. They took their name—Freemen or Franks—from their ruling passion, a love of liberty; and their Fatherland, the region traversed by the Rhine, the Neckar and the Main, was called Franconia to distinguish it from the Latin Francia or France.

The most important tribes were the Ripuarian Franks, who dwelt near Köln, and the Salian Franks, who dwelt near Frankfurt.

As a nation, the Franks came into prominence in the fourth century A.D., and, about the year 420, they conquered and settled in that part of Gaul now called Flanders, losing thereafter many of their Teutonic racial characteristics.

HISTORICAL DATA

418. Pharamond, son of Marcomir, was their chief. They soon established the principle of hereditary succession (420), and the first chief or prince to be elevated on the buckler (a ceremony which was equivalent to a coronation, and conferred supreme command of the army) was Clodian the Long-haired (428).

Clodian's elder son became the ally of Attila. The younger, named Merovee or Merwig ("mer" = great, and "wig" = a warrior), had been sent to Rome in his youth, and became later king of the Franks, with his capital at Tournay. He assisted General Ætius at the battle of the Catalaunian Plains, and defeated Attila. It is from his name of Merovee that this race of kings, lasting three centuries, takes its designation as the MEROVINGIAN DYNASTY.

At his death in 458, he left a goodly inheritance to his son Childeric, who was driven from his throne by Ægidius, general of the Roman forces in Gaul. Ægidius was chosen king of the Franks in his place. After a time Childeric was recalled to the throne, and he died in 481.

481. Clovis or Chlodowig (Latin: "Clovig"; German: "Lodovic" or "Ludwig"; French: "Louis"), called Clovis the Great, succeeded. He is known as one of the most bloodthirsty and treacherous tyrants in history. None the less he was very popular, and possessed superior merits which attracted the respect and allegiance of all the Frankish tribes. He subjugated the Alemanni, and annexed their territory of Alsace, Lorraine, and a large part of Germania.

---

[1] Tacitus wrote of " Germania," A.D. 98.

He married (492) a Christian princess, Clotilde, daughter of Chilperic, king of the Burgundians, and was baptised in 496. He vanquished Syagrius, son of Ægidius, took Soissons and transferred his capital to that place.

501. Gundobad, king of the Burgundians, having murdered the father of Clotilde, was attacked and defeated by Clovis, who annexed the territory of the fallen Gundobad to his own.

507. Expedition against Alaric II., king of the Visigoths, whom he slays at Poitiers, completely destroying the Visigothic power in Gaul.

508. Clovis is attacked by Theodoric the Great and defeated by him at Arles. The subsequent treaty of peace secured practically the whole of the Visigothic territory to Clovis, with the exception of a small strip near the Gulf of Lyons, which they were allowed to retain. Clovis makes Paris his capital.

S. Geneviève (432–512) the patron-saint of Paris.

511. Death of Clovis, " The most Christian King." He and his wife are canonised. Ripuarian and Salian Franks combined under Clovis.

The sons of Clovis were: Thierry, King (at Metz) of Austrasia, succeeded by Theodebert (534) and his grandson Theodebald (548); Clodomir, King (at Orleans) of Burgundy; Childebert, King (at Paris); Clotaire, King (at Soissons) of Neustria.

The descendants of Clovis were weak—puppet kings—and left the government to the Mayors of the Palace or " Major Domus."

538. Franks invade Italy under Theodebert.

554. They invade and invest Milan, but are driven back by Narses.

558. Clotaire sole ruler. At his death (561) he left four sons, and his kingdom was divided between them. Charebert ruled at Paris; Gontram ruled over Burgundy at Orleans; Siegebert ruled over Austrasia at Metz; Chilperic I. ruled over Neustria at Soissons.

566. Brunhildis marries Siegebert, and he is assassinated (575) by Fredegundis, wife of Chilperic I.; Childebert obtains Orleans.

581. Clotaire II. at Soissons.

584. Chilperic I. assassinated at Chelles near Paris.

593. Supreme power in the hands of Fredegundis.

596. Thierry II., son of Childebert, and Theodebert II. at Metz.

610. Brunhildis obtains full power. Later she is seized, tied to the tail of a wild horse and kicked to death.

613. Clotaire II. sole monarch.

628. Dagobert I., called the Great, son of Clotaire II., king of all the Franks. The second most important sovereign of this dynasty. He divided his kingdom (638) between his two sons: Clovis II. taking Burgundy and Neustria; Siegebert, Austrasia.

656. Clotaire III., son of Clovis II.

670. Childeric II., king of the whole realm of the Franks, assassinated with his queen and son. Thierry III. reigns in Burgundy and Neustria; Dagobert II., son of Siegebert, in Austrasia; Dagobert is assassinated; Thierry reigns alone.

691. Clovis III. Pepin of Heristal, Mayor of the Palace, rules in his name. He made the office of " Major Domus " hereditary.

695. Childebert III., his brother, called the Just.

711. Dagobert III.

716. Chilperic II. governed and eventually deposed by Charles Martel (the Hammer), Mayor of the Palace.

719. Clotaire IV., of obscure birth. Raised to the buckler by Charles Martel. He died the following year, and Chilperic II. is restored to the throne. He dies; is succeeded by Thierry IV., son of Dagobert III., who dies in 737, and Charles Martel rules alone as duke of the Franks.

742. Childeric III., son of Chilperic II., surnamed the " Stupid." Carloman and Pepin, sons of Charles Martel, share in the government.

752. Pepin, surnamed the " Short," becomes sole ruler and is the first king of the CARLOVINGIAN DYNASTY.

Costume of the Early Franks

Fourth and Fifth Centuries

Our earliest knowledge of the Franks after their settlement in Gaul is gained from the historian Sidonius Apollinaris (430–488). He describes them as "monsters," and "from the top of their red skulls descends their hair, knotted on the front and shaved in the nape of the neck. Their chins are shaven, and instead of a beard they have locks of hair arranged with the comb" (moustaches) (*see* Fig. 99). He relates that they had large strong limbs, and wore a tight-fitting tunica to the knee, with a wide girdle round their "lean stomachs." To hurl their two-edged axes, turn their shields round and round, and to bear down the enemy before their spears was child's play to them.

He also tells us he saw the Franks enter the city of Lyons in 470, attired in close-fitting tunicas reaching to the knee, with exceedingly short sleeves scarcely covering the shoulders, made of some striped material. Over this they wore a cloak (sagum) of green cloth with a red border. They were girt with a broad belt, ornamented with metal studs, and wore their swords suspended on the left side by a baldric crossing the breast. Their thighs and legs were bare,

Fig. 99

but they had laced boots of undressed leather reaching to the ankles.

The tunica of their young King Sigismer was of white silk, and his sagum was of a brilliant scarlet.

> Like the gold that gleamed upon his dress, was his hair.
> Beautiful in hue as the vermilion of his sagum was his complexion.
> The fairness of his milk-white silk attire was rivalled by his skin.

He had come to celebrate his nuptials with the daughter of a Burgundian chief.

Agathias, writing in the early sixth century, tells us that they fought with their chests and backs bare. Their legs were girt with linen or leather bracco of the same style as those worn by the Teutonic auxiliaries seven hundred years earlier.

The bracco was the distinctive dress of the Teutonic tribes, but after their arrival in Gaul this garment was more or less discarded by the upper classes. Later, they adopted *pedules* (*see* Byzantine Empire, p. 191), which became a familiar feature of Frankish dress.

Other authors of this time mention "bright striped dresses," and "bright striped mantles," so the art of the dyer must have reached a high standard. Also "bright dress stuff which the Friesians spred as merchandise"—evidently a primitive woollen material which afterwards became known as "frieze." This is a curiously early record of its existence, as it was undoubtedly considered a novelty when introduced into England in Edward III.'s reign.

THE NOBILITY

The dress of a Frankish noble was a narrow tunica of soft material, cut like Diagram 13. It reached just above the knees, was striped or plain, with a bright colour as a border. Over this would be worn sometimes a short jacket of fur, without sleeves. A belt with a buckle was

fastened round the waist, set with precious stones and studs of gold, and from it was suspended a small sword on the right side. A larger sword hung on the left side, by a baldric of leather, ornamented with studs, crossing the breast.

The legs were bare from the thighs downward, and on the feet were shoes of undressed leather laced on the instep and turning over at the ankles (see Fig. 100). It was very usual to have the shoes open at the top, exposing all five toes as far as the joints (see p. 200).

Tattooing was still a prevalent fashion, common to both nobles and people as late as 785, and the short sleeves and tunicas worn showed off this decoration to advantage.

Cloaks, with borders of different colours, were fastened either in front or on the right shoulder with a fibula.

Fig. 100

At the end of this period, the nobility ceased to wear the short over-tunic of fur or skin. It was worn only by freemen and serfs, with whom it remained in fashion for several centuries longer.

The *hair* of princes and nobles was worn long and flowing, it being a distinguishing mark of nobility. Young men shaved their faces, leaving only a small moustache, but among the aged and learned long beards were at all times reverenced.

A peculiar style of dressing the hair was in vogue among some of the tribes which formed this race. The men shaved the back of the head, allowing the hair on the front to grow to a very great length. This they tied up in a knot on top, with the flowing ends falling down on both sides like a horse's tail. The fashion appears to have been borrowed from the Aquitanians, a tribe inhabiting that part of Gaul which lies between the Garonne and the Pyrenees, among whom it remained in fashion until the eleventh century.

Jewellery of the early Franks. Articles of personal adornment consisted of fibulæ, ear-rings, bracelets, belt-buckles, and plates of metal for decorating skin jackets, waist-belts and sword-belts. Bronze, often gilded, was the chief metal used, and, among the wealthy, ornaments of gold.

The fibulæ were of especially beautiful designs, and made of gold or bronze, inlaid with pebbles and semi-precious stones.

Bracelets, often worn by men on the right arm, and ear-rings were of the same materials. Necklaces of coloured glass beads were in common use. The buckle fastening the waist-belt was an important item, and was richly chased or inlaid. *See also* Jewellery, p. 237.

STATE COSTUME—MEN

Sixth, Seventh and Eighth Centuries

The rise of the Frankish nation in the fifth century gave no little concern to the officials of the Eastern Empire; and it was deemed wise to add their barbarian chieftains to the lengthy list of similar worthies whose propitiation appeared to be expedient. After the success of Clovis in his war (507) against the Goths in Gaul, the title of " Augustus " was conferred upon him (510) by the Emperor Anastatius, who thereby gave tacit sanction to the usurpation of Gaul. Gregory of Tours narrates that on the day the insignia of his honours were delivered to him, Clovis set aside his barbarian attire, and robed himself in tunica palmata and paludamentum, placing a jewelled diadem upon his head. He adopted with alacrity the Byzantine mode of dress and, his example being followed by most of the nobles and Court dignitaries, the customs, costume and etiquette of Byzantium speedily displaced former modes and practices at the Court of Clovis and his successors. Long hair, however, continued to be worn by Frankish notabilities, and a few other variations from Byzantine models will be referred to in connection with the examples which follow.

The *State costume of a Frankish king* of the Merovingian Epoch is shown in Fig. 101. In general appearance it is of the familiar type described in the preceding chapter.

The tunica, save for a slight variation in its decoration, is in every way the same as that worn by Byzantine nobles. The paludamentum likewise; but it is simplified and without ornament except for the fibula of Frankish workmanship which fastens it.

The leg-coverings are characteristic of Frankish dress. This king wears bracco tied at the knees, and over them pedules (*see* p. 191) cross-gartered from the ankles upward. Shoes of a simple form, in leather or cloth, are worn.

A touch of barbarism remains in the *hairdressing*. It was the custom among members of the Frankish reigning house to allow the hair to grow to a great length, as a sign of royal birth. The first to attain to the title of king was "Clodian of the Long Hair," and the fashion originated thus. It is shown in Fig. 101, braided in long plaits on either side of the face, and with the extremities rolled up and fastened.

The crown is of Byzantine design, but wrought in rather a clumsy manner by a Frankish goldsmith. A spear is held in the hand, in imitation of Byzantine emperors and their Holy Lance, and as part of the Frankish insignia as a chief.

Fig. 101

Some examples of goldsmiths' work came from Constantinople in the early days of this epoch. Later, when Clovis overthrew the Visigothic power in Gaul (507), the Franks obtained possession of large quantities of masterpieces of the goldsmiths' and other arts, stored in different strongholds by Alaric I.—loot which he had deposited there after the sack of Rome in 410. These priceless treasures accumulated by the Romans comprised gold and silver cups, plates, dishes, furniture, jewellery, textiles, and "twenty cases to hold the books of the Gospels." This wealth was distributed by the successors of Clovis among the churches which were afterwards built in Christianised Frankish Gaul. Chilperic I. encouraged the arts, and sent to Constantinople for craftsmen whom he established in the vicinity of his palace.

Goldsmiths' Work

The *Bishop-Saint Eloi,* or *Eligius,* was born at Cadillac, near Limoges, in 590. As a child he showed great artistic talent, and was placed later with Abbo, Master of the Mint at Limoges, where he made rapid progress in goldsmiths' work. He became coiner to Clotaire II. (613) and treasurer to Dagobert the Great (628). He is famous as a master-goldsmith, and is responsible for the creation of many works of art, especially furniture. He made two chairs of gilded bronze set with jewels, and one of them, known as "Dagobert's Chair," is still extant (*see* Fig. 101 and compare with Figs. 69 and 131). A back and sides were added by Abbot Suger in the twelfth century. S. Eloi became a very important personage at Court, and dressed very magnificently, "more for propriety than taste." His under-garments were made of the finest linen, and his outer ones were of the richest silk, embroidered with gold and jewels. Having amassed great wealth, he acquired a distaste for worldly life and became a priest, conforming strictly to the Irish monastic rule of S. Columba. He was appointed Bishop of Noyon (640), and died in 660. He is the patron - saint of goldsmiths and metal-workers.

Fig. 102

Fig. 102 shows a *Frankish noble* or official at the Court of a Frankish king where Byzantine influences have considerable sway. Compare this with Fig. 71. Attention is directed to the pocket attached to the waist-belt, to the bracco, and pedules already described (*see* p. 191). The foot-coverings exposing the toes are of Byzantine origin.

This type of costume remained in use from the sixth century to the ninth, and was worn at the Court of Charles the Bald (842–877). During the reign of Dagobert the Great, lavish display was manifested in the costume and accessories of a Court which rivalled in magnificence that of the Eastern emperors.

Frankish chieftain or noble in war dress, fifth to the ninth century. In battle the nobles put on a short jacket of fur over their cloth or linen tunica. These fur jackets had no sleeves, reached to just above the hips, and were very often covered (thickly or thinly) with metal bosses.

Fig. 103 shows a chief wearing, instead of this fur jacket, the lorica of leather, and above it a cuirass of mail composed of linen or leather thickly sewn over with scales of leather or horn, invariably gilded. It was made more secure by leather straps passing over the shoulders and around the chest—a distinctly Teutonic device.

The helmet bears evidence of its Teutonic origin (*see* Fig. 109); but it was also very general for a warrior of this period to go bareheaded.

A large knife or dagger, called a "scramasaxe," was carried on the right side, suspended from the waist-belt. A large sword hung on the left side, by a baldric of leather and studs, or a chain, crossing the breast; these long swords were only used by princes and chiefs.

Fig. 103   Fig. 104

A round convex shield was carried, generally made of the wood of the lime tree, strengthened with a boss, studs, and rim of iron. The shield occasionally had devices painted on it. A spear was nearly always carried in the hand. To these were often added an axe, called a "francisque," either stuck in the belt or carried in the right hand by a loop at the end of the handle.

COSTUME OF THE MIDDLE CLASSES—MEN

An ordinary warrior of this period wore a tunica of cloth with short sleeves, a belt with a buckle of bronze at the waist to carry the scramasaxe, and a pouch containing a firestone, eating-knife, comb, steel, money and similar necessities.

Short bracco, just showing beneath the tunica, left the knees bare. Coarse pedules of white wool on the lower leg, cross-gartered with leather bands, and shoes of leather, completed the dress (*see* Fig. 104).

A spear was carried in one hand, and the francisque in the other. A basin-shaped helmet of metal and leather might be worn, but the head was sometimes uncovered, the hair flowing, and the face clean shaven with the exception of the upper lip.

LOWER CLASSES

The lower order of Franks all wore the drawers of linen or leather similar to Fig. 107C, but unlike other races at this period, they cross-gartered them all the way up the leg to the waist with straps of hide.

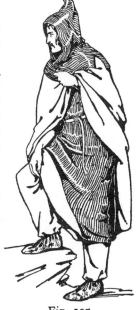

The chest and back were bare, or jackets without sleeves, made of skins laced together with thongs of leather, might be worn.

Hair. The Frankish chronicler, Gregory of Tours, says that the common people were commanded by an express law to cut their hair close round the middle of their foreheads, in contrast to the nobility. The beard and moustache were allowed to grow long.

Fig. 105 shows a man of the people. His tunica is much longer than as hitherto used, and could only have been worn so on exceptional occasions. The Franks were an active people, and garments of this kind were cumbersome. The bracco are not in this case cross-gartered; but the wearer evidently prefers a costume suited to relaxation and comfort in a cold climate. The cloak is surmounted by a cucullus or hood, which descends

Fig. 105

over the shoulders, forming a cape. The shoes are of primitive make, in untanned hide (*see* p. 12).

THE GLOVE

First mentioned on p. 46 as a covering for the hand. Known in very early times. Rebecca put skins on the hands of her younger son to secure for him his elder brother's birthright. Latin: "Manica," meaning a sleeve over the wrists and knuckles. The manica with separate fingers attached was used by the Romans.

Low Latin: Wantus	Celtic: Golof = to cover
Scandinavian: Vottr and Glofar	Anglo-Saxon: Glof

Swedish: Wante   French: Gant

Spanish = Visigothic: Guando   English: Glove, gauntlet

The existence of the name in different languages proves that the glove in its primitive form—a bag—was used by these nations.

During the Merovingian Period the "wantus" came into general use with the wealthy. In shape it was a bag, with a separate compartment for the thumb. It was made of finely-dressed skins with the fur inside, ornamented outside with gold and set with jewels on the back. Sometimes the fur was worn outside, and the glove lined with a warm material. Gloves were used only for cold weather.

Frankish warriors of this period wore bags of skin on their hands as a protection against cold weather when fighting in northern countries. (Continued in Vol. II, p. 89.)

Fig. 106

COSTUME OF THE NOBILITY—WOMEN

The Frankish ladies' costume of the period evolved under the influence of Rome and Constantinople, but was carried out on slightly different lines. It would be the model for any fashionable British lady of the time; but the chaotic disorder in Britain was not conducive to much interest in the vagaries of fashion.

Fig. 106 shows a noble lady of this epoch. She wears the dalmatica with the clavus, confined at the waist by a belt of goldsmiths' work. Over this is draped a semicircular cloak, woven with a gold pattern in circles, and on the head is placed a veil attached to the hair by a large ornamental pin. Reference should be made to Fig. 54, depicting the dress of a Roman lady of the fourth century, from whose costume this Frankish lady has sought inspiration in every particular except the palla contabulatum.

MIDDLE-CLASS WOMEN

For the most part, the costume described under Teutonic freemen's wives, blended with that described under Roman-British, was the prevailing mode for women of the lower orders.

JEWELLERY OF THE FRANKS

At the time of their migration, the Franks, like most of the tribes of Teutonic stock, were well acquainted with the metalworker's craft.

In their early days the Teutons had come under the influence of the Sarmatians, an ancient nomadic and warlike people possessing many characteristics of the Scythians, an older race from whom they are supposed to have descended. From these sources the Teutons acquired a taste for articles of adornment of original character, and a technique in craftsmanship unlike all Classic practice.

When the Franks were established in France, they maintained their national traditions, and their metalwork ornaments were of solid, indeed clumsy, construction. In their design, natural objects were discarded, and high-relief modelling avoided. They covered the whole surface with a diffuse pattern very much akin to Eastern types of work. By the sixth century the work of Frankish goldsmiths compared very favourably with that of Byzantine artificers, and much of it was fashioned on Byzantine lines.

Frankish jewellery owed a great deal to the energy, taste, and practical knowledge of S. Eloi, and it is due to him that the native work of the Merovingian Epoch equalled and often excelled the goldsmiths' work of any other nation.

Mosaic work in stones, glass, and paste was used freely by them for decoration, in a style corresponding with the Byzantine— both came from the same source, Persia.

Crowns. When the long-haired Frankish kings adopted the crown as a royal emblem, they copied it from those worn by contemporary Byzantine emperors. This applies also to the rest of their regalia.

Necklaces and *bracelets* of Teutonic origin gave place to those in fashion at Byzantium, but they retained an individual taste with regard to *fibulæ* and *buckles*.

Fibulæ of the safety-pin type almost lost their original shape. The one shown here is an elaborated version of it.

Fibula

The flat diamond-shaped part which catches the point of the pin is incised with scroll work. The bridge is divided with an opening, and the part which holds the spring of the pin is highly developed and ornate.

The particular design associated with Frankish fibulæ has a semi-circular head with radiating ornaments, and a long end, slightly curved

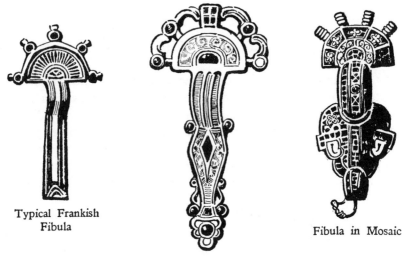

Typical Frankish
Fibula

Fibula in Mosaic

Large Fibula highly ornamented

at the top and then flattened to take the pin. These tall fibulæ are of infinite variety, but all have the semicircular head.

Circular Mosaic Agrafe

Mosaic work and incised scrolls on gold form the decoration of other shorter and wider fibulæ, but these follow the same lines as the preceding examples.

Circular-topped brooches or *agrafes* offered tremendous scope to decorative artists, of which they took full advantage. They were very much used by Frankish nobles of the Merovingian and Carlovingian Epochs for fastening their rich cloaks.

Smaller brooches, intended for pure ornament and not utility, were of various shapes, sizes and designs, a favourite one being a bird. These were minute specimens of enamel or mosaic set with jewels. Small gold ornaments, with pins attached, supposed to represent flies or bees, were used for numerous purposes, chiefly for fastening the veils worn by ladies of this time. Long pins, with quaint ornamental heads, were worn in the hair (*see* Fig. 106).

Brooches

Pin

Buckles were an important and useful item of jewellery, and were used for fastening the waist-belts of the men, both in civil and war dress. They were made in two pieces, the tongue in one and the slot in the other, one of which—the tongue—is shown here. It is of fairly simple design when compared with one of the Mid-Merovingian Epoch. Beside being much larger—six, eight or even ten inches in length—the latter, illustrated here, is very ornate.

Half of Buckle

Half of Buckle
Mid-Merovingian Epoch

GERMANIC PEOPLES

Jutes, Saxons, Angles, and Goths, 200 b.c.–a.d. 768

HISTORICAL INTRODUCTION

At the end of the first century A.D. Tacitus refers to the territory north of the Roman Empire and extending to the Baltic as "Germania."

In the third and second centuries B.C. there was a tribe, called later by the Romans "Teutoni," who inhabited that part of modern Germany which is situated round about the lower Elbe.

Increase of population necessitated an expansion of their territories. In order to achieve this, they entered into a league with the neighbouring Cimbri with the purpose of amalgamating forces for the invasion of northern Italy and expansion of their frontiers. These hordes of fierce barbarians descended the Alps into Illyria, and defeated the Roman army in the year 113 B.C. After various successes, they were completely routed by the Roman general Marius in 101 B.C.

This is the first heard of the Teutons, the ancestors of the Germanic peoples. At a later date they were divided into many tribes, the most important being those enumerated in the Historical Data relating to the Franks (p. 225), together with:

The Vandals, who lived between the Warthe and the Baltic.
The Gepidæ, who lived around the mouth of the Vistula (Danzig).
The Lombards, who lived on the east bank of the lower Elbe between the Elbe and the Oder (Saxony).

An attempt to invade Teutonic territories was made by Roman armies under Varus in A.D. 9, but they suffered a most ignominious defeat at the hands of the Teutons, under the leadership of a chief of the Cherusci named Hermann, or Arminus.

In the fifth century A.D. a great migration of these people into Gaul and Britain took place. Those tribes who remained behind on their native soil founded the Frankish kingdom of "Austrasia." Under Charlemagne (768) it became the principal part of his kingdom, although its name was dropped, and under his successors formed part of Germany proper (840).

(For further historical data of these tribes, *see under* Imperial Rome, the Goths, Byzantine Empire, and the Franks.)

Costume of the Teutonic Tribes—Early Period—Men

In the earliest times, the Teutons, like the Britons, went naked.

At a later stage a primitive dress was worn, consisting of a tunica made of two pieces of skin, joined on the shoulders and from under the arms to the bottom edge. This reached to just above the knees, leaving the arms and legs bare save for one or two bracelets.

On the head, in some cases, they would wear a round cap of skin or fur (*see* Fig. 107).

Later still, they wore coverings of linen or woollen stuff. These consisted of two rectangular-shaped covers, one worn in front and the other behind, covering the body from the shoulders to the knees or lower (*see* Fig. 107A).

In battle-array they presented an awe-striking appearance, chiefs and the most important men wearing on their own heads those of wolves, bears, and oxen (the last with horns), using the rest of the skin as a cloak

Fig. 107   Fig. 107A   Fig. 107B   Fig. 107C

(sagum: *see* Fig. 107B). Others had the spread wings of eagles fastened to iron caps or helmets.

For *arms* they carried spears and knives, and occasionally shields.

At an early period in their history the use of iron was unknown. By degrees they acquired the use of it, and supplies were obtained from the Romans, probably in return for the amber which was found on the shores of the Baltic. They headed their spears with sharp and narrow iron points, and used darts with pointed iron tops, which were thrown in great numbers into the ranks of the advancing foe. Their cavalry were simply armed with a spear, and carried shields of wood or osier. Their *hair* was long and flowing on the shoulders; in colour a light gold or a red gold. It was sometimes worn in the manner shown in Fig. 107C and referred to under Franks of the same period.

During the second century A.D. they adopted a practice of binding pieces of skin under their hitherto bare feet, piercing the edges, and drawing them tightly on the instep with a thong (*see* Celtic Shoe, p. 12). In the century following, the lower part of the calf was bound with skin, a custom which continued until the tenth century.

Costume of the Teutonic Tribes—Early Period—Women

In early days the women followed the example of the men, and used as a garment two rectangular pieces of skin or stuff; but about the be-

Fig. 108   Fig. 108A

ginning of the Christian Era they adopted Roman dress (which was not altogether unlike their own), except that the material used was spun hemp, whereas the Romans used very fine linen, or wool. Sleeves were added to this dress if required, and borders of different colours were used to edge these garments of natural tinted fabric.

They were very fond of ornamenting their dresses with stripes, spots, and even animals and birds, of brilliant hue (*see* Figs. 108 and 108A). The Roman mantle, practically the semicircular cloak, was very popular with these women.

Hair. In general, the hair of these people was fair, varying from pale yellow to red. In early times, it was worn flowing on their shoulders, but later it was parted, wound round the head, and secured by a band of coloured material.

Costume of the Teutonic Tribes—Fifth Century—Men

When the Angles and Saxons under Hengist and Horsa made their first appearance on the shores of Britain they wore, so a chronicler tells us, tunicas of leather and four-cornered helmets; and one chief in command of the Angles had long hair flowing down his shoulders, and wore a wreath of amber beads, with a golden torque about his neck, the skin of a large beast forming his cloak or sagum. It is also related that Hengist himself wore scales fixed all over his leather tunica, and a sagum of fur. He was armed with a piercing weapon—a spear—and carried a shield of split wood.

The costume of Hengist seen in Fig. 109 has been reconstructed from these details. He wears a tunica of flaming red woollen stuff, partly covered by a " lluryg " or cuirass of gilded scales fixed to a leather foundation. It descends well over the hips. A belt of leather, ornamented with iron bosses and pendent pieces, surrounds the hips, and to this smaller weapons could be attached. Over the left shoulder are two leather straps, supporting an ornament and chains of polished iron which suspend the scabbard, made of wood covered with skin, and fitted with bronze blade-slot and terminal. The sword blade is of iron, with a bronze hilt. The skin of a large animal hangs from the shoulders. A spear and a wooden shield elaborately decorated with bronze and polished iron are carried. This type of cuirass and four-cornered helmet of gilded bronze, with comb and the spread wings of eagles attached to flanges, were worn only by the most important chiefs. The legs are bound with leather-studded straps, and primitive skin shoes are worn on the feet.

Fig. 110

Men of importance wore tunicas with very short sleeves, reaching to half-way above the knee. Over this was often worn a deep body-belt of hide, with the hair turned either inside towards the body, or outwards. It extended from under the arms to below the waist, or lower, and was kept in place by straps of leather, passing over the shoulders and buckled in front. The body-belt was decorated, according to the taste of the wearer, with bosses of bronze and ornaments of metal. Over it again, to carry the sword and knife, were often worn both a waist-belt and a hip-belt, sometimes one, sometimes neither (*see* Fig. 110). On the legs, if they were not bare, they wore bracco (a very characteristic part of barbarian costume, including that of the Teutons), tied at the ankles and, later (about the end of the fifth century), cross-gartered up to the

Knives

FIG. 109. HENGIST, CHIEF OF THE ANGLES (A.D. 449)
Some of the details are taken from contemporary records, and some from the researches of German archæologists.

knees or above. This cross-gartering of leather was sometimes interlaced with a cord or small leather thong: no doubt to make the cross-gartering more secure. Shoes were of untanned hide, shaped like those worn by the Celts.

The *hair* was worn long and flowing on the shoulders, and moustaches and beards were allowed to grow long. Beards were held in great esteem among these people, and to touch the beard stood in lieu of an oath. The name "Langobard" (Longbeard) was given to a branch of this tribe on account of the unusual length of their beards. Later, the name developed into Lombards, and the tribe inhabited that part of Italy now called Lombardy.

A *chieftain in battle* would add to this dress a helmet with

horns. Some helmets had side-flaps and were surmounted with a metal representation of an animal, usually a wild boar. He would carry a spear and a shield of wood, which might be covered with hides, bound and ornamented with iron or bronze, or painted in various colours (*see* Fig. 110).

It must be understood, unless otherwise mentioned, that cloaks of cloth or skin could be worn with any of these early costumes, according to the circumstances and taste of the wearer.

The followers of these barbarian chiefs have been described as wearing garments of linen that could be called anything but clean. Possibly this is a reference to the colour, the linen used by the barbarians at that time being of a fawn or putty colour.

Bracco were much worn by the common people, with the sole addition of a cloak of cloth or skin, fastened as usual on the right shoulder. These garments comprised their dress (*see* Fig. 107C).

Costume of the Teutonic Tribes—Fifth Century—Women

The *wives of chieftains* wore a straight garment with short sleeves of a more or less fine material, and over it a sort of supertunic composed of two oblong pieces of stuff, back and front, attached on the shoulders with brooches, and confined at the waist with a belt. The short sleeves of the under-dress showed on the upper arm (*see* Fig. 111). Round the hips was worn a girdle of leather, very richly decorated with metal ornaments,

Drinking vessel & jug.

many of which were suspended by small chains from the belt, besides various articles for personal use, such as pouch, knives, scissors, keys, etc.

The *hair* was allowed to flow on the shoulders, and great ladies would wear fillets of gold or silver twisted wire round their heads, with wide metal collars and necklaces at their throats. They wore ear-rings, and on their arms bracelets of gold twisted work.

More often than not, they used mantles of fur, particularly the long-haired skin of the bear, lined with a brilliant colour, or cloth cloaks draped from their shoulders, fastened with ornamental bosses.

Fig. 111   Fig. 112

MIDDLE-CLASS WOMEN

The women of the middle class would either wear the same style of dress, not so elaborate or costly, or they would have a skirt of cloth, kept in place round the waist and hips with a broad leather belt, ornamented with bronze bosses, and a short jacket of cloth, with short sleeves fastened down the front with clasps and brooches of bronze (Fig. 112).

The *hair* was worn flowing on the shoulders, or else braided in plaits, hanging on either side of the face.

The *peasant women* were clothed in a style similar to those of Celtic Britain.

COSTUME OF THE GOTHS

Sidonius Apollinaris mentions that the most important garment of the Goths was a tunica of home-spun linen, in its natural colour—fawn. It reached half-way down the thigh, and was ornamented at the edge with a band of bright colour or fur. These tunicas would be cut on the plan of Diagram 13 with long sleeves to the wrist, sometimes long enough to extend over the hand for warmth. When not so required, the sleeve was pushed back in folds or rucks over the wrist. The tunica sometimes took the shape of a short overcoat, wrapped across the front and belted. Hoods were frequently worn, in shape something between

Fig. 113

Fig. 113A

the Phrygian cap and the Roman cucullus. On the legs were bracco, tied at the ankles and, drawn over them, ankle boots of hide, secured round the ankles by thongs (see Fig. 113).

Goths adopt the bracco. In the land of their origin, the Goths were not in the habit of covering up the legs. They appeared in the civilised world at a time when the barbarian had acquired considerable culture, and was a barbarian only in name. In accordance with barbarian dictates in fashion, they adopted the characteristic bracco. When they migrated into Gaul, they retained their national views on dress, tempered to some extent by Roman ideas. As time progressed, they became more and more Romanised, adopting fashions first from Rome and, in the fifth century, from Constantinople. When Theodoric the Great became master of Italy, they assumed the dress of the Italians in every detail, except that they retained the bracco. Short bracco were worn by the Goths and Langobards, as well as by the Franks. They were like our modern knickerbockers, and copied from the hip-coverings worn by soldiers of Roman garrisons stationed in cold climates. Below these, the legs were covered with pieces of linen or leather, resembling gaiters, cross-gartered with straps of leather, often studded with metal—a fashion inherited from the Franks and described under that section.

Fig. 113A is from an ivory portrait of an Italian nobleman of the sixth century, and shows the costume worn by the Gothic nobles attending Theodoric the Great after his assumption of the title of King of Italy. The tunica is entirely Byzantine, as worn in Rome at that date, and the same applies to the cloak. The distinguishing features of Gothic nationality are the long-curled hair with beard, the bracco, and the curious leg decoration, consisting of pedules cross-barred with cord.

Furs of different kinds—otter, marten, sable, lamb, goat, and even cats and dogs—were used as trimming to the tunicas, or pieced together to form the sagum. Important personages had these skins made into tunicas with or without sleeves. These skin tunicas or coats reached to the hips, sometimes lower, and were often elaborately decorated with metal ornaments, very finely worked.

Arms carried by the Goths included the sword, spear, bow and arrow, and knife. Shields, oval or hexagonal in shape, were generally made of wicker-work covered with hide, and made more substantial by metal fittings.

JEWELLERY OF THE TEUTONS

As has been stated, the Teutons were skilled metalworkers, and their inheritance of craftsmanship is mentioned in connection with Frankish jewellery. They made their weapons (undecorated) and their sword-hilts, scabbards, helmets and ornaments from iron introduced to them by the Romans. Bronze was also much used, and these metals were treated in a very artistic manner. Their designs were very similar to those employed by the Celts and Northmen, and show very intricate interlaced patterns, combined with grotesque and contorted figures of men and animals associated with Norse mythology. Their articles of personal adornment can scarcely be called jewellery. Head-bands, necklaces, torques, bracelets, and the numerous small ornaments of utility attached to the girdle of the Hausfrau were forged from iron, which was highly polished and had the appearance of steel or even oxidised silver, or from bronze burnished to look like gold. Gold was rare, being reserved for the ornaments of chiefs of the highest rank. Mosaic work, described earlier, was frequently employed for decoration.

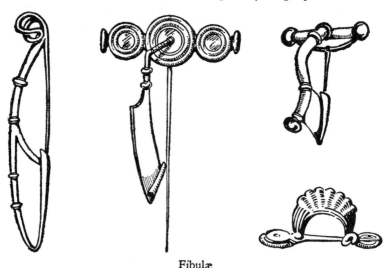

Fibulæ

Fibulæ were very graceful in form, many of them following the safety-pin type. The T-shaped fibula composed of three circular plaques on a bar has the catch for the pin-point rigid. The pin and catch are bent together for fastening. The smaller one is made of bone or ivory with bronze knobs, and the pin is fixed to a spring. The arch fibula was frequently worn for fastening parts of clothing, but was of small size and usually made of bronze. The pin was riveted at one end, and a twisted wire kept the point in place at the other.

Clasps were very generally used as fasteners for belts or the sagum, besides many ornamental discs, perforated with patterns, and often with separate pieces

Clasp

of metal attached, for holding belts and chains. Ornamental plaques, to serve all purposes of decoration, either hung on chains or were used

Ornamental Disc and Plaque

as tops to circular brooches, and were of many designs worked in various ways. This one shows the eight-legged horse of Woden, executed in enamel, incisions, or repoussé. Many other objects of personal adornment, of great barbaric beauty, were made by these skilled Teutonic craftsmen. An ornament of curious shape is seen at the neck of the Varangian Guard (*see* Fig. 86), and many such were hung about the persons of superior chiefs.

Bracelets of great variety were worn by both sexes on their arms, and by some important men also on their ankles. The spiral form was very popular. Sometimes the ends were twisted spiral fashion into a solid circular piece (*see* Fig. 7),

Bracelet

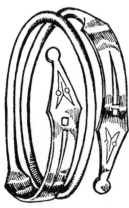

and often the round wire was flattened at the ends and worked to represent animals' or snakes' heads. Many bracelets were so massive that they had the effect of a vambrace or gauntlet (*see* Fig. 109).

Necklaces were chiefly composed of amber beads or polished pebbles. The more uncivilised people living in remote parts still used the teeth of wild animals.

Bracelet

Note.—It is interesting to see that in many details of dress, ornament and design, the Teutonic tribes closely resembled the Celts of Britain in pre-Christian times.

LIST OF AUTHORITIES CONSULTED FOR CHAPTER VI

THE BRITONS
F. W. Fairholt
S. R. Gardiner
J. R. Planche
York Powell

THE FRANKS
Agathias
Anuerin
Sidonius Apollinaris
M. Barrera
Dr. Brewer
Eginhard
Edward Gibbon
S. Baring Gould
Arthur Hassall

Fr. Hottenroth
Paul Lacroix
Deacon Paul
C. H. Read
Ary Renan
Strzygowski
Gregory of Tours

THE TEUTONS
Sidonius Apollinaris
Edward Gibbon
S. Baring Gould
Thomas Hodgkin
Fr. Hottenroth
T. W. Rolleston.

CHAPTER VII

THE ANGLO-SAXONS AND THE ENGLISH

TOGETHER WITH

THE FRANKS OF THE CARLOVINGIAN EPOCH AND THE CAPETIAN DYNASTY

AND

THE GERMANS OF THE CARLOVINGIAN AND SAXON DYNASTIES

FROM A.D. 700 to 1066

CONTEMPORARY EMPERORS AND KINGS

	ENGLAND	FRANCE	GERMANY
752		Pepin the Short	
758	Offa the Mighty		
768		Charlemagne	
800			Charlemagne
802	Eagberht II.		
814		Louis le Debonnaire	Louis le Debonnaire
837	Æthelwulf		
840			Lothaire
843		Charles the Bald	
855			Louis II.
857	Æthelbald		
860	Æthelbert		
866	Æthelred I.		
872	Ælfred the Great		
875			Charles the Bald
877		Louis the Stammerer	
879		Louis III. and Carloman II.	
880			Charles III. le Gros
884		Charles le Gros	
887			Arnulf
888		Eudes Comte de Paris	
898		Charles the Simple	
899			Louis the Child END OF CARLOVINGIAN DYNASTY IN GERMANY
901	Eadward the Elder		
911			Otto, Duke of Saxony, and Conrad, Duke of Franconia.
918			Henry the Fowler, first of Saxon Dynasty
922		Robert	
923		Rudolf of Burgundy	

ENGLAND	FRANCE	GERMANY
925 Æthelstan		
936	Louis IV.	Otto I. the Great
940 Eadmund I.		
946 Eadred		
954	Lothaire	
955 Eadwy		
958 Eadgar		
973		Otto II. the Bloody
975 Eadward the Martyr		
979 Æthelred II. the Unready		
983		Otto III. the Red
986	Louis the Indolent	
	END OF CARLOVINGIAN	
	DYNASTY IN FRANCE	
987	Hugh Capet	
996	Robert the Pious	
1002		Henry II. the Holy
		END OF SAXON DYNASTY
1013 Sweyn Forkbeard the Dane		
1014 Canute the Mighty		
1015 Æthelred restored		
1016 Eadmund Ironside		
1016 Canute again		
1024		Conrad II.
1031	Henry I.	
1035 Harold I.		
1039 Hardicanute		Henry III. the Black
1042 Eadward the Confessor		
1056		Henry IV. (aged 10 in 1066)
1060	Philip I.	
1066 Harold II.		

THE ANGLO-SAXON PERIOD

HISTORICAL DATA OF THE ANGLO-SAXONS, THE FRENCH AND THE GERMANS
A.D. 700–1066

BRITAIN

A.D. 700. At the opening of this period the kingdoms of Northumbria, Mercia and Wessex were pre-eminent.

A.D. 716. Æthelbald succeeded his uncle, Penda, as king of Mercia and built up a great power. Bede, the monk of Jarrow, born 673. The greatest scholar of his time. Wrote *Ecclesiastical History of England*. Died 735.

S. Boniface, "the Apostle of Germany," born at Crediton in Devonshire about 680. Archbishop of Mainz (752). Murdered by the pagan Frisians in 755.

Offa succeeded Eagberht I. and became the most powerful king of Mercia. He brought Britain into close relationship with the Continental powers. Alcuin, a highly cultivated scholar, born at York (735), of a British noble family, was sent by Offa with other scholars to the Court of Charlemagne. Offa died 796.

Cenwulf, the last important king of Mercia (796–815).

A.D. 787. The first of a succession of raids made by the Northmen. For about one hundred years the West Saxon kings continuously endeavoured to check the ravages of these Vikings or sea-rovers.

802. Eagberht II., king of Wessex, brought the whole of Britain (with the exception of Wales and part of Cornwall) under his sole subjection in 829. With this date the Heptarchy may be said to have ended; but the old seven kingdoms were not thoroughly welded together until the Norman Conquest. King Eagberht, by Order in Council held at Winchester in 829, called his country "Angle-lond" (Saxon for "country") or "England."

GERMANY

By the Treaty of Verdun in 843 the empire of Louis le Debonnaire was divided between his three sons. Louis "the German" became king of Germany; Charles le Chauve, of France; and Lothaire, of Italy.

ENGLAND

871. Ælfred, the son of Æthelwulf and grandson of Eagberht. He spent some part of his youth at Rome. Many years of his glorious reign were spent warring against the Danes. He rehabilitated London, and laid the foundations of the British Navy.

GERMANY

The final separation of Germany, France and Italy took place in 887.

FRANCE

France was reduced to the narrow territory between the Loire and Seine. Ravages by Northmen and Saracens on the coasts of Germany, France and Italy.

In 888 Eudes Comte de Paris was raised on the buckler in reward for his defence of Paris.

GERMANY

A.D. 899. A wild race of Magyars or Avars invaded Germany. They were called Hungarians by the Germans, who believed them to be descendants of the Huns.

A.D. 900. At the beginning of the tenth century Germany was divided into five independent territories, ruled by dukes, who were also appointed to offices in the emperor's household:

Saxony with Thuringia
Franconia, whose Duke became Chief Sewer
Swabia   ,,   ,,   ,,   Chief Butler
Bavaria   ,,   ,,   ,,   Master of the Horse
Lorraine   ,,   ,,   ,,   Grand Chamberlain

The death of Louis the Child in 911 ended the Carlovingian Dynasty in Germany.

FRANCE

A.D. 912. Rollo the Northman or Norwegian was allowed to settle in France, and established the Duchy of Normandy.

ENGLAND

A.D. 925. Æthelstan was famous for his deeds, and his friendship was sought eagerly by many foreign kings and princes. He received from the ruler of the Franks many relics (including a piece of the True Cross), which were deposited at Malmesbury Abbey.

GERMANY

A.D. 933. The savage Hungarians ravished the borderlands of the empire. They were expert horsemen, and to encounter them on equal terms Henry the Fowler greatly strengthened his cavalry. He instituted meetings of his subjects who were knights and gentlemen for the practice of military exercises, partly for training and partly for pleasure. These gatherings proved very popular and were the origin of the *tournament*.

The Hungarians made a formidable attack, but were defeated at Merseburg on August 10, 955. The Holy Lance of S. Maurice was brought into action on this occasion.

ENGLAND

The Great Dunstan; born at Glastonbury, the son of a wealthy Thegn; he became a Court favourite with Æthelstan, Eadmund and Eadred. He took the cowl, and was celebrated for his great learning, accomplishments and skill at handicrafts. He became abbot of Glastonbury in 943, but was deprived of his various offices by Eadwy. At the accession of Eadgar, he was appointed Archbishop of Canterbury, and became chief minister during the reigns of Eadgar and of Eadward the Martyr—the young king who was assassinated at Corfe Castle by order of his step-mother. Dunstan died in 988.

FRANCE

The reigns of Charlemagne's successors were disturbed by constant civil warfare. This period is also conspicuous for a dearth of learned men. During the tenth century every province had its own ruler, whose authority was supreme.

Burgundy was ruled by a king; Aquitaine, Normandy and Brittany, by dukes; Champagne, Flanders and Toulouse, by counts.

A.D. 987. End of the Carlovingian Dynasty. Hugh became king, but was never crowned or invested with royalty. He was also abbot of S. Martin of Tours, and his costume as such was a monk's frock, cope and cowl. From the last garment, *cappetus*, he derived his surname of "Capet." He was the first of the Capetian Dynasty.

The Duchy of Gayenne and Countships of Roussillon, Auvergne, Vermaudois, and Anjou were now created. From this time German traditions and nationality lost all hold on France. The Feudal System was definitely established.

ENGLAND

The Danes made repeated attacks upon England during the years 990, 994 and 997. A great massacre of these marauders took place in 1002, but in 1013 they were triumphant, and their king, Sweyn Forkbeard, became king of England.

Prior to this latter date (1003) the most distinguished man of the civilised world at that time had died—Pope Sylvester II. (930-1003). A Frenchman by birth, he was famous for his wisdom and talent.

A.D. 1014. Canute, son of Sweyn Forkbeard, succeeded as king of Denmark and England. The death of Eadmund Ironside left him sole ruler (1016). Under his excellent rule of mercy, wisdom and judgment, England recovered from the lengthy period of disorder. He married Emma, daughter of the Duke of Normandy, and widow of Æthelred II. the Unready.

GERMANY

The founder of the house of Guelph lived in the reign of the Emperor Conrad II.

ENGLAND

A.D. 1042. Eadward the Confessor, son of Æthelred and Emma. He lived in exile at the Norman Court until called to the throne on the death of Hardicanute, his half-brother. He married Eadgyth, daughter of Godwine, Earl of Wessex. His Court was frequented by Norman nobles, to whom he showed great favour, and many of whom he appointed to offices in Church and State.

In A.D. 1051, Duke William of Normandy, his cousin, visited him at Westminster, and a compact was made between them that William should succeed to the crown.

A.D. 1066. Harold II., the last king of the English, son of Godwine, Earl of Wessex, and of Gytha, a Danish lady. Pierced in the right eye by an arrow at Senlac, and died October 14, 1066.

ARTS AND CRAFTS

THE art of the Anglo-Saxons is not characterised by any marked individuality: artists of these times were imitative rather than creative. The limited number of works of art brought to England during the early part of this period inspired, amongst primitive Anglo-Saxon craftsmen, a desire to produce similar works, and the results of their efforts were willingly acquired for their own use by the nobility and wealthy.

Monuments and crosses appear to have been the first objects to which the newly-awakened sense of artistic appreciation was applied. These show intricate geometrical and interlaced designs, partly Celtic and partly Byzantine in character.

10th Cent.

Glass-blowing was practised by Teutonic tribes, but their work was of an inferior kind. The Anglo-Saxons were by no means expert in this craft, even although Benedict Biscop provided them with excellent samples of foreign make. In the eighth century glass-blowers were brought from France to teach them the craft. Thereafter they were able to produce glass for windows, vessels, and other domestic utensils.

Drinking vessel.

The Teutons were proficient in *metal work* and in the *goldsmiths' craft,* and this ability was inherited by the Anglo-Saxons. Their bronze, enamel, inlay, silver and gold work compares very favourably with that produced on the Continent. A carved whale-bone casket, known as "The Franks' Casket," of Anglo-Saxon workmanship, dating from about A.D. 700 and now in the British Museum, shows primitive decoration and figures in costume. It is a creditable effort in this branch of art.

Cup, temp. Alfred.

The Teutons were also excellent *carpenters,* and among other things made moderately good boats, capable at least of conveying numbers of heavily-equipped warriors across the North Sea. This legacy of talent in the Anglo-Saxons proved very useful when Ælfred the Great inaugurated England's navy.

Great progress was made in *architecture,* stone now taking the place of wood in the building of churches. Examples of Anglo-Saxon architecture are to be seen to-day at Monkwearmouth and Jarrow, co. Durham; Bradford-on-Avon, Wilts; Sompting, Sussex; Earls Barton, Northants; and other places.

The art of *illuminating manuscripts* began in England in the early eighth century, inspired by various religious books illustrated by Byzantine artists, which were brought to this country, notably by Benedict Biscop. Comparison will show, in almost every detail, the very great influence of Greek art upon the work of the Anglo-Saxons. The *Lindisfarne Gospels* and the *Durham Book* are clearly Byzantine in treatment, especially the former, yet they were executed by Anglo-Saxon artists.

Literature is almost entirely represented by epic poetry; another mode of expression inherited from the Teutons, who were renowned for their sagas. The *Beowulf,* dating about the eighth century, is the most important, and follows very closely in style and construction the earlier sagas of the Teutons. Cynewulf (born about 720; died 800) was a Northumbrian who chiefly composed religious poetry. In prose, the *Anglo-Saxon Chronicle* is the most important work. Scanty records of Britain's earlier history were collected together by King Ælfred and compiled under his superintendence at Winchester. He appointed officials to carry on the duty of recording future events.

By this time (about 800) the use of the Celtic and Latin languages in Britain had practically ceased. They were almost entirely replaced by the numerous dialects spoken by the conquering Angles, Jutes, and Saxons; and it was a blend of these from which the root-stock of English in due course took form.

Incorporated bodies of persons called "guilds," from the Anglo-Saxon "gild," a money payment, came into existence during this period. They were formed for religious purposes, each member contributing a fixed sum to the common fund for paying fines, singing masses for souls, for burial, and for assisting others of the guild in times of need. Frith guilds were afterwards formed by bodies of artisans to protect themselves from violence and theft.

7th Cent.

REGAL COSTUME AND THE NOBILITY, A.D. 700–1066

The year A.D. 700 is a suitable date for opening this chapter. It was a period of comparative relaxation after the many years of strife described under the Dark Ages. A resuscitation of the arts and civilisation had taken place in Britain, following the gradual absorption of the various races who had invaded and ravished the land during the preceding three centuries.

Dating from this time also, Roman influence on dress in Western Europe entirely disappeared. Fashions adopted by those of great wealth and position were inspired by Byzantium, and the materials of which their clothes were made were supplied by Byzantine manufacturers.

Garments have been referred to in Chapters III. and IV. by their Latin names. Henceforth the Anglo-Saxon and French names will be used for the same garments.

Latin		Anglo-Saxon	French
Tunica	(Dia. 13)	Tunic (Dias. 22, 23, 24)	Cotte
Colobium		Sherte	Camise
Dalmatica	(Dia. 15)	Dalmatic (Dia. 18)	Dalmatique
Bracco	(Dia. 3)	Bracco	Braies
Hosa		Hose	Hose
Pedules		Socca	Socque
Stola		Gunna	Gown (Dia. 25)
		(*Celtic :* Gwn)	
Sagum		Cloke	Manteau
		Poell (Dia. 21)	
Lorica		Corium	Cuirasse
		(*Saxon :* Lluryg)	("Cuir" = leather)

In Gaul, or as it was now called, France, the Merovingian Dynasty came to an end. For 170 years the mayors of the Palace had virtually ruled, but in 751 Pepin ascended the throne as undisputed monarch. He was descended from a long line of ancestors—the Arnulfings, a noble family of the Frankish kingdom of Austrasia. Important to him, and to the future of his country, is the fact that he received the title of "Patricius of the Romans," *i.e.* Protector of the Romans and the Pope. He died in 768, and was succeeded by a son destined to be the most important man in Christendom during the latter part of the eighth and beginning of the ninth century:

Carl—Charles—Carlos Magnus—or Charlemagne.

He became joint king of the Franks with his brother Carloman in 768 and, at Carloman's death in 771, sole ruler.

Appearance of Charlemagne. A description of him is given by his secretary Eginhard (born 770 in Austrasia; died 844). A man of commanding presence and unusually tall—he was nearly seven feet—with large and lustrous eyes, a long nose, and a fine head of yellow hair; grave, dignified and moderate in his taste for dress, except in later life, when keeping Imperial State. Then his ambition was to imitate Constantine the Great. Not content with that, he even tried to surpass him in his patronage of the arts. A man of high culture such as this must have been a model for all well-dressed men of his epoch throughout the civilised world, and it is fortunate that Eginhard has given us a description of his dress.

Fig. 114

Ordinary dress of Charlemagne. He says that on ordinary occasions Charlemagne adopted the costume of his nation, the Franks—very simple, and as worn by the people. A description of the costume is as follows (*see* Fig. 114): A linen under-tunic was worn next the skin, with braies of the same material cross-gartered up to the knee with thongs of leather, often coloured and sometimes studded with metal. On his feet he had shoes of leather or cloth. Shoes were now of better workmanship than formerly, and were sometimes worked and set with stones. The over-tunic of linen or cloth was edged with a border of coloured silk or silver, with sleeves cut rather wide at the armhole, but narrowing at the wrist. This tunic was confined at the waist by a belt, the tunic slightly pouching over it in front; and at his side hung the ever-present sword. On the shoulders was draped a short semicircular cloke of cloth, bordered and lined with silk (in the winter with fur), fastened on the right shoulder by an ornamental agrafe. A collar of gold, set with stones, was sometimes worn round the neck. For extra

warmth a short jacket of otter skin or marten, without sleeves, was added
to this dress. (The fashion of wearing these little jackets of fur was
dropped by the nobility towards the end of the Merovingian Period,
and they were used only by the lower classes; but Charlemagne brought
them back into fashion again for a short time.) On his head he wore a
round cap, something like a Scot's bonnet, of cloth, with an embroidered
head-band, and raised in front with an ornament.

Charlemagne was on very friendly terms with Britain. He owed
much to King Offa for the introduction to Alcuin, the scholar who
inspired a literary revival at the Carlovingian Court, and in return
Charlemagne made costly presents to the British monasteries. He also
made a gift of two silk tunics to Offa (790), from which we gather that
the British king, on occasion, was well-dressed.

During this time (787–802) Charlemagne entertained at his Court
a royal refugee from one of the kingdoms of the Heptarchy—*Eagberht*;
and it is stated that Eagberht accompanied the King of the Franks to
Rome for his coronation in 800. When Eagberht was called to his
kingdom of Wessex two years later, there is no doubt that he took
back with him a wardrobe of the latest Frankish and Byzantine cut.
This, of course, helped to stimulate the tastes of his subjects for more
up-to-date garments.

Charlemagne as emperor. Charlemagne had already received the
silver crown of Germany at Aachen (Aix-la-Chapelle) in 768; and in
774 he was crowned at Milan with the Iron Crown of Lombardy. In
December 800, Charlemagne proceeded to Rome, accompanied by a
large retinue of chieftains and nobles, to settle a controversy between
Pope Leo III. and his enemies. To celebrate the occasion, High Mass
was held at the ancient basilica of S. Peter on Christmas Day, and, as
the king knelt at the altar, the Pope, either spontaneously or, as some
suggest, with premeditation, set the crown of the Cæsars upon his head
and hailed him:

Romanorum Imperator semper Augustus,

words which carried a noble tradition and were acclaimed by a huge
concourse of peoples.

The Empire of Rome, which had died at the hands of one German,
was resurrected for another as THE HOLY ROMAN EMPIRE. Emperors,
by election, continued to rule this empire until it was dissolved in 1806,
when Francis I. of Austria formally resigned the crown.

State dress of Charlemagne. On State occasions Charlemagne,
with a degree of reluctance, arrayed himself in all the magnificent
paraphernalia befitting an emperor (*see* Fig. 115). His Imperial robes

consisted of a tunic with tight sleeves and bordered with gold, and over it the dalmatic, now worn as a garment symbolising his protection of the Church. It is of white silk or linen, with heavy borders in scarlet and gold, and belted at the waist by a gold and jewelled girdle from which is suspended the State sword. Over the dalmatic is worn the lorum and the paludamentum. They are put on by first placing the lorum in position in front at the waist, and over the right shoulder. Before proceeding further, the front top corner of the paludamentum is temporarily fixed on the right shoulder, leaving the back part hanging at the back. The lorum is then arranged in the usual manner (see Fig. 70). The back part of the paludamentum is brought across the back, over the lorum, and attached to the front corner on the right shoulder by a jewelled ornament. The paludamentum is of a very rich brocade manufactured at Constantinople,[1] and the design is composed of large floriated circles in green, blue and gold, enclosing green and gold elephants. The circular designs between the larger circles are in green, blue and gold leaves and scrolls, the whole upon a ground of brilliant vermilion, and bordered with heavy gold. The lorum is in cloth of gold, brocaded in squares, with jewels—rubies or emeralds—set in each. The crown is made up of eight plates of gold, profusely set with rubies, emeralds, pearls and diamonds, most of them in clear settings. Four of the plates have enamel centre subjects surrounded by jewels, and all are hinged together. The front and back plates are a little taller than the rest, and each is rounded at the top. On the front plate stands a jewelled cross.[2] The sceptre and orb are carried. The shoes are of scarlet leather embroidered with gold squares, with a gold band up the front set with three emeralds and finished above the instep by a trefoil tongue. They are laced close to the ankle.

In the year 1165 Charlemagne's tomb under the dome of the cathedral[3] of Aix-la-Chapelle was opened. The body of the emperor was found seated upon an ivory throne, clad in his Imperial robes. The crown, already described, was on his head, and he was girt with the great sword of State, the book of the Gospels lay on his knees, and a pilgrim's pouch was by his side. The Holy Lance of S. Maurice was held in his hand.[4] Fragments of the paludamentum which hung from

[1] By Peter, the superintendent of the Imperial factory.
[2] The arch was added at a later period. The crown is now in the Imperial Treasury at Vienna.
[3] The basilica built by Charlemagne. He used much material, pillars, etc., taken from ruined temples in Greece and Rome, and marbles from Ravenna. The building was the first in the new style called Romanesque.
[4] Either this or the one used by Henry II. (see Fig 119) must have been a replica.

FIG. 115. THE EMPEROR CHARLEMAGNE IN FULL STATE DRESS (A.D. 800)

The costume is modelled on the Court dress of Byzantine emperors. The design in the background is from a contemporary source.

the shoulders of the dead emperor exist to-day, and the design of the brocade described above and illustrated in Fig. 115 is taken from one of these pieces.[1]

The portrait of Charlemagne in his Imperial robes, painted by Albert Dürer, and now at Nuremberg, although sixteenth century in treatment, is very interesting, as the costume may have been painted from many original details to which Dürer had access, since disappeared.

The dress of *Anglo-Saxon kings* is exemplified in the three Figs. 116, 116A and 116B. The tunics vary slightly in decoration, but are similar in shape. For their cut, refer-ence must be made to Diagrams 19 and 22. The cloke, called "Poell" in Anglo-Saxon, is semicircular and worn after the manner of the paludamentum. The leg-coverings of each figure differ. Fig. 116 wears hose, and above them is seen the bottom of the under-tunic. Simple shoes are worn on the feet.

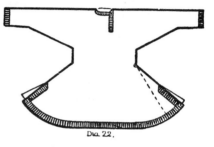

Dia. 22.

This is the costume of a king of the ninth century and the style worn by Ælfred the Great. The statue to this hero at Winchester shows him in war-dress, armed with helmet, sword, and shield, and is an excellent authority.

Fig. 116A is King Æthelstan, taken from an illuminated MS. in the library of Corpus Christi College, Cambridge. His tunic is yellow, bordered with gold; his cloke indigo, and his hose, with foot part combined, are red-orange.

Fig. 116B represents King Eadgar, whose dress is very similar, but his legs are bare at the knee: the lower parts swathed with bands of coloured or gilded leather, tied with elaborate knots, and shoes, cut in a V at the sides, on his feet.

The crowns show the gradual development from the Byzantine style (*see* Fig. 116) to the more floral variety which came later into general use.

Dress of Anglo-Saxon nobles. Four noblemen are shown in Figs. 117, 117A, 117B and 117C. The early Anglo-Saxon name for a noble of the highest rank was "Æthel," and the title of "Ætheling," meaning "King's Kin," was bestowed on those of royal blood. "Thegns" (Anglo-Saxon: "Thegnian" = to serve), and later "Gesith," were nobles of large estate, and were often in personal attendance on the king. Later still, the name "Eorl" meant the same thing.

[1] Pronounced by some authorities to be of the tenth or eleventh century!

Fig. 116   Fig. 116A   Fig. 116B

Fig. 117   Fig. 117A   Fig. 117B   Fig. 117C

This title was also conferred upon the headman—Ealdorman = older or elderman, a civil magistrate (modern alderman), especially of a shire. When Canute came to the throne, the name "Eorl" was changed into "Earl" (Scandinavian: "Yarl"; Danish: "Jarl"). A "Staller" was also a noble holding the office in the royal household equivalent to the marshal of a later date.

Fig. 117 is a thegn of the ninth century in war-dress. Comparison with Figs. 97, 98 and 103 will make the development clear, and the Frankish influences will be noticed. The legs are clothed in hose, socca and shoes.

Fig. 117A shows a head-dress worn by Anglo-Saxons. It is a Phrygian cap, with an upstanding brim.

Fig. 117B is a young eorl of the tenth century, wearing a *new-shaped tunic*. It was during this century that the skirt part was worn fuller, an effect produced by it being cut more on the circle at the sides, from a centre at the waist-line (*see* Diagram 23). This gave the folds a radiating effect, and the edge a zig-zag appearance. Often the lower ends of the side seams were left open for about eight to ten inches, to give freer action. This tunic shows a decorated opening at the neck where it is buttoned or laced. It is bound at the

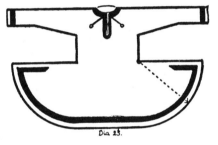

Dia 23.

waist by a belt, not always seen, as the material of the upper part bulged over it. Waist-belts were not always worn, and, if none were used, the tunic was fastened so tight at the waist-level that the looser material above slightly bulged, and gave the same effect. This young eorl is in the act of fastening his cloke on the right shoulder by means of an agrafe. His legs are covered with hose, and socca all in one with the foot-piece, ornamented at the top with a decorated band. Clokes were of three shapes. That in most general use was the semicircular. Others were oblong, and some square. With very few exceptions they were all fastened on the right shoulder and draped over the left arm.

Fig. 117C is an ealdorman, one of the wise men, or chiefs temporal and spiritual, who formed the highest "husting" or council of the king, called the "witena-gemot."

He is wearing a long tunic, quite exceptional among Anglo-Saxons, with decorations at the knee. Over this is a cloke, fastened in front, and on his head a pointed cap peculiar to his office.

Dress of French kings, eleventh century. During his reign, Charlemagne promulgated many severe edicts against luxury in dress, and had a great aversion to clothes of a foreign nature; but his successors, kings of France and emperors of Germany, had different opinions, and dressed almost as extravagantly and richly as the emperors at Constantinople.

The rich silken fabrics and brocades of gold and many colours which gave distinction to the Court costume of Carlovingian and Capetian courtiers, all came from the "Gynæzeum" (factories and workshops for weaving silk) on the shores of the Bosphorus, as did also various items for its trimming and decoration. The costumes of kings and princes of France during the tenth and eleventh centuries therefore differed considerably from those of the Anglo-Saxons.

Fig. 118 shows one of the early kings of the Capetian Dynasty—Robert the Pious. A richly embroidered tunic descending to the ankles is worn (often over another which showed only below the over-tunic). The circular decoration, of course, has its origin in the segmentæ of the Empire Period in Rome. The cloke having lost its original shape, as shown in Diagram 17, is a semicircle (*see* Diagram 21), fastened on the right shoulder with a jewelled agrafe. The crown is Byzantine, with the exception of the floral decoration just coming into favour.

Eadward the Confessor had a great partiality for Norman manners, customs, and costume. Fig. 118 shows the type of dress he very likely wore when he came to the English throne.

A throne of the ninth, tenth, eleventh and twelfth centuries. The seat or throne is typical of those in use at the time, and variations of it are seen in illuminated MSS. of the ninth, tenth, eleventh and twelfth centuries. It is made of wood entirely overlaid with gold plate, and decorated with enamels. Many examples are profusely decked with gems and jewels. They are obviously copied from Byzantine work.

Cushions were shaped like a modern bolster, with embroideries at the ends.

Origin of the Fleur de Lys. Attention is called to the increasing use during this period of the "Fleur de Luce" as an ornament. Heraldry was scarcely thought of, and was not introduced until the middle of the twelfth century. The design is derived from two originals—the conventionalised *Iris blossom* and the outline of the *spearhead* javelin or lance (*see* Figs. 114 and 117). In the early days of the Frankish Monarchy it was the custom at a royal investiture to place a reed (the practice may

FIG. 118. A FRENCH KING OF THE CARLOVINGIAN OR CAPETIAN DYNASTIES

The seat, of gold and enamels, is typical of those in use from the ninth to the twelfth centuries.

Fig. 119. THE EMPEROR HENRY II., THE HOLY
(1002–1024)

(*see* p. 265)

be noted earlier in the act of placing a reed in the hand of Our Lord), with an iris blossom, in the hand of the king, in place of a sceptre. It has been stated already that the lance was held by a Frankish king to symbolise his headship or chieftainship of a warrior clan.

Dress of German emperor, eleventh century. Fig. 119 is the Emperor Henry II., the Holy (1002–1024), in full State. The tunic is Byzantine, but the side seam is cut at right angles under the armpit, giving the effect seen in the illustration. His cloke is obviously the paludamentum. The socca or hose are embroidered, and the shoes are cut into straps which all join to a band at the ankle, and are a reversion, although of superior workmanship, to the type of primitive skin shoe worn by the Celts, Teutons and Early Franks.

The crown is a circular band about three inches in height, sur-mounted by four leaves and an arch springing from the front to the back. This is a new detail added about this time to Imperial and Regal diadems.[1]

The State sword is held in the left hand, and the Holy Lance of S. Maurice (*see* p. 187), enshrining the nail from the True Cross in an enamelled reliquary, is held in the right.

Dress of German noble, eleventh century. A German noble of the eleventh century is shown in Fig. 120. The tunic is cut like Diagram 22, but with this exception—the bottom edge is quite straight and meets the side seam at an acute angle. This arrangement produced a much longer seam at the side, which hangs in a long point. The cloke can be distinguished easily as a semicircle by the angle at the bottom corners, in contrast with that of the paludamentum, which would be much more pointed. Hose and socca with em-broidered bands are worn on the legs. The head-dress is quite new in shape; it has a domed embroidered crown, not unlike the Byzantine (see Fig. 89).

Fig. 120

Canute the Mighty is represented in Fig. 121. The second son of Sweyn, he succeeded him as King of Denmark and England in 1014. He created an empire comprising, besides these two nations, the Wendish coast of the Oder and Norway, and the Scots owed him allegiance.

---

[1] The arch seen on Charlemagne's crown may have been added at this time.

FIG. 119. THE EMPEROR HENRY II., THE HOLY (1002–1024)
He is holding the Lance of S. Maurice in one hand, and the sword of State in the other
The details of costume and decoration in the background are from Henry's missal.

Bloodthirsty and savage in youth, he became a mild and religious monarch and a great patron of the Church.

Fig. 121

The Danes. Danish supremacy did not influence fashion in England. The Danes were a little behind the English in refinement, and the nobility attending Canute eagerly adopted the manners, customs and costume of the new kingdom.

Canute was simple in his tastes, but a man of some culture. He had travelled a good deal and had visited Rome, on one occasion attending the coronation of the Emperor Conrad II. (1024) there, so he knew something of regal pomp and splendour. His costume shown in the Liber Vitae (British Museum), a register of the New Minster, Hyde Abbey, Winchester (1016–1020), is unpretentious and without decoration except for plain borders round the neck, wrists and bottom edge of the tunic; but, in accordance with the general fashion of the times, these borders were frequently worked with patterns, as the illustration (*see* Fig. 121) shows. The cloke is here shown with a portion caught up into a knot tied by the cords normally used for holding the cloke on to the shoulders. These cords have curious ornamental ends. The knees are bare, after the Anglo-Saxon and Danish custom. He wears the socca with decorated tops and ordinary shoes. The crown is a good example of Anglo-Saxon design.

House-carles. An important innovation was the introduction of a king's bodyguard numbering from two to three thousand picked men of Danish nationality. They were called "huscarls" or "house-carles," and formed a regular force of armed soldiers, in contra-distinction to the "fyrd" or levy of the

Fig. 122

people. "Butsecarls" were the fighting men who manned the ships.

The Huscarls shared with their contemporaries, the Varangian

Guard, the reputation of being the finest body of soldiers in the world. They always followed Canute, and remained as a bodyguard to succeeding English kings until they perished, overwhelmed by numbers, at Senlac.

Anglo-Saxon noble, eleventh century. A distinctive costume is shown in Fig. 122; it represents an Anglo-Saxon earl of the eleventh century. A plan showing the shape and arrangement of decoration of the tunic is given in Diagram 24.

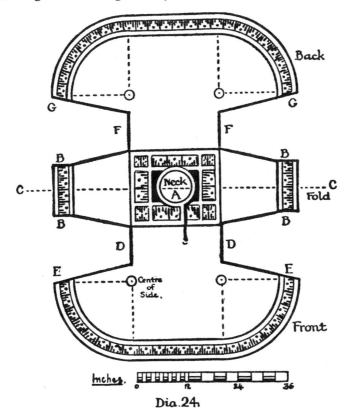

Dia. 24.

This new tunic was made all in one piece, if the width of the material allowed; and Diagram 24 shows it in plan when opened out flat. A is the hole for the head to pass through. It is surrounded by an almost square piece of embroidery. BB are the wrist-bands. The dotted line CC indicates the fold over the shoulder and down the sleeves. The centres from which the side circles are set out are marked on the plan. The lines E D B–E D B on the front portion are seamed to the back portion G F B–G F B, and the tunic is complete. When the skirt was left partly open up the sides E D–G F, the embroidery was continued to outline the opening. A semicircular cloke might be worn as usual, or could be dispensed with altogether. The legs in this figure are clothed in cloth socca, ornamented with bosses of gold and cross-gartered with gilded leather. This earl holds the rod of office as chamberlain.

MEN OF THE MIDDLE CLASS

Fig. 123 is a very superior man of middle class. He wears a tunic with slightly different shaped sleeves, wider in the upper arm (*see* Diagram 22). During the whole of this period, two or even more tunics were worn, the outer one obviously being the best and most ornate. The under-tunics were of woollen and linen material, cut on lines similar to

Fig. 123   Fig. 124

those of the outer one, but perhaps not so full. These under-tunics were called in Anglo-Saxon "sherte," or "sceort," meaning "short." The small semicircular cloke is fastened in a new way. A corner is pushed through a ring fixed to the straight edge about three or four feet from the opposite corner. The leg-coverings display no novelty, but are typical of this period.

Fig. 124 is an *Anglo-Saxon warrior* of the ninth, tenth, and eleventh centuries. The leather lorica was called by the Anglo-Saxons, "corium." The Roman manner of cutting the part surrounding the hips and armholes into straps has now gone out of use, and in its place the different layers are shaped into points or scallops, and often resemble leaves. A plain or striped tunic with short sleeves is worn under it, and a cloke used if necessary. The coverings of the legs are essentially Anglo-Saxon. The helmet has the comb (*see* Fig. 117), but the square-shaped brim has disappeared, and in place of it a studded band is used. A spear, sword and shield, and often in addition a bow and arrows, were carried. This is the type of warrior who met the Normans at Senlac.

MEN OF THE PEOPLE

Figs. 125, 125A and 125B are typical of the people in general. The tunics and clokes followed the lines already described.

Fig. 125   Fig. 125A   Fig. 125B

Fig. 125 shows the dress of a man at the beginning of this period. He has fastened up his tunic after the manner shown and described under Fig. 90B. (This last figure is Byzantine and much later in date, which shows how very generally this practical method was adopted.) The cloth boots worn over hose are cut in an unusual manner at the top.

Fig. 125A is from an illuminated MS. of the tenth century. The most noticeable feature about the costume is that the rather loose socca are attached at the back of the leg, presumably by sock suspenders!

This was quite a usual custom, as many illustrations show this pronounced loop effect below the knee.

Fig. 125B is a man of the lower orders wearing a plain tunic cut in the older fashion, as shown in Diagram 19; but the sleeves are rather wide and short on the upper arm, showing the sleeves of his sherte. Cloth hose are fastened at the ankles, leaving the foot bare—a very usual practice with this class of person, who worked very frequently in damp fields. For walking on rougher ground, the foot was slipped into an easy-fitting shoe, fastened with buckle and strap across the instep.

MEN'S HAIRDRESSING

The hairdressing of men of the Anglo-Saxon Period was quite simple, as will be seen by the illustrations given.

The upper classes were considerably influenced by the fashion in hairdressing prevalent in Byzantium. The styles worn by Charlemagne and the kings shown in Figs. 116, etc., differ only slightly from the emperors and nobles shown in Chapter IV. The young eorl (see Fig. 117B) has decidedly flowing locks, and the hair of the ealdorman (see Fig. 117C) falls upon the shoulders, and these two may be quoted as typically Anglo-Saxon. Canute wears his hair a moderate length, although it is said he wore it hanging in profusion over his shoulders. This was also a Danish fashion, worn by him only when a young man. The earl (see Fig. 122) has adopted the German or French fashion of a fringe on the forehead, and the head bound with a fillet.

The hair of the French king (see Fig. 118) is dressed in the same way as the Anglo-Saxon kings.

The Germans (see Figs. 119 and 120) show the same style, but the hair is not quite so full.

It is in the middle classes that the typical Anglo-Saxon style of hairdressing is seen to advantage. Long, fair, waving hair, sometimes parted, sometimes not, flowing about the ears and on the shoulders, was the usual fashion. Beards of all shapes—forked, pointed, curled—were worn, with long or short moustaches; or beards alone, without any hair on the upper lip.

LEG-COVERINGS AND FOOTGEAR

The general type of leg-covering worn by the Anglo-Saxons was the old-fashioned bracco—the loose-fitting drawers seen in Diagram 3. The French name for this garment, when fitting *closer* to the leg, was "braies." The name of the tight-fitting hosa of the Byzantines was changed into Anglo-Saxon and Teutonic by replacing the "a" by an "e"—hose. All three of these leg-garments were worn by the Anglo-Saxons, with cross-gartering over the bracco and the braies, and sometimes over the hose.

Pedules of Frankish origin, described under "Byzantine" (see Chapter IV., p. 191), were re-named by the Anglo-Saxons "socca," and of these there were many varieties. Most of them are shown in the illustrations (see Figs. 114, 117, 117B, 120, 121, 122, 124, and 125A).

Boots and shoes of the Anglo-Saxons were made to the natural lines of the foot. Improvements in the cobbler's craft have been noted from time to time. During the early part of the ninth century the shoe-wrights were able to cut the uppers so well that the right shoe could be distinguished from the left.

The usual style of shoe was very like a modern bedroom slipper, but with a strap attached to the back part, fastening round the ankle with a buckle.

The drawings on this page show four varieties of shoes in use at this time.

The materials used for making boots and shoes were leather, dressed or undressed, cloth and felt. Fine cloth, coloured or gilded leather, and silk, ornamented (though moderately) in various ways, with gold embroideries, often set with jewels, were used for making the footgear of the nobility and wealthy. Black was usually worn by the commonalty.

The soles were composed of leather of various thicknesses, plaited straw, or wood. The wealthy did not despise the use of wood for the soles of their elegant footwear.

High boots were not general, but Fig. 125 shows a curious pair, of the ninth century, made in black cloth or leather.

ANGLO-SAXON WOMEN

During the hundred and fifty years between 450 and 597, the moral and social conditions of the antagonistic peoples in Britain were deplorable.

However barbarous in their habits the invading Jutes, Saxons, and Angles might be, they must be commended for at least one quality —the high esteem in which they held their women-folk. With the introduction of Christianity into Kent, at the end of the sixth century, civilisation and culture came again to Britain. The rise of womanhood to a high and dignified position dates from this time. To the list of noble women headed by the solitary Boadicea, may now be added the following:

Bertha, the first Christian "Queen,"—the Saxon title for the king's wife, meaning "the king's companion," from which the word "queen" is derived.

The wife of S. Oswald (634).

S. Hilda, Abbess of Whitby.

S. Ætheldrytha, Queen of Northumbria (670), who had a convent on the site of Ely Cathedral.

The Abbess Ælfleda (680) of Whitby, King Oswy's daughter.

Judith, step-mother of King Ælfred (850).

The Godly Ælswitha, wife of Ælfred (870).

The Lady of the Mercians, Æthelflaed (918), Ælfred's daughter.

These and many other great ladies of the Anglo-Saxon Period not only served God and their country well, but, what is more to the point, they thoroughly looked after their own homes; and it is at this time that the foundations of the "Good old English Home" were laid.

Outside influence must in justice be credited with a small share in the development of house-pride, as an example was set to Western civilisation by the empresses of Charlemagne (he had four wives, and four who were not), who superintended in every detail the domestic arrangements of the royal palaces.

Weaving and embroidery. The art of weaving in England, during the Anglo-Saxon Period, made very great strides under the tutelage of some Greek weavers who emigrated to this country. The ladies in attendance at royal residences, and those of the households of the nobility, were highly skilled in the art, and also in embroidery. Their fabrics, woven from linen, wool, and a little raw silk mixed with gold or silver, and embroideries carried out in gold, silver, and coloured threads of silk or wool, sometimes set with jewels (chiefly of Byzantine design), achieved a world-wide reputation. The borders of tunics worn by well-dressed men were worked by their wives or lady friends. Although the Franks of the Carlovingian Epoch were proficient in both these arts, they sent their craftsmen to England to learn weaving, and many Frankish ladies came here to finish their studies in needlework and embroidery.

Cambric. In the ninth century a fine make of gauze-like linen was woven in Eastern Europe. A similar material made at Amorgos is referred to on page 54. It is not impossible that this, as well as gauzes made of silk, were used by the wealthy for their veils, etc. A hundred pieces of this material formed part of a rich gift from a Greek lady to the Emperor Basil I., and it is described as being so fine that each piece could be enclosed in the joint of a reed. This material, at a later date, was introduced into France, and manufactured especially at Cambrai, whence it takes its name.

REGAL COSTUME AND THE NOBILITY—WOMEN

Eighth and ninth centuries. The costume of a noble lady is shown in Fig. 126, worn at the beginning of the eighth century. It was the

Fig. 126   Fig. 127

fashion following the type of dress shown in Fig. 106, and remained in use until the middle of the ninth century. This lady is wearing a "gwn"—now called in Anglo-Saxon a "gunna" or "gown"—with moderately wide sleeves to the elbow, and ornamented with a band of embroidery round the neck, down the front, and round the hem of the skirt and the sleeves. The gown is cut as shown in Diagram 25, but with shorter sleeves, and worn without any girdle. Under this is another gown, with sleeves fitting close to the wrist, and under this again another garment of the same shape, called a "camise." A square veil of transparent soft material, embroidered with a small design, is placed over the head. The Byzantine element in this costume will be noticed on referring to Fig. 83.

Dia. 25

Ninth century. The costume worn by the Empress Judith (*see* Fig. 127), wife of Louis le Debonnaire and daughter of the Count of Bavaria, is very similar to that just described, except that the sleeves are considerably wider and longer. The gown, which here resembles a supertunic, is hitched up at the sides to give a draped effect, and this makes the garment appear shorter. It is woven or embroidered with large circles of gold, a fashion which continued in use irregularly until the eleventh century. It is stated that this empress had gold plate upon her dress to the weight of three pounds. The under-gown of some rich material has tight sleeves, long enough to ruck on the forearm, with a band of gold round the wrist. This is a very usual form of sleeve.

Waist-girdles were almost entirely out of vogue during the whole of this period. The gowns either hung in folds, straight from the neck, or were hitched in such a way as to make radiating folds from the sides to the front of the dress, as shown in this illustration.

From the shoulders hangs a semicircular cloke, worn in a new way, being fastened in front with a jewelled agrafe, and enveloping the figure; but it was the usual mode to throw the front back over the shoulders to show the lining of some rich fabric. It has a band of gold all round the edge.

The veil is small, arranged over the head in a manner peculiar to this period, which gives zig-zag folds on the forehead and at the sides. This one is caught by the agrafe which holds the cloke. It is surmounted by a diadem of gold and jewels.

Ninth century. Fig. 128 represents Queen Judith, wife of King Æthelwulf and step-mother to King Ælfred. This costume is like the

FIG. 128. QUEEN JUDITH

Wife of Æthelwulf and step-mother of King Ælfred. She wears the typical costume of a queen of this period.

one just described, but the centre band of the last century has been retained. The supertunic is very gracefully draped, being pinned or held close by the right arm, which is enveloped in the ample semi-circular cloke. The whole costume is much simpler, and displays more beautiful lines than that worn by the German empress, and this graceful simplicity, which extended to their use of colour, is a distinguishing feature of the dress of Anglo-Saxon ladies. The veil has now taken a new shape. It is a circle, with a circular hole cut, not in the centre, but about twelve to fifteen inches from the edge (*see* Diagram 26). The larger portion was draped on the head, the face and throat being revealed through the hole. Care was taken to arrange the edge in graceful flutes. Above the veil

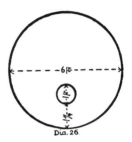

is placed the crown, a band of gold, set with jewels and ornamented with floral motifs.

The costume of a *princess or noble lady of the ninth, tenth and eleventh centuries* is given in Fig. 129. Here again the super-

Fig. 129   Fig. 130

tunic is draped, but this time it is attached to an invisible cord girdle. The cloke is of a new shape, being cut on the principle of the paenula (*see* Diagram 12), but instead of the hole for the head being in the centre, it is so placed as to make the front portion much shorter than the back. This forms a kind of shoulder-cape, which is worn draped over the forearms. This lady is wearing an oblong veil, the right end of which is draped round the neck and falls over the left shoulder under the left side of the veil. The coronet keeps the veil well in place.

The lady shown in Fig. 130 is wearing the same kind of circular cloke, and with it the circular veil described under Fig. 128. The drawing is treated in the manner of an illumination in a tenth-century manuscript. MSS. of this time furnish many examples of ways of wearing the circular veil. The hair was dressed low down on the nape of the neck to show the natural contour of the head. The veil was then somewhat bunched on the head so as to hang in many small folds and form a goffered edge over the face, in the centre, and on each side above the ears; the remaining part of the veil was thrown over the shoulders, evidently more than once, as there seem to be many folds and zig-zag edges. Her gown hangs straight from the neck, and has tight rucked sleeves to the wrist.

Materials and patterns. Silk or soft woollen fabrics were the materials used by the wealthy for veils, gowns, and under-dresses, as the drapery is always delineated in a graceful manner.

Gowns at this time were very much decorated with patterns, generally spots, groups of spots, and circles. The fact that these ornamentations do not interfere with the lines of the drapery suggests that they were woven into the fabric, not embroidered on it.

In many illuminated MSS: of this time, the ample under-gowns are so long that they lie upon the ground, and this surplus is represented in illuminations as twisted rolls.

German empress, eleventh century. The saintly Cunigunda, Empress of Henry the Holy, is shown in Fig. 131. She is wearing a distinctly Teutonic type of dress, on similar lines to that shown in Fig. 111. The supertunic worn by the empress is cut very much on the lines shown in Diagram 18. The same garment ungirded is seen in Fig. 132. Two bands of ornamentation encircle the skirt part, and two the sleeves, and a piece forming a collar, with pendent decoration, encircles the neck. The sleeves are quite different from any hitherto seen. They are cut close to the upper arm, widening out at the elbow, until they become very long and open at the wrists. This supertunic is girded at the waist, and has other points of resemblance to the garment worn by the lady in

FIG. 131. THE EMPRESS CUNIGUNDA

Wife of Henry the Holy (1002–1024). The design in the background is from the same source as that shown in Fig. 119.

Fig. 131. THE EMPRESS CUNIGUNDA
(1002–1024)

Fig. 92. The veil is the circular one first seen in Fig. 128. The crown is a reversion to the Byzantine type. The Empress Cunigunda holds a model basilica in her left hand, a method adopted by artists of illuminated MSS. to denote that she was a builder and benefactress of churches.

German noble lady, eleventh century. Fig. 132 shows a German noble lady of the early eleventh century, wearing a supertunic very like that of the Empress Cunigunda. It is ungirded, and worked or woven with a design of the period. Being a young girl, her hair is left undressed and simply flowing, confined with a fillet of gold or silk. The under-gown only reaches to the ankles, and shows her feet clad in shoes which button up the front.

A seat and curtains of the period. The seat is a very usual one,

Fig. 132

Fig. 133

framed on the X principle, terminating at the top with animals' heads and at the bottom with claws. In the background, curtains of embroidery, for which the Anglo-Saxon ladies were famous, are draped in the prevailing manner. They are looped round the columns, and the ends passed between the columns and the upper part of the curtains. This arrangement of curtains was used by the Byzantines of the sixth century and copied by the Anglo-Saxons. It remained in general use in England during the Anglo-Saxon and Norman Periods.

English queen, eleventh century. The unrelieved simplicity of the costume of Emma, Queen of Canute (*see* Fig. 133), is a striking contrast to the costume of the four previous ladies. The queen wears a loose gown fitting the neck and bust, but very much widened out and forming ample folds at the feet. She has caught up part of it in her right hand. The sleeves are wide at the wrists, and one is turned back to show the lining of another colour. A cloke is attached across the shoulders by cords, tied on the right side under the veil. The ends of the cords are finished with ornaments of goldsmiths' work. The veil is a circle with a hole for the face, and is placed on the head before the crown; a portion of the veil is then draped over the left side of the crown, and attached to the veil on the top of the head. The crown is a band of gold, set with jewels.

MIDDLE-CLASS WOMEN

Fig. 134 shows a woman of middle class, clad in a long gown fitting moderately close on the shoulders and bust, but widening a little towards

Fig. 134

the feet. The sleeves are wide at the wrists, but are fairly close-fitting at the upper arm. The habit of turning the sleeve back at the wrist to show the lining should be noticed as a vogue of this time (end of tenth and first part of eleventh century). The embroidered sleeves of the under-gown show, and are tight to the wrists. This gentlewoman wears a small circular veil drawn up close under the chin, and over it is placed a hat, something like a bee-hive, of plaited straw.

The women of the people during the Anglo-Saxon Period were dressed exactly like the contemporary Byzantine woman shown in Fig. 94B.

Materials and colouring. The supertunic, with wide open sleeves, was often worn over the gown by women of the burgess class. The materials used by them were linens, cottons, and woollen stuffs, woven at home. The colourings used for the clothes of women of this class were all shades of greys, dull greens, browns, natural hues and subdued tones, all characteristic of the Anglo-Saxon commonalty, and relieved here and there by touches of brighter colour in the modest amount of needlework with which they decorated their serviceable garments. This principle also applied to the men.

HAIRDRESSING OF THE ANGLO-SAXON WOMEN

Scarcely any representations of women without a head-covering are seen in illuminations of this period. It was customary among them to keep the head enveloped in a veil, sometimes very voluminous, at others quite small. Under these circumstances it is to be inferred that they dressed the hair in a very simple manner, by parting it in the middle, waving it on the temples, and fixing it in a knot or coil at the nape of the neck in the manner seen in Fig. 37.

Young girls of all classes wore their hair flowing on the shoulders, bound by a "snöd," or band, if necessary, to keep it in place. The band varied with the social position of the wearer. The highest had them made of gold, set with precious stones; others wore plain bands of gold, silver or silk. The poorer classes used bands of cotton material.

Ornamented hairpins were worn by Anglo-Saxon ladies, although usually hidden by their veils; and many examples have been found in various parts of Western Europe.

Long flowing hair was worn by women of all classes in the privacy of their homes, as the story of the wooing of Duke William of Normandy testifies. The Lady Matilda, daughter of the Count of Flanders, made disparaging remarks about the man of her father's choice. William came to hear of them, and making hot haste to Lille, found the lady at needlework, attended by her women. Seizing her by *her long tresses,* he dragged her about the apartment, beat her, and finally flung her at his feet; after which she consented to marry him!

10th Cent.

JEWELLERY OF THE ANGLO-SAXONS

The jewellery worn during the seventh century by a personage of high estate was a mixture. Part of it would be heirlooms of Roman workmanship, formerly the treasured property of some slaughtered Briton; and part of it of Teutonic origin, worn and brought from the Fatherland by an ancestor—one of those chiefs who came marauding during the invasions of the fifth and sixth centuries.

Jewellery to the Anglo-Saxons was an unimportant branch of their arts. In character it was like that of the Franks, who were of the same Teutonic stock as the Saxons and the Angles, but it contained also a Scandinavian and a Celtic strain, due to the coalescence of the various races now populating the country. In Anglo-Saxon graves a variety of articles of jewellery has been found—ear-rings, finger-rings, crosses, and circular pendants for hanging round the neck, agrafes for fastening clokes, and buckles of bronze, silver, gold and enamel. The designs most frequently encountered are the Celtic vermiculate, and the Scandinavian type depicting heads of animals.

Enamelling was not done by the Anglo-Saxons until about the end of the tenth century, and was then copied from foreign examples.

Many objects of goldsmiths' work made before the end of the seventh century are described by chroniclers, from whom we gather that the work produced was very creditable. Bracelets, rings and necklaces of

Crown—Otto III.

Crown—Anglo-Saxon

gold, set with precious stones, and "a golden fly adorned with gems" (*see* Frankish Jewellery, p. 236) are mentioned. When Ælfred came to the throne he encouraged foreign skilled goldsmiths to settle in England, and their advent gave an impetus to the native craftsmen, who reproduced articles of jewellery with a technique almost approaching the best Frankish and Byzantine work.

Crowns. Many examples of Anglo-Saxon and French crowns have been shown already, and their evolution from the band to the floriated style has been described on p. 259.

A curious square crown worn by the Emperor Otto III. (983) is shown. It has its prototype in the four-cornered helmet of an earlier age. A particularly beautiful yet simple Anglo-Saxon crown of the eleventh century has tall leaf-like motifs standing straight up from a narrow head-band.

Necklaces of gold chains and supple twisted wire work—some being set with small jewels at intervals—were worn by Anglo-Saxon noblemen. With the ladies, the prevailing vogue of wearing the veil in folds about the neck obscured necklaces from view, so they were not essential to well-dressed women.

Necklaces of terra-cotta beads, with coloured ornament and incisions filled in with colour, were worn by women and men of the middle classes. Beads of amber and garnets were in use, besides pendant-drops (like the pear-shaped pearl, for which there was such a rage at Constantinople) cut from crystal, amethyst and garnet.

Ear-rings were very small, usually only a plain gold ring, but sometimes the gold ring had a small ornament or jewel threaded on the gold wire.

Ear-ring

Bracelets were not very generally worn until the Danes came. Then bracelets were adopted by both men and women of the nobility. Like their kinsmen the Jutes and Angles, the Vikings considered gold and bronze bangles a sign of honour,[1] and for some long period bracelets in the form of massive gold rings were worn by the Anglo-Saxons.

Rings were another item of jewellery worn by the upper classes to indicate their superior position. The ring—copied from Byzantine models—was usually worn on the third finger of the right hand. A gold finger-ring, decorated with gold twisted wire and granulations, is shown here.

Pins for the hair were often used by great ladies. Their beauty and richness were of little advantage, as they were nearly always covered

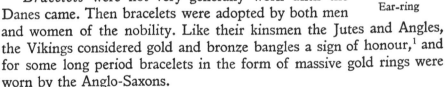

Hair-pin

by the veil. Many, precisely the same as described under Frankish Jewellery, were in use. This also applies to the curious little fly

---

[1] "Here Æthelstan, King, lord of earls, bracelet-giver to heroes."—*Anglo-Saxon Chronicle*, A.D. 937.

ornaments, which found favour with Anglo-Saxon as well as Frankish ladies.

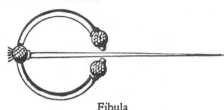

Fibula

Fibulæ and *agrafes* were replicas of those described under Frankish Jewellery. A very simple fibula on the penannular plan is of gold with ornamentation suggesting a thistle.

Circular-topped agrafes were executed in mosaics and engraved gold set with jewels—copies of those worn by Frankish nobles.

A large pin with a jewelled and decorated circular head was a

Circular-topped Agrafe

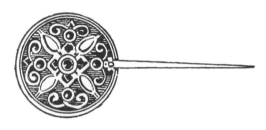

Ornamental Pin

useful and ornamental article for pinning a cloke, or fixing the draped over-gown so fashionable among Anglo-Saxon ladies.

Crosses, pectoral and reliquary, were very much worn and were in every respect identical with those already described. The example shown here is of seventh-century workmanship, and is now in Durham Cathedral. It was found in the coffin of S. Cuthbert; it is of gold set with enamels, mosaic and jewels, the large red stone in the centre covering a small reservatory for a relic.

A cross of gold, richly enamelled, was found in the chest containing the body of Eadward the Confessor. It was suspended round the neck by a gold chain twenty-four inches in length.

LIST OF AUTHORITIES CONSULTED FOR CHAPTER VII

Asser
Bede
Dr. Brewer
F. W. Fairholt
E. E. C. Gomme
J. R. Green
Thomas Hodgkin
Inger

J. S. Mann
J. R. Planche
York Powell
W. F. Reddaway
T. W. Rolleston
Alexander Speltz
H. D. Traille

Oct.14.1066

FINIS

GENERAL INDEX

NOTE.—*Page references in heavy type refer to Illustrations*

INDEX OF NAMES